America

Fights Back

America Fights Back

Armed Self-Defense in a Violent Age

Alan Gottlieb
and
Dave Workman

Merril Press
Bellevue, Washington

AMERICA FIGHTS BACK

is published by

Merril Press, P.O. Box 1682, Bellevue, WA 98009.

www.merrilpress.com

Phone: 425-454-7009

Distributed to the book trade by

Midpoint Trade Books, 27 W. 20th Street, New York, N.Y. 10011

www.midpointtradebooks.com

Phone: 212-727-0190

Cover Photos by Mark A. Taff

FIRST EDITION

LIBRARY OF CONGRESS CATALOGING-IN-PUBLICATION DATA

GOTTLIEB, ALAN M.
  AMERICA FIGHTS BACK / ALAN GOTTLIEB AND DAVE WORKMAN. -- 1ST ED.
      P. CM.
  ISBN 978-0-936783-50-5
  1. GUN CONTROL--UNITED STATES. 2. FIREARMS--UNITED STATES. 3. FIREARMS
OWNERS--UNITED STATES. I. WORKMAN, DAVE. II. TITLE.
HV7436.G675 2007
613.6'6--DC22

                                        2007033742

PRINTED IN THE UNITED STATES OF AMERICA

Dedication

To the servicemen and women who are out there every day on the front lines, in far-off places, defending the rights that we enjoy here at home and far too often take for granted, including the right of self-defense. These heroes make it possible for Americans to sleep secure in the knowledge that when they wake up, it will be in a nation where we enjoy the right to vote, to worship as we choose, to say what we believe and disagree without fear.

We also dedicate this book to every armed private citizen who has unselfishly risked his or her life so that their neighbors, friends and family could be safe from criminal harm.

Finally, we want to thank all the people who have generously sacrificed to support organizations that staunchly defend our Second Amendment rights. Without your devotion to liberty, there might not be a full Bill of Rights, and America would be a mere shadow of the nation we call home.

CONTENTS

PROLOGUE

"This (type of) thing doesn't happen in Cheshire. We're the type of community where people go to bed and they don't lock their doors."—**Cheshire, Connecticut Police Lt. Jay Markella, speaking to CBS News, July 28, 2007.**

Cheshire, Connecticut is a peaceful upscale family community described by Wikipedia to be the center of population in the state.

In the 2000 census, the community showed 28,543 residents, 9,349 households and 7,254 families living within the town limits. The largest ethnic groups living in the community are of Irish and Italian descent, and the median income – again according to Wikipedia – was $80,466 with the median family income set at $90,774.

It is what some might describe as a "Ward Cleaver kind of town," where one might expect the popular television series *Leave it to Beaver* about the fictional Cleaver family that ran from 1957 to 1963 to have been based.

All of that has changed now, and not for the better. It will never again return to the way it was prior to Monday, July 23, 2007. Sometime after 3 a.m., according to various published reports, two men broke into the home of prominent diabetes specialist Dr. William Petit, Jr., medical director of the Joslin Diabetes Center affiliate at the Hospital of Central Connecticut, and his wife, Jennifer Hawke-Petit, co-director of the Cheshire Academy's Richmond Health Center. The couple's two daughters, Hayley, 17, and Michaela, 11, also live at home. The Petits had been married for 22 years.

Hayley had graduated in June from the prominent Miss Porter's School and had been accepted to Dartmouth College – her father's alma mater – where she was reportedly planning to study medicine and presumably follow in the footsteps of her parents. While at Miss Porter's, she had been involved in athletics, playing on the basketball team and running in cross country. She had also been co-captain of the crew team.

None of that mattered to two men identified by the Hartford Courant as 44-year-old Steven Hayes and his partner, Joshua Komisarjevsky, 26. They are not interested in the exemplary professional lives of the Petits, nor are they concerned with the bright future of the eldest Petit daughter. At this writing, Hayes and Komisarjevsky were far more interested in their own futures, which appeared rather bleak.

For the next several hours, the Petit family was held hostage. Shortly after 9 a.m., one of her family's captors accompanied Jennifer Hawke-Petit to the Maplecroft Plaza branch of the Bank of America, forcing her to make a cash withdrawal. Reportedly, Hawke-Petit was able to tip a bank employee that her family was being held hostage, and police were alerted. They responded to the family home and surrounded it.

Dr. Petit had been badly beaten and tied up in the basement. Upstairs, his wife and daughters were tied to their beds and assaulted. Hawke-Petit was strangled. The daughters died from smoke inhalation after the house was set on fire by their killers, possibly to destroy evidence of what had transpired there over the previous several hours.

Dr. Petit managed to free himself and escape as his home went up in flames.

Hayes and Komisarjevsky flee in a station wagon as police arrive and the fire erupts. The vehicle rams three police cars and crashes, and they are taken into custody.

According to the August 10, 2007 edition of the Courant newspaper, Komisarjevsky and Hayes were both on parole, the younger man having been released in April and his older partner hitting the streets in May. Both have been listed by the Connecticut Department of Corrections as "nonviolent offenders."

This probably surprised a judge who had reportedly noted of

Komisarjevsky before sending him to prison in 2002 that the young man standing before him is a "cold, calculating predator." The newspaper reported that Komisarjevsky, in order to steal money to support his drug habit, would slash through screen doors of homes in Cheshire at night, while wearing night-vision goggles.

Meanwhile, Hayes is the kind of criminal suspect one might imagine showing up in the script of a detective drama. He has made a long career of burglary, larceny and check forgery.

Hayes and Komisarjevsky reportedly met in 2006 at a residential drug treatment center in Hartford. They subsequently spent five months living in the same halfway house.

As this book was going to press, both men faced charges of murder, kidnapping, aggravated sexual assault, robbery and larceny. Under our system of justice, they were to be presumed innocent until found guilty beyond a reasonable doubt in a court of law, by a jury of their peers.

In the wake of this monstrous crime, the state of Connecticut wept.

Well, perhaps that is not quite fair or accurate. At least one Connecticut resident, Republican Governor M. Jodi Rell, took what she probably thought was a real swipe at violent crime. She signed legislation requiring gun owners to report lost or stolen guns within 72 hours of discovering them missing, or face penalties ranging from an infraction to a felony, according to a news release touting the measure.

Meanwhile, the Connecticut Network to Abolish the Death Penalty quickly made it clear where its priorities lay. It issued a statement expressing "hopes the (Petit) family is receiving all of the support they need in this time of profound tragedy."

"All of us wish to support the survivors in their healing."

If anyone were to ask "What happened to the American dream," the aftermath of the Petit family outrage would be the answer. Three members of a family are slaughtered in their home, and the best lawmakers could do in an effort to prevent this kind of thing from happening is pass gun legislation penalizing law-abiding citizens who had, themselves, been victimized by crime?

A mother and her daughters are brutalized and murdered in their beds, and an organization of hand-wringing simps issues a diatribe against subjecting the perpetrators to the highest degree of punishment available under existing law, while whining that "violence is pervasive in our society and it must stop?"

There can be but one rational, reasoned, sensible response to such nonsense and the people who preach it: Go to Hell and take the shortcut.

Connecticut, despite the presence of such American icons as Colt's Manufacturing Company in Hartford, Marlin Firearms Company and O.F. Mossberg & Sons in North Haven, and Savage Arms in Suffield, is not a state where one would find firearms in most homes.

In the days following the Petit murders, however, newspapers reported a spike in firearm sales. WFSB News quoted firearms dealer Scott Hoffman, operator of Hoffman's Gun Center on the Berlin Turnpike, who said people had been buying shotguns, thanks to a shorter waiting period than they would have to endure if they tried to buy a handgun. In Connecticut, you must have a pistol permit to buy a handgun, and that can take up to 90 days. There is a lengthy waiting period on handgun purchases.

Noted Hoffman about all of his new customers: "They're scared for their own personal safety and their family's safety, their children's safety and they want a way to protect themselves."

Of course, to the casual observer, this reaction might seem senseless, because the suspected perpetrators were already behind bars, and not out there somewhere, waiting to strike again.

But it is quite possible that Connecticut residents were acting not simply out of blind fear, but with the clear understanding that the suspects in the Petit case are not the only career criminals who have ever gotten out of prison only to victimize someone else. They realize that what happened to the Petit family could just as well happen to them.

As close to making sense as might be possible for the Connecticut Network to Abolish the Death Penalty, that group acknowledged, "We are not sure what exactly motivates people to walk into a house, brutalize four people and leave them to die in a burning house."

Neither does anyone else, but of course, psychoanalyzing human predators is perhaps the last thing a homeowner should think about when such monsters are kicking in their doors and attacking their families. In a nation that claims to be the bastion of freedom and liberty, where every citizen should be able to excel at "the pursuit of happiness," the first and foremost thing they ought to be thinking about is survival and, at least according to the more laconic gun rights activists, "where to aim."

Lt. Markella of the Cheshire Police Department is wrong. This type of thing *does* happen in Cheshire. It can happen anywhere in America when citizens become complacent enough to elect people who will erode their sacred right of self-defense. It has been happening in communities like Washington, D.C., Chicago, New York and elsewhere that political correctness and philosophical condescension has replaced common sense. It can happen in any community where absent parents are replaced by gangs as a family structure, where public defenders and deputy prosecutors engage in an ongoing game of expediency, with the support of apathetic judges whose own sense of justice should have them standing before the bench, and not sitting behind it.

It happens in environments where citizens are lulled into a false sense of security by pompous police administrators who caution people to "avoid taking direct action and let the police handle it."

Worst of all, it happens all too frequently right in front of us, in communities from Connecticut to California and from the Gulf of Mexico to the Gulf of Alaska. And we have let it happen, through years of staying home on election night, while we were too busy to attend a PTA meeting, and when we went to the taverns, bowling alleys and cocktail lounges instead of "meet the candidates" nights and city council sessions.

All too many of us do not even know the names of our state legislative representatives, much less our congressmen and women. Stop people on the street and ask them if the know who Julia Roberts is, and they can identify her as the famous actress, but ask them who John Roberts is, and less than half will be able to identify him as the Chief Justice of the United States Supreme Court.

In the process, we have turned over far too much of the American dream to the so-called "Nanny Statists" who have come to the conclusion that they are far more capable of making decisions for us than we are. Highest on their list of things to do in order to establish communities like Cheshire, Connecticut is to have made it increasingly difficult for us to fight back.

They have done it through passage of restrictive gun laws,

adoption of statutes that impair our right to defend ourselves and the perpetuation of a court system that seems to have lost sight of what justice really should be.

But from this morass are emerging an increasing number of true heroes; Americans who remember that this country was built on self-reliance, and that one always has not merely the recourse, but the responsibility, to resist.

These people are just like us. They are our neighbors, our friends, fellow workers, and more often than not, people we don't even know, but would like to. They don't think of themselves as heroes, just average people who grew up believing that they have a right to achieve whatever dream they can, and that once they have earned what they have through hard work, sweat and perseverance, it is worth protecting.

Such people do not seek public recognition. They merely wish to be left alone so they can live their lives in peace.

They never think of themselves as particularly courageous. More often than not, they recall how terrified they were, not only for themselves, but for their loved ones. Indeed, their actions suggest that they considered their own safety far less important than the safety of others they were defending.

Some may believe that America has reached a turning point, but we think differently. As we researched the book you are about to read, it became clear that America has never gone around any bend, nor as a people have Americans really lost their moral compass.

The American spirit is alive and well, even though far too many have mistakenly concluded that we are no longer what we once were. Within us there remains the fortitude to do the right thing, to take a stand against evil, and do our part to see that good prevails.

We were reminded of Robert Frost's poem "The Road Not Taken." We are not so much at a turning point in this country as we are at a fork in the road. We can look at horrendous acts of savagery as the murders of the Petit family and accept this in our stride, or we can damn well do something about it.

As you are about to read, some of us already have made the decision. The road they have chosen is fraught with obstacles, and the journey down that road may be far less comfortable, and far more risky than had they chosen to remain with the flock and, like all the other sheep, depend upon shepherds and sheep dogs to protect them from the wolves.

We are not sheep in America, we are people. And the fork in the road we face is the decision, as a society, to stand on our feet or crawl on our knees.

We would never meekly surrender our country to foreign invaders, and we must never surrender our neighborhoods to predatory criminals. Above all, we must never give up the means to defend our homes and neighborhoods for some false sense of security.

Realizing that the awful thing that happened in Cheshire can happen anywhere is not the signal for us to give up our means of self-defense, but instead to strengthen our resolve to defend our communities by defending our right to possess the very tools that make it possible to fight back.

CHAPTER 1

'This is America'

Bobby Earl Hardy of Gulfport, Mississippi was what many in law enforcement would call "a scumbag." Born February 21, 1975 in Mississippi, he stood five feet, eight inches tall and weighed 145 pounds, evidently all of it bad. An African American with black hair and brown eyes, he was first arrested at the age of 18 years by the Gulfport, Mississippi Police Department on a charge of aggravated assault on Dec. 5, 1993

His life would go down hill from there with future legal troubles, to the point that Harrison County, Mississippi Sheriff George H. Payne, Jr. would eventually describe him as "a predator; simply a predator."

Two years after his first scrape with the law, Hardy was arrested again, for aggravated assault, according to the Mississippi Department of Corrections. This occurred on the day after his 20th birthday; a hell of a way to celebrate.

Hardy became what is known in police jargon as "a model citizen" with convictions for assault and armed robbery, so when he was released from prison in May 2006 after having served two years for armed robbery stemming from an incident in Gulfport at a store called the Lyman Quick Stop, he had established a behavior pattern. It was a safe bet that he would get in trouble again on the outside sooner or later. It was sooner.

His last criminal act occurred on the night of October 16, 2006. Having become something of a casual customer at a convenience store operated by Tommy and Elizabeth "Beth" Greer, that evening Hardy showed up about 9 p.m. asking what time the Greers would be closing. Recognizing the man as a past customer, Tommy advised that closing time would be about an hour later. Hardy departed.

After closing, the Greers drove the eighteen miles to their home outside Saucier, where they had had to leave the garage door slightly open to accommodate the longer cargo bed of Beth's new pickup truck. Tommy went inside and Beth began retrieving some things from the trunk of their car, only to hear a chilling voice behind her say "Hey."

Beth straightened up to be confronted by a man wearing a ski mask and gloves, with a semiautomatic pistol in one hand. Trying to remain calm, she twice pleaded with the assailant not to kill her, but the masked man seemed more interested in her husband, so he stepped around her and followed Tommy into the house.

Confronted by the masked intruder in his own home, and believing he was about to be murdered, Tommy Greer did a remarkably brave thing: He attacked the man with just his fists, igniting a life-or-death battle that seemed to echo throughout the house. As the two men crashed around inside, outside Beth cautiously made her way to the door of her car and reached inside for the one thing she desperately wanted to get her hands on: The loaded .38 Special pearl-handled revolver that she always kept inside.

A memento from her first marriage to a Mississippi constable who had died many years before from a heart attack, it was her late first husband's revolver for which she had purchased the pearly white grip panels before he passed away. It was still loaded with the same ammunition that had been in the gun all those years before, cartridges with roundnose lead bullets.

Inside, as her husband struggled with the masked gunman, a single shot rang out. Beth immediately feared the worst. Her husband was dead, she thought, and there appeared to be enough blood to confirm that. Fortunately for Tommy, the head wound he suffered was only a grazing shot, but head wounds bleed profusely.

Perhaps thinking he had killed Tommy Greer, the gunman turned his attention back to Beth. He emerged through the doorway back into the garage, the pistol still in his hand, evidently preparing to gun down the woman who, only moments before, had not interested him enough. In a moment, she would be the only thing on his mind; a potential witness.

Bobby Earl Hardy was about to make what veteran firearms instructor Massad Ayoob calls "a fatal error in the victim selection process." Ayoob, founder of the Lethal Force Institute in New

Hampshire and part-time police officer, expert witness and investigator, has made a career of studying people like Hardy, and training private citizens and fellow police officers how to survive deadly encounters with such men.

Ayoob is one of the leading authorities on gunfights, and he has a keenly-developed sense for analyzing a gun battle and determining what went right and what went wrong at a given moment. His LFI, while established and based in New Hampshire, is something of a traveling educational opportunity, offering firearms and self-defense courses all over the country. It has become one of the more renowned "shooting schools" in the United States, and it attracts students from all over the world.

Hardy took one step toward Beth Greer before she raised the snub-nosed revolver and, aiming at the center of his wiry body mass, shot him. The lead bullet crossed the short distance of the garage in a heartbeat and slammed into Hardy with a jolt, punching a hole through his stomach and grazing his liver, knocking him to the floor, but not out of the fight. At that point, Tommy Greer had regained his feet, and he yelled at his terrified wife to fire again.

"I'm sure he was coming out to do away with me so there would be no witnesses," Beth recalled to one of the authors in chilling detail.

As he fell, Hardy had fired a shot that sailed past Beth and lodged in the door post of her car. She fired at least three more rounds before the mortally-wounded gunman managed to get on his feet and stumble out of the garage, down the driveway and climb into a waiting getaway car. As he fled, Beth fired the last rounds in her small revolver.

Beth threw her empty gun into the trunk and grabbed her badly bleeding husband, and then raced down the road to a hospital. Unknown to her, neighbors had already called the Sheriff's Department and a patrol car arrived minutes after the Greers sped away.

A short time later, Bobby Earl Hardy, lying on a gurney and being prepared for emergency surgery, gasped his final breath. He had been dumped at a hospital by his accomplice to die all alone, surrounded by strangers.

To hear Sheriff Payne tell it, nobody in the community, and certainly nobody on his department, lost any sleep over the departure of Bobby Hardy from this life. In the vernacular, the shallow end of the gene pool had been cleansed of one more germ.

Later, after learning of the event, a national gun rights organization, the Second Amendment Foundation – an educational and legal action citizens group based in Bellevue, Washington – would create a special award to honor Beth Greer and women like her who use firearms to defend themselves or their loved ones. The Eleanor Roosevelt Award is named in honor of the late First Lady who, according to her own account, frequently carried a handgun even while living in the White House, and later during her travels in the South as she campaigned for civil rights.

Beth Greer, as would any normal person, struggled with the incident and came to know Sheriff Payne as a genuine friend, upon whose experience and understanding she would lean over the next few months. Payne believes she is a hero.

One thing the incident taught Beth is that she needed to upgrade the ammunition she carries in her gun, from lead bullets to expanding hollowpoints.

"I don't go anywhere without a gun," she said in retrospect three months later. "I'd hate to think what would have happened had I not had that gun in my car that night. I was able to get through this and I will never hesitate to use a gun again."

Fed Up, Fighting Back

Americans are fed up with crime and they are fighting back. Frustrated after years of social experimentation with early release, sham rehabilitation, crime after crime committed by recidivist felons who seem to wind up back on the street with alarming regularity, they have fought for, and passed, concealed carry laws that allow them to be armed, and are now fighting for stronger self-defense statutes that allow them to stand their ground and defend their lives, without fear of legal prosecution afterward.

If September 11, 2001 taught Americans anything, it was that the façade of security with which this nation had been living so long proved to be a hologram. The government could not prevent an attack by terrorists anymore than police and sheriff's departments – no matter how dedicated and courageous their officers and leaders are – can protect communities from criminals like Bobby Earl Hardy.

Perhaps Sheriff Payne, upon whom some in high places might

look at as a "sheriff from Mayberry," the fictional town in the old Andy Griffith television program, proved himself wise beyond his age in the common-sense, ground level approach that rural lawmen seem to frequently exhibit.

"This is America," he observed matter-of-factly in an interview with WLOX news in Gulfport, "and we're not going to be intimidated by these thugs that think they can come to our homes and rob us or shoot us, and we're not just going to be intimidated and roll over for them. Quite frankly, there was a gun battle there and she won the gun battle and this outlaw lost his life."

Sheriff Payne is hardly alone in that philosophy. Following a string of armed robberies late last year that ended in justifiable homicides in the Cincinnati, Ohio area, oft-quoted Cincinnati attorney Richard Goldberg told the Cincinnati *Enquirer* that citizens in his city are fed up with crime.

"People in this day and age are sick and tired of violent crime," he told the newspaper. "There's a general attitude in society that police are there after the crime occurs. People are going to take it on themselves to defend themselves."

Police Chief Tom Streicher amplified the attorney's statement when he told the newspaper that the shootings were not "vigilante justice" but self-defense under existing law. However, he issued the almost obligatory statement that "Our advice to the victim is let it go and call the police. We'll come. We'll find the bad guy."

That comment brought almost universal guffaws from gun rights activists on KeepAndBearArms.com (KABA), possibly the most active internet gun rights forum in the country. It is a forum that gets thousands of visits every day from gun owners.

One man responded to the police chief's remark sarcastically mimicking his words: "We'll eventually come, and most likely all we'll find is your dead body."

Others cited studies that suggest resistance to criminal attack reduces one's chances of being harmed, and still others expressed the sentiment that they would "be damned if I will roll over and show my belly to any criminal scum."

According to the *Enquirer*, Cincinnati police reported at least nine justified self-defense killings during 2006, because the citizens who pulled the triggers were fighting criminals who intended to harm them.

Hamilton County Prosecutor Joe Deters was quoted by the newspaper noting, "People just want to protect themselves and their families."

Across the country, citizens in state after state have been campaigning through their state legislatures for several years to return America to a level playing field. First, the effort was to restore a citizen's right to bear arms in his or her own defense. Gun rights organizations, especially the National Rifle Association and Citizens Committee for the Right to Keep and Bear Arms, supported passage of concealed carry laws. As this book was written only two states did not have some form of concealed carry for private citizens: Illinois and Wisconsin.

But in 40 others, the laws have been written to require that citizens who meet the statutory criteria *must* be issued a concealed carry license. In Alaska, lawmakers took an even bolder step by passing a statute that eliminated the need to have a carry license to carry a handgun openly or concealed inside the state.

Vermont is the only other state with this kind of latitude, its Supreme Court more than a century ago ruling that citizens have the right to carry firearms openly or concealed so long as they do not intend to harm another person.

An increasing number of those states have adopted "reciprocity" agreements, which recognize and allow citizens from one state to carry concealed handguns in another state, under their state-of-resident licenses. A few states have passed blanket "recognition" statutes that recognize all out-of-state gun licenses, while others, such as New York, California and Oregon, refuse to recognize anyone else's carry license. Of those three, only Oregon issues licenses to non-residents who want to carry inside Oregon borders.

With adoption of carry statutes, the next legislative step has been passage of "stand-your-ground" laws. Such laws are designed to protect private citizens who defend themselves from lawsuits filed by their assailants or a criminal's "bereaved" family in the aftermath of his death at the hands of an intended victim.

Over the years, horror stories about homeowners being sued by burglars or their families have become legend in self-defense circles. The stand-your-ground laws remove this liability, while making it clear that a private citizen has a right to defend himself or herself against criminal attack in a place where that citizen has a right to be.

This includes shopping malls, restaurants, parking lots; any public place where the public normally would be expected to be able to come and go. These statutes are not "Castle Doctrine" laws, which only recognize the concept that "a man's home is his castle" and that intruders could be dealt with.

The stand-your-ground philosophy gives the private citizen broader latitude in the arena of self-defense. Under so called "duty to retreat" laws that have infuriated private citizens for years in more than 25 states – because it makes them vulnerable to criminal and civil prosecution if they defend themselves without first having attempted to retreat or flee from an attack, even in their own homes – the legal system has been arguably tilted in favor of the criminal.

Another, darker "down side" to such laws is that people compelled to turn and run can be, and sometimes have been, shot in the back.

But having endured years of failed social programs that seem to have created a bold, perhaps arrogant criminal element that believes it can ignore not only the law, but everyone else's right to be left alone, Americans have obviously had enough. Although the campaigns to pass such laws were subject to attacks of hysteria by gun control proponents claiming that it would open the door to "Wild West gunfights," the legal track record of such statutes has actually been very good.

The rhetoric has become almost predictable over the years, with spokespersons for organizations like the Brady Campaign to Prevent Gun Violence to repeatedly predict vigilante-style justice meted out by armed private citizens. One Brady Campaign spokesman, Zach Ragbourn, was quoted by *USA Today* in the March 20, 2006 edition insisting that such statutes "are more accurately called 'Shoot First' laws. They allow a person who just feels something bad is going to happen to open fire in public."

That's not accurate, and the Brady Campaign knows it. Traditional self-defense statutes and stand-your-ground laws are written to allow the use of force, up to and including lethal force, only in cases where there is an immediate and unavoidable threat to one's life. Under the law, citizens can defend against attacks that can reasonably be defined as threatening grave bodily harm as well as death, such as a beating that might leave someone permanently disabled. And so far, responsible armed citizens seem to be living up to that standard.

In fact, none of the bloody predictions tossed about from one legislative battle to another by self-defense opponents such as the Brady Campaign have ever come true. The rhetoric from gun opponents eventually began wearing thin with lawmakers who were being hammered by their constituents and educated by gun rights organizations that increasingly seemed to have the facts on their side.

Even sheriffs in some communities, after watching the law at work for perhaps six months to a year or more, publicly changed their opinions from initial opposition to support.

Law enforcement's attitude about fighting back may go beyond even the level of mere acknowledgement that concealed carry laws work. In Albuquerque, N.M., after a series of home invasion robberies that resulted in the shooting deaths of three suspects, a spokeswoman for the Albuquerque Police Department identified by World Net Daily as Trish Hoffman told a reporter, "Hopefully, this is going to send a message to people who are breaking into homes. They're engaging in very dangerous behavior, not only to the people they're robbing, but to themselves."

Permanently Deaf Ears

But that message is usually ignored by the criminals at whom it is aimed. If the message falls on deaf ears at first, often those in the criminal element wind up with permanently deaf ears by the time the dust settles on a crime scene.

While some special interest groups and social do-gooders wring their hands in anguish over such cases, Americans in general are solidifying their long-held belief that criminals who die in the commission of a crime generally get what they deserve. This philosophy is regaining traction from the Carolinas to California, wherever bad people confront good ones and come out the losers.

In the early hours of August 12, 2006, three men identified as Tavaras T. Pittman, Larry Donnell Williams and Tomarae D. Brinkley stopped by the home of Leroy Thorpe in Whitakers, North Carolina. Claiming that Thorpe owed them money, the trio began beating him and a friend, identified by the Rocky Mount *Telegram* newspaper (August 15) as Thurman Pitt.

The newspaper said the three attackers beat Thorpe and Pitt

with a baseball bat and at some point during the vicious altercation, one of them threatened to go get a firearm. When Pittman, Williams and Brinkley went outside, it gave Thorpe an opportunity to grab his shotgun, and when they came back, Thorpe fired. The shot charge hit Pittman in the chest, fatally wounding him, and his companions immediately fled.

Williams returned a short time later, but investigating police had to track down Brinkley at another residence. Not surprising in a society in which the criminal element seems to take full advantage of "turnstile justice," it was revealed that both Williams and Brinkley had prison records. Brinkley had spent time in prison for drug violations, car prowling and possession of stolen property. Williams had done time for assault with a deadly weapon, hit-and-run, auto theft, driving while his license was revoked, communicating threats and possession of stolen goods.

Trying to beat a man whose apartment he had invaded in Sacramento, California brought a man identified as James Robinson to an untimely end on the night of Nov. 14, 2006. Acting with an accomplice, Robinson dragged the unidentified apartment dweller outside and the two thugs began beating their victim.

At some point, according to a published report, the apartment owner managed to break free, get back inside and arm himself. When Robinson continued the attack, he was shot and killed.

In Indianapolis, Indiana on the night of December 4, 2006, a man named Mark D. Yant, 22, made his own "fatal error in the victim selection process" much like the poor decision of Bobby Earl Hardy. In this case, according to the Indianapolis *Star* newspaper account, Yant should have learned from a previous error, but he didn't. Criminals often ignore warning signs, and wind up on the wrong end of a gun. So it went for Yant, who had been arrested in September of that year for disorderly conduct and impersonating a public officer.

The intended victim in this case was a homeowner identified as Eric Williams. He had earlier been robbed by two armed intruders who had curiously acted at first as though they were police officers. The difference between Williams and Yant is that Williams had learned from a bad experience, and as a result of the October home invasion, had purchase a .40-caliber semiautomatic pistol.

Whether it has any connection with the Williams case, Yant's earlier arrest was the result of a traffic stop following a hit-and-run accident. Yant was a passenger in that car, and he identified himself to responding officers as a sheriff's deputy in Indiana's Marion County, the newspaper reported.

On the fateful night, Yant appeared at Williams' home, armed with a 9mm handgun. He fired once, putting a bullet into the door frame of Williams' house, bringing a lethal return volley from his intended victim. Yant died from multiple gunshot wounds.

A common denominator in nearly all of the self-defense cases stemming from attempted home-invasion robberies is that Americans are accepting the notion that the dead or seriously wounded perpetrators made the decision to commit a criminal act, and only they set in motion the series of events that led to their downfall.

Ample evidence of the public's growing lack of sympathy for criminals who find themselves on the receiving end came in the aftermath of a case in Shreveport, Louisiana in January 2007.

According to the *Times* newspaper of January 12, 2007, two brothers identified as Leonard and Jeremy Ellison, both city residents, tried to pull a late-night home invasion, but their intended victim, identified as Emmanual Henery, fought back.

The newspaper and police reports said the brothers broke into a house late one evening only to find all too late that Henery was at home. Also in the house were two other men and a younger woman.

The 56-year-old Henery opened fire on the two Ellison brothers. Leonard, 24, hit the floor in the kitchen, fatally wounded with a single gunshot wound to the head. He would die later at LSU Hospital. His brother, wounded six times with bullets in both legs and two more wounds in the side, was hospitalized at the same hospital, and charged with armed robbery with a firearm.

Public reaction was strongly supportive of Henery. Shreveport *Times* readers noted in a public response section such things as "criminals who kill/attempt to kill should be executed immediately."

"Why should they have the luxury of rotting in jail all their lives or most of their lives," the reader questioned. "My house/car/person is always armed and you can bet without a doubt in my mind I will shoot to kill of some crazy ass person is going to try to hurt my family. I will make sure they are dead before I call 9-1-1. It is well within my right and I will use my rights to the full extent."

Another wrote, "Now this is the old Shreveport that I know and love. We're all in agreement that bad guys deserve bad things happening to them…Shoot them, stab them, burn them or just run over them…I don't care, just eradicate the scum."

Others also wrote supportive comments, but one remark summed up best how *Times* readers seemed to feel: "I sure wish I had that homeowner's exact address so I could send them a thank you card and some more ammunition."

Each month in its magazines *The American Rifleman, The American Hunter* and *America's First Freedom*, the NRA runs a column called "The Armed Citizen." This has been a staple of the magazines for a couple of generations, and it is quite probably the most read section in each publication. This single-page has carried thousands of stories about incidents of legal armed self-defense, which no doubt many in the Shreveport area read regularly because there are a high number of NRA members in Louisiana.

There is no way of knowing whether any of the *Times* newspaper readers are NRA members, but their published remarks reinforce the sentiment that the time is long overdue for Americans to be fighting back; not taking the law into their own hands, as self-defense opponents constantly assert, but acting within the law as it was intended to be used by law-abiding citizens who firmly believe they have a right to not be victimized.

A 'Natural Right'

Long before the United States Constitution, long before English Common Law, even before the Ten Commandments, the first natural law, and the first natural right, was the right of self-preservation. Even dinosaurs understood this concept, fighting back against predators eons before man ever walked on the planet.

Up through man's evolution over hundreds of thousands of years, the right of a sentient being to live free from the threat of bodily harm or death has been understood even by the most primitive civilizations. Attacked, one can fight back, if not to preserve one's self, then at least to preserve one's family or offspring.

A mother bear will turn savagely violent if she feels her cubs are threatened, while the female deer will try to draw predators away from her fawns when danger approaches. Ant colonies wage war against one another, or unite to defend the nest and the queen and her eggs if the nest is attacked.

Man, the "civilized beast," is no less defensive of his own life, the lives of his children and mate when a lethal threat looms. It is a natural reaction, far more natural than submitting meekly to slaughter.

There is in all creatures a "fight or flight" instinct that has its roots in the natural law of self-preservation. If an attack seems overwhelming, "run for your life" is as natural and sensible reaction as fighting for your life.

However, in all too many cases, running has been found to simply encourage more predatory attacks. And where many social engineers seem to have been "running" for years from a hard truth – that predatory criminals have no concept of mercy – average citizens have reached that "moment of clarity."

In addition to defending themselves and their families, private citizens are growing more convinced that what they own, their personal belongings and their property, is worth defending as well. After all, they reason, "I worked hard for that, I earned it, I paid for it, and I am not about to let some thug take it from me."

While most states do not recognize a right that extends to defense of property, some states do. Colorado's infamous "Make My Day" law, which was decried by the same detractors who perennially attack self-defense and concealed carry statutes, clearly established the tenets of the modern "Castle Doctrine." Simply put, the principle makes it abundantly clear to criminals of all stripes that if you set foot in someone else's home without their invitation, you do so at your own peril.

Some years ago, the Second Amendment Foundation produced a remarkable window sticker for which public demand has only grown. It bluntly warns: "The owner of this property is armed. There is nothing inside worth risking your life for."

Roundly blasted as "redneck rhetoric" by gun rights opponents, there has curiously never been a counter-message distributed by the political Left that declares, "There are no firearms in this home." Even those who may bitterly oppose the notions of gun ownership and self-defense are not so self-delusional as to believe they would be safe from the criminal element if they were to so post their property.

Instead, one might argue, such people live in the safety sphere of their armed neighbors. Where it may be suspected, or even apparent, to burglars and other criminals that a property owner may be armed, it is not atypical that such miscreants avoid entire neighborhoods where they have even the smallest fear that they may encounter an armed citizen during the commission of a crime.

Just how deep is someone's personal convictions against guns and self-defense can be readily measured by their conduct after natural disasters or man-made chaos. During the Rodney King riots in Los Angeles, and in the aftermath, gun stores were flooded with people who had never before owned a firearm, but desperately wanted to get their hands on one at the time. When they learned of lengthy waiting periods, many of those people became outraged. They had previously supported tough gun laws, but evidently convinced themselves that such laws would only prevent criminals from quickly buying firearms. Only now did they realize that such laws applied to all citizens.

In the days following the 9/11 terrorist attack, even more Americans who had never owned guns bought them. The authors learned of sudden spikes in activity at many gun shops around the nation, and requests for training in the defensive use of handguns. Reality is a hard teacher.

Who can forget the image of the armed Florida homeowner standing guard over the rubble of his destroyed home in the aftermath of Hurricane Andrew, in front of a hand-painted sign that simply explained looters would be shot?

All of this is part of the social epiphany through which Americans have traveled during the past few years. While the Utopian ideals of the 1960s may have seemed fine at the time and even up through the years when Bill Clinton was president, the social and political realities of the 21st Century have caught up to people, who are learning perhaps for the first time that in a serious situation, whether it be a massive disaster or a home invasion robbery, help may not be coming in time, if at all, and we are on our own.

And so, Americans are fighting back. They are fighting to defend themselves, their families, and even their neighborhoods. And perhaps they are fighting to regain the dignity of self-reliance from an earlier age that was, and remains, uniquely American.

CHAPTER 2

The Deterrent Factor

Former National Rifle Association President and Academy Award-winning actor Charlton Heston put it thusly: "When what you say is wrong, that's a mistake. When you know it's wrong, that's a lie."

In today's divided culture – gun owners versus people who dislike guns and gun rights – there has erupted an unavoidable conflict over what is right for American citizens; to be legally armed and able to defend themselves, or to be prevented from owning and carrying firearms for that purpose, through various regulatory schemes, local ordinances or state and federal statutes. Such statutes appear to gun rights activists to be written more for the purpose of harassing law-abiding citizens than they are to deter criminals.

It is in this environment that gun rights activists with the support of the NRA and other gun rights groups have pushed concealed carry laws in more than 30 states since the mid-1980s, and in each one of those campaigns, self-defense opponents used the same rhetoric.

"Concealed carry will lead to gunfights at traffic stops!"

"Such laws will endanger children!"

"It will be like Dodge City on a Saturday night!"

"This law will lead to OK Corral-type shootouts!"

"This law will put our police in danger!"

There is only one problem with all of these arguments. They're not true and there is plenty of data to prove it.

For starters, let's take a look at the "Wild West shootout" arguments. Opponents of concealed carry legislation use this argument so often that it has become part of the pop culture vocabulary. It is also thoroughly discredited by historians, most prominent being career journalist Richard Shenkman, author of *Legends, Lies and Cherished Myths of American History.* In that book, he wrote that in 1878 – the heyday of cattle drive boomtowns in Kansas – Dodge City recorded just five homicides.

In a February 2004 essay that can be found on the Internet, Colorado writer Ryan McMaken noted that "All the big cattle towns of Kansas combined saw a total of 45 murders during the period of 1870-1885. Dodge City alone saw 15 people die violently from 1876-1885, an average of 1.5 per year." Wouldn't it be nice if the streets of today's American cities were all that safe?

During the time that Wyatt Earp was a town marshal and city policeman in places like Wichita and Dodge City, he was involved in just one fatal shooting; hardly the image portrayed in the television series about the legendary lawman.

There were two notable incidents in Old West lore that might be accurately described as wild shootouts, one occurring on September 7, 1876 in Northfield, Minnesota – not even three months after the battle of the Little Bighorn in Montana – and the other on October 5, 1892 in Coffeyville, Kansas.

The Northfield incident involved a gang of heavily armed outlaws led by Jesse and Frank James. Accompanied by Cole, Jim and Bob Younger and fellow robbers Bill Chadwell and Charlie Pitts, they attempted to rob the town's bank. But the good citizens of Northfield, suddenly aware that their bank was being robbed of *their* money, responded as good citizens of that era would: They armed themselves, or were already armed out of habit, and opened fire. When the shooting started, the notorious outlaw gang suddenly found themselves facing a hail of bullets in a town full of armed private citizens defending their community, in an era long before there were such notions as a "duty to retreat" and "civil liability" or "vigilante justice." Citizens of that era understood that they were ultimately responsible for their own safety, and even the safety of the community, and they frequently went armed in public, and with the rare exception of the Northfield raid, they lived in relative tranquility. Concealed carry opponents tend to overlook that kind of detail because it does not fit their agenda of citizen disarmament.

In the gun battle that erupted on the streets of Northfield, Miller and Chadwell were killed almost outright, while the Younger brothers were all wounded. The gang fled but within hours, it seemed the entire state of Minnesota was alerted to the outrage, and every citizen with a horse and gun was out looking for them. Eventually, near the town of Mankato, the gang split up with the Youngers and Pitts heading west, while Frank and Jesse managed to head west and south, eventually eluding the various posses.

Near the town of Madelia, Minnesota, the Younger brothers and Pitts were cornered in a gun battle. Pitts was shot dead, and the Youngers were all freshly wounded but survived and surrendered, and were subsequently sent to prison, after pleading guilty to murder so as to avoid being hanged. While it might be argued that the Youngers had acted stupidly, there were not crazy.

But what happened that day in Northfield sent a signal to outlaw gangs still operating in the West: Stay out of Minnesota. In that era, would-be desperados were of no mind to try their luck in the state that shot the James-Younger gang to pieces.

The Coffeyville incident occurred somewhat after the "Wild West" of big cattle drives and Indian wars in Kansas, but close enough so that local residents were still well aware of the need for personal protection even when one might be convinced "civilization" had arrived.

In this case, a gang led by Bob Dalton, with his brothers Emmett and Grat, plus Dick Broadwell and Bill Power, attempted to pull the nation's first daylight robbery of two banks simultaneously. According to some historic accounts, Bob Dalton was enamored with the prospect of "out-doing" the James gang. But when their plan went horribly wrong, shooting broke out and once again, armed citizens responded and in a flurry of gunfire, brought down all the robbers, who shot and killed some of the citizens. Only Emmett survived. Here, again, opponents of private gun ownership conveniently overlook the details of this incident.

But what do these historical anecdotes have to do with today's social environment?

In the real "Old West," and even in parts of today's "Modern West," there were and remain individuals who understand that violence does not erupt on a schedule and criminals do not make appointments in advance. Therefore, prudent people are, as the Boy Scout motto suggests, always prepared. This does not mean law-abiding, armed Americans get up every morning looking to fulfill some fantasy of heroism. Instead, they get up every morning determined that they will return home every night and sleep safely in their own beds.

Take, for example, the case of Ohio resident and sexual assault victim Cathy Lindsey, whose story was told by WEWS in Cleveland, carried on the Associated Press and eventually reported in the September 20, 2006 issue of *Gun Week*, a newspaper published by the Second Amendment Foundation that covers firearms-related news all over the country.

In the summer of 2006, Lindsey applied for an Ohio concealed carry license because of concerns that the two monsters who attacked her 23 years before, Richard Reed and Robert Hogsten, were being released from prison.

At the time she was attacked, Lindsey was the divorced mother of three children, attending college and working part time to support her young family. Then one night, three men broke into her Middletown residence, raped her repeatedly while holding a gun to her head, and then made her beg for her life and the lives of her children.

But her attackers did something incredibly stupid during the course of their vicious assault. They took turns wearing the same pillowcase over their heads, apparently thinking that this would prevent Lindsey from later identifying them.

After the rape, the trio left Lindsey alive and she drove to a hospital, the news services reported. She identified two of the rapists and police later arrested the third after Lindsey identified him in a lineup.

In the days leading up to the release of Hogsten and Reed from prison, Lindsey revealed that she was taking precautions against the possibility that either man could show up back in her neighborhood. Reed was originally a neighbor of Lindsey.

While Reed and Hogsten took plea bargains, the third rapist, Hogsten's brother, went to trial and was convicted. He was sentenced to a longer prison stretch and will not be eligible for parole until 2011.

Lindsey was not shy about her feelings in the days before their release when she spoke to a reporter.

"They're arrogant and violent and they can think of only one thing – revenge," she told the reporter. "I feel like a walking target. I walk down the street like I've got a bull's eye on me."

But today, this target can shoot back. A licensed practical nurse, Lindsey is driven to and from work by her husband, Michael, a corrections officer and military veteran who taught Cathy how to shoot. She reportedly is proficient with a revolver and his .45 ACP pistol. The couple filed for protective orders to keep both rapists at a distance.

The Buckeye Firearms Association, a grassroots gun rights organization in Ohio, observed on its website at the time that cases like Lindsey's are exactly what their campaign to pass the state's concealed carry statute was all about.

If the Old West taught us anything as a society, it was that individualism had its virtues. America, unlike any other culture in world history, was largely founded on the labors of individuals and individualists; people who left the confines of civilization to first explore and then settle a vast new continent. In their wake came the inventors and entrepreneurs – people like Henry Ford, Samuel Colt and Oliver Winchester – who at first risked whatever personal fortunes they had, and then made fortunes.

But always first were the individuals who did not simply risk their fortunes, but also their lives as they moved west, away from the early settlements to the new frontier. They learned a truth that, despite society's best efforts and the finest intentions of rank-and-file law enforcement, when trouble comes calling, it is up to the individual citizen to deal with it. Whether the nearest lawman was two days away on the prairie, or five minutes away after calling 9-1-1, by the time they arrive, the crime is typically over and what remains is to handle the aftermath.

The real Old West taught us something else: In the absence of law enforcement, private citizens must act immediately to defend themselves and protect innocent lives. Outlaws were dealt with, often harshly, and that created a deterrent factor that today's jumbled, perhaps irreparably broken legal system is woefully unable to provide.

Cops and Kids

What about the argument that police would be made more unsafe by concealed carry? That certainly has not proven to be the case in state after state where concealed carry statutes have been passed.

A study by University of Georgia researcher David B. Mustard, writing in the October 2001 *Journal of Law and Economics* suggests that right-to-carry statutes have not increased the danger to police officers.

In his report entitled "The Impact of Gun Laws on Police Deaths," Mustard studied data from 1984-1996 to learn how right-to-carry laws and waiting periods affect the number of police fatalities. His opinion: "Allowing law-abiding citizens to carry concealed weapons does not endanger the lives of officers and may help reduce their risk of being killed."

Barely a month after Mustard published his report, in November 2001, the National Association of Chiefs of Police released the results of a national survey that showed over 60 percent of the nation's sheriffs and police chiefs support concealed carry by private citizens. That survey polled more than 23,000 top cops, asking this question: "Do you agree that a national concealed handgun permit would reduce rates of violent crime as recent studies in some states already reflected?" Sixty-two percent of the respondents said "Yes," according to the NACOP report.

Street cops have figured out that armed career criminals do not go through the process of obtaining gun permits. The primary reason for this would be that they would be identified during the screening process and their applications would be rejected, quite possibly at the same time they found themselves being arrested. Criminals just carry their guns illegally, putting a lie to the notion that one more gun law might be the answer to violent crime. If thousands of existing federal, state and local gun laws have not yet prevented a single crime – and there is no evidence that they have – then passing yet one more law, or preventing passage of a law that puts citizens on equal footing with predatory criminals will not provide the watershed panacea that gun rights opponents seem always to be looking for.

Adding legally-armed citizens to the mix does not make things worse, because such people are not in the habit of shooting police officers. There are documented cases where armed citizens have come to the aid of police or other crime victims.

Don't take the authors' word for it. Instead, pay attention to what H. Sterling Burnett, senior policy analyst for the National Center for Policy Analysis wrote in May 2000, as Texas observed five years of concealed carry by its residents. By that time, more than 200,000 Texans had been licensed to carry, and Burnett observed that they were "far less likely to commit a serious crime than the average citizen."

"Many predicted that minor incidents would escalate into bloody shootouts if Texas passed a concealed-carry law," Burnett wrote. "That prediction was dead wrong."

What about the perceived threat to children? That seems largely to be a myth invented as part of the anti-self-defense playbook rhetoric, tossed out for consumption by an ignorant press to be repeated in print and on the airwaves as though it was credible.

There is not a single concealed carry statute in the United States that allows children to carry guns. The majority of these statutes put the minimum age at 21 years for even applying for a carry permit or license, and it is rare to find a licensed citizen involved in an illegal shooting. The few exceptions wind up being prosecuted, and most assuredly lose their carry permits, if not their gun rights.

For example, two years after Michigan passed its concealed carry reform statute in the 1990s, authorities in St. Clair County, provided a text book example of how officials all over the country frequently reassess their initial fears after they've seen such laws at work for a while. There, according to a report carried at the time in the Port Huron *Times Herald*, more than 2,500 gun permits had been issued and there had been virtually no trouble with legally-armed citizens.

Yet self-defense opponents consistently argue that such laws would arm gang-bangers and other juvenile criminals simply by putting more guns on the street. It is a preposterous argument not supported by any credible data.

Youthful gang members cannot legally purchase handguns, and cannot legally carry them. They obtain their firearms through illicit means, either from street acquaintances, illicit sales, and burglaries or from family or "friends." None of these transactions or acquisitions is legal, and gun control advocates know it.

Yet they would prevent, through emotional rhetoric and political pressure, law-abiding citizens from having firearms. While their arguments might be supported by police administrators, whose opinions are often reflections of the anti-gun mayors who hire them, rank-and-file cops are not so quick to dismiss a citizen's right of self-defense.

During the debate on concealed carry legislation in Wisconsin a few years ago, Milwaukee Police Association President Bradley DeBraska testified in favor of the bill, reportedly stating, "The good law-abiding citizens deserve every opportunity to defend themselves against persons committing heinous crimes."

Wisconsin lawmakers twice passed concealed carry legislation, but it was twice vetoed by anti-gun Gov. Jim Doyle, a liberal Democrat.

The Deterrent Factor

Much has been written on both sides of the debate about whether the presence of legally armed citizens contributes to or erodes public safety. Remember, we are discussing citizens who are legally armed, not recidivist violent predatory criminals who carry guns illegally. The problem with opponents of self-defense and concealed carry is that they seem to make no distinction between the two, and instead presume that all armed people have criminal intent, and subliminally portray them as such in their rhetoric.

But in the 1980s, an academic researcher named John Lott, then at the University of Chicago, turned the world upside down with a landmark study that asserted states and even communities with higher rates of armed citizens had lower rates of violent crime. Lott examined years' worth of crime statistics and data, and not just from a handful of selected states to form a "cross section" of the country, but from every county in every state of the country. Such an undertaking had never been attempted in the past, and when his work was completed – with the participation of David Mustard – Lott's conclusions both horrified and infuriated gun control proponents from coast to coast.

The Lott-Mustard study was the foundation for a 1998 book, *More Guns = Less Crime*. It ignited a new and furious debate about the relevance of firearms in a modern society, and their value as a "deterrent factor" against violent criminals. Naturally, Lott's work was criticized and openly attacked by anti-gun organizations and researchers most often linked to such groups.

But Lott's book became a powerful revelation for gun rights advocates and provided solid arguments supporting passage of concealed carry statutes in many states.

Lott had been preceded by another study, done by Prof. Gary Kleck, a criminologist at Florida State University. His data suggested that American citizens use firearms for personal defense perhaps 2.5 million times each year, and in most cases a shot is not even fired.

The prospect of deterring crime appears to be on the minds of citizens in states where concealed carry is legal. In Arkansas, where an estimated 50,000 residents have obtained their carry permits according to a December 28, 2006 report carried on KATV in Little Rock that quoted data from the state police, twice as many people had signed up for concealed carry classes in 2006 as had taken the course in 2005.

People interviewed for that report noted that citizens had obtained carry licenses because they were "afraid of being carjacked, afraid of being abducted…being broke into their houses, cars, whatever." Many of those people are single females.

A cornerstone to the "deterrent factor" is when police reacting to a justifiable shooting, tell reporters that they hope such an act "sends a message to other robbers."

On November 22, 2006, a thug entered Ray and Wendell's Barber Shop in Cleveland, Ohio with gun in hand. He ordered everyone to give up their wallets, jewelry and watches. But the robber turned his attention away from his crime long enough for shop owner Ray Williams to draw his licensed, concealed handgun and open fire.

The robber dropped his gun and ran out the door, only to be arrested by police later.

Williams told WEWS news in Cleveland that he fired to protect his business and his customers.

Incidents like this cause would-be robbers to reconsider their activities, or at least their intended targets.

However, throughout the debate on whether concealed carry may have some community benefit, or be of benefit to society at large, cases like the barber shop incident are systematically avoided and ignored by opponents of self-defense.

Perhaps the biggest problem with the Deterrent Factor is that it is impossible to gauge accurately. Or is it? While it is impossible to provide a single example of a crime that was prevented by a gun control statute – though there are thousands of crimes that were not prevented by restrictive gun laws – Prof. John Lott's data tends to show that violent crime is less likely to occur in regions of high gun ownership.

This may be no more vivid than in a comparison the authors did between two similarly-sized cities, Milwaukee, Wisconsin and Seattle, Washington in early 2006 when the debate was raging in Wisconsin over concealed carry.

Washington is the smallest western state at 71,303 square miles, yet it is larger than Wisconsin's 65,503 square miles. Both states have large, and largely liberal, urban population centers while they also boast thousands of square miles of rural farm and forest land.

In 2005, Milwaukee, a city of approximately 583,600 residents – where it is illegal to carry a concealed handgun – there were 110 homicides. That same year in Seattle, a city of approximately 571,500 people, there were a mere 27 murders. In surrounding unincorporated King County, Washington there were less than a dozen criminal slayings that year.

Washington residents can carry concealed handguns and a lot of them do, more than 240,000 at last count. It is, on a per capita basis, the fifth leading state for the number of licensed armed citizens among its overall population of any state in the union. The Evergreen State has had a concealed carry statute for more than 50 years and a state constitutional right to bear arms that is rock solid. An armed Washington citizen might look at the murder statistics in Milwaukee, shake his or her head and wonder why Wisconsin's citizens are treated as though they are "second class" and not allowed the means to defend themselves.

Overall in Washington, violent crime is comparatively low, and crimes involving firearms that are reported frequently involves gang and drug activity, recidivist criminals who cannot legally possess firearms, and juvenile thugs. All of the gun control laws combined have not kept firearms out of the hands of these individuals, and experts concede that even if gun ownership were suddenly banned, the criminal element would still be armed.

Yet knowing this, anti-gunners adamantly refuse to acknowledge that citizens have a right to defend themselves, and that when they fight back it sends a message to other would-be criminals. Sometimes, the deterrent factor is specific, and even if criminals are not discouraged from continuing their crime streak, at least they know enough to leave armed citizens alone.

The Case in Wilmette

Actor and NRA President Charlton Heston, who taught us the difference between making a mistake and deliberately telling a lie, may be remembered by citizens of upscale Wilmette, Illinois for having grown up there and attending that community's New Trier High School.

But Wilmette has another claim on history, not nearly as appealing but certainly more colorful, perhaps even notorious.

Many years ago, Wilmette became one of a handful of communities to ban handguns. It was, one Chicago newspaper editorialist admitted, largely symbolic. In the "new" America where people are beginning to fight back, that ban also became a cause for public scorn and ridicule after an incident that unfolded the night of December 29, 2003 and held headlines for weeks to follow.

A habitual criminal named Morio Billings chose the night of December 28 to burglarize a home owned by restaurateur Hale DeMar. On his first nocturnal visit, Billings had taken several items including a set of house keys. Much has been written about Billings, not only by the authors but by others, including Robert VerBruggen, writing for *Reason*. VerBruggen noted that Billings, driving a stolen BMWX5 sport utility vehicle had been staying with his mother in nearby Chicago. He was AWOL from the Army at the time, and in violation of probation.

Apparently figuring he'd made such an easy score on his first visit, Billings went right back to the same house the following evening. This time, however, things went decidedly less smooth for the 31-year-old burglar who had already been arrested a half-dozen times that year for residential burglary, auto theft, driving with a suspended license, receiving stolen property and possession of a controlled substance.

This time, DeMar was home and armed, with a handgun, a .38 Special Smith & Wesson he had owned for years and reportedly had never before so much as loaded. Instead, he had kept the gun, and another revolver, locked in a safe. DeMar, fearing for the safety of his children who were staying with him following a separation with his wife, shot Billings and wounded him. When the police arrived, the homeowner suddenly found himself in trouble for having violated the handgun ban, and for not having a current, valid Illinois Firearms Owners Identification Card in his possession.

The case exploded across the national talk radio airwaves and became an overnight sensation with gun rights chat groups, all of which claimed this was a text book example of gun laws that punish the wrong people. That DeMar was facing any kind of charge at all outraged the public. Outside of Illinois, and even in most areas outside Chicago, the ridiculousness of the symbolic handgun ban passed so many years before suddenly became a sharply focused issue among Americans who had had enough.

Amid protests and bad publicity that was made even worse when DeMar was criticized for not having changed the locks on his home fast enough following the previous night's burglary, Wilmette Police Chief George R. Carpenter put his foot firmly in his mouth when he said DeMar put himself at unnecessary risk "on multiple levels."

Carpenter's rhetoric reached the point of hypocrisy when he told reporters, "It would be unfortunate and potentially tragic to conclude from this incident that Wilmette families would be safer if they keep a handgun in their homes. The opposite is true. Wilmette families are in greater danger if they keep a handgun at home." The nation's gun owners quickly demanded to know whether Carpenter kept a handgun at his own home. The question was never answered.

In the end, DeMar was fined $750 for having violated the handgun ban. He was also initially charged for not having an FOID card, which had expired in 2000, but faced with overwhelming public sympathy for DeMar and no small amount of anger over the technical violation, the Cook County state's attorney dropped that charge a few weeks later, and also determined quickly that DeMar had acted in self-defense.

There is a post script to this story and it illustrates what is so terribly wrong with the legal and political systems that punish homeowners like Hale DeMar for defending their homes and families from people like Morio Billings.

In August 2004, Billings pulled a seven-year prison sentence for the DeMar home burglary. But he was released after having served less than three years.

Was he out on good behavior? You be the judge. According to the *Chicago Tribune*, just eleven days after his prison release, Billings once again found himself under arrest, for robbing a house...in Wilmette. This time around, he had taken a 2004 Volvo parked in a driveway, plus a purse and keys.

It was not, however, Hale DeMar's house.

CHAPTER 3

Stopping Rape and Abuse

Rape. The mere mention of the word will justifiably make most women feel uneasy, for themselves, their daughters, their mothers, sisters and friends.

Of all the violent crimes one can commit, rape is perhaps the most personal, but in a cold, vicious, ruthless sense. Rape is not about passion. It is brutal, terrifying, personally and – for many victims – spiritually agonizing, physically and emotionally degrading and a crime from which some victims never recover. It is the act of a person for whom, according to some people, there can be no earthly redemption. In prison, rapists find themselves on the social scale only slightly above child molesters.

With the onset of the AIDS (Acquired Immune Deficiency Syndrome) epidemic, rape can also literally be a death sentence for the victim, should the AIDS virus be transmitted.

According to the Rape, Abuse and Incest National Network (www.rainn.org) a sexual assault occurs every two and a half minutes somewhere in the United States. One in six women may find themselves victims of sexual assault, and one in every 33 men may suffer the same degradation.

According to the National Crime Victimization Survey, in 2005 there were 191,670 reported rapes, attempted rapes or sexual assaults.

About 44 percent of rape victims are under age 18, according to the RAINN website, and 80 percent are under age 30.

There is good news of a sort. Since 1993, according to RAINN, rape has declined by more than 69 percent.

There is better news. Because rape victims are fighting back, sometimes rapists never make it to jail. Occasionally, they don't even make it to the hospital, and there are not a lot of crocodile tears shed over their loss.

Serial killers Theodore Robert Bundy and Gary Ridgway were rapists who took their monstrous crimes to the extreme. Bundy raped and murdered his way from the Pacific Northwest to Florida, where he was captured, tried and executed in the electric chair. This after he had been arrested in Utah and convicted of kidnapping, and escaping from jail twice in Colorado, where he was on trial for murder. Ridgway, the infamous "Green River Killer" of Washington State, will rot in prison for the rest of his unnatural life for his barbaric crimes. It may never be known how many women Bundy and Ridgway truly killed, but at least they will never kill again.

But like all predators, Bundy and Ridgway will be replaced by other monsters. That is one reason why an increasing number of women, many singles who have never been married or single mothers who may be divorced or legally separated, or are effectively "single" because their husbands may be deployed overseas in the military, are arming themselves.

One wonders even now, years after Bundy and Ridgway committed their murderous killing sprees, what might have been the outcome had just one of their victims been armed. Bundy and Ridgway, like most serial killers, did not use guns. They strangled their victims or, as Bundy did on occasion, bludgeoned them, and Ridgway – in a chilling confession to King County Sheriff's investigators – said he chose strangulation as his method of killing his victims because he was "good at it." Had just one of the 49 women Ridgway murdered, or the eight Bundy was known to have killed in Washington State in the 1970s, been armed and had been able to use her gun, a lot of those women just might be alive today.

Where do such predators come from? Bundy came from a middle class neighborhood near the University of Puget Sound campus in north Tacoma, Washington, although his childhood was rather bizarre. Born out of wedlock, he grew up believing that his mother was his older sister, and he and his mother lived with his grandparents for a time, before moving from Philadelphia, Pennsylvania to Tacoma,

Washington.

Ridgway was born in Salt Lake City but his working class family moved to the town of Auburn, Washington, several miles south of Seattle, when he was a youngster. His mother was reportedly domineering, and even as a young man he exhibited an odd obsession with prostitutes. Ridgway was married twice and was a father, yet of all serial killers, he appears to have been the most prolific, eventually confessing to 48 murders.

Both Bundy and Ridgway not only were killers, they were necrophiliacs, having sex with the dead bodies of their victims.

Most sexual predators do not achieve the notoriety of a Bundy or Ridgway because the degree of their depravity doesn't approach that level, but they do come from neighborhoods all over the country. But simply because someone is not a Bundy or Ridgway does not mean that he may be any less dangerous to the community at large, and especially threatening to an intended victim.

However, instead of cowering in fear of such individuals and waiting in dark corners or closets while praying for the police to arrive in time, many Americans take control of their fears and act decisively.

Such might be said for Lisa Pelland of Santa Fe, New Mexico. Her frightening experience was detailed in the pages of the Albuquerque *Journal* on April 19, 2002, about 36 hours after she confronted a man named Jay P. Medina. Both Pelland and Medina were 42 years old at the time, but they apparently had never met.

What Medina was doing outside Pelland's bedroom window on the night of April 17 could lead one to draw several conclusions, all of them bad. Pelland heard noises outside her window at about 11 p.m., the newspaper account explained, so she prudently grabbed her handgun before going outside to investigate. That's where she discovered Medina, stacking bricks on the ground outside her window.

Medina had no criminal background, but at the time he was estranged from his wife, Dena Ashley-Medina, who had coincidentally filed for a protection order against her husband only two days prior to his late-night confrontation with Pelland. The protection order was sought after Medina allegedly had a physical confrontation with his wife, during which he reportedly threatened to burn down her house and destroy everything before he killed her. He never got the chance to follow through on those threats. Of course, Pelland had no way of knowing about Medina's alleged violent outburst against his estranged wife, or the fact that Ashley-Medina had filed for the protection order 48 hours earlier.

Jump ahead two days to the yard outside Pelland's home, where she has just met Medina for the first and last time of his life. Pelland told investigating police that she yelled at the stranger to stay away from her, but instead he began advancing. Perhaps thinking to change his attitude, Pelland then warned the man that she was armed, but he kept coming. He "said something that caused her to be in fear," the newspaper account explained, and at that point, Pelland raised her gun and fired. Medina died at the scene. Responding police officers discovered that Medina was not armed.

Under New Mexico's self-defense statute a private citizen may use lethal force "…in the necessary defense of his life, his family or his property, or in necessarily defending against any unlawful action directed against himself, his wife or family" and "when committed in the lawful defense of himself or of another and when there is a reasonable ground to believe a design exists to commit a felony or to do some great personal injury against such person or another, and there is imminent danger that the design will be accomplished…"

Not that Pelland understood any of this at the time, but the New Mexico statute – like similar justifiable homicide laws in other states – is grounded in what is generically called "the reasonable man doctrine." That is, a person may take an action that "any reasonable person" would take, faced with similar circumstances, knowing what he/she knew at the time. It became quickly evident that what Pelland knew at the time was that her life was in grave danger, and that the threat was imminent. Indeed, the threat was just a few feet away, aggressively moving toward her.

Hours later, she told a reporter, "It was completely horrible, my life was in danger."

The newspaper also interviewed Pelland's neighbor, Ted Peña, who heard both gunshots. Another woman, identified as Priscilla Quintana, told the newspaper, "I don't blame her for what she did. Who knows, the guy could have been trying to get in her bedroom. I wouldn't want anyone looking in my window."

Two and a half months later, a grand jury reviewed the facts of the case, and ruled that Pelland's actions were justified. According to a report in the July 3, 2002 edition of the Santa Fe *New Mexican*, the Pelland case was "screened and staffed internally by most of the senior attorneys within the district attorney's office." Translation: The best and brightest in the First Judicial District Attorney's office examined Pelland's case. It is highly unlikely that if there had been anything questionable in the facts of this case that it would have not been found under such scrutiny.

At this writing, only one magazine – *Women & Guns*, published by the Second Amendment Foundation – devoted itself to women who have found that firearms are not evil, but equalizers, perhaps even emancipators. From personal protection to plinking, sport shooting and hunting to education, *Women & Guns* caters to women who have decided that they are ultimately responsible for their own safety.

Some of the top female writers and firearms experts have written for the magazine, sharing their experience and knowledge. A typical edition of the magazine carries columns by Defensive Strategies expert Lyn Bates and attorney Karen McNutt, who writes about legal affairs from a woman's perspective in "Legally Speaking." Nationally-recognized firearms instructor Gila Hayes is a frequent contributor. This publication is unique in a field where most women's magazines tend to caution against owning guns or avoid the subject altogether.

But don't many of the pop culture experts warn women that guns are dangerous? Shouldn't guns only be carried by police and soldiers, or kept under lock and key if not removed completely from the home?

Perhaps the best authority on that subject would be someone like Adrian Rodricka Cathey, but alas at this writing, Mr. Cathey is not available to share his personal perspective on firearms kept by women for personal protection. He's dead, and by all accounts of his activities, it might be said that he was asking for it.

The UNCC Rapist

Twenty-six-year-old Adrian Cathey was a serial rapist who terrified the neighborhood around the University of North Carolina's Charlotte, N.C. campus in the fall of 1998, to the point that the hysteria created by his nocturnal activities even made the national news. His criminal record included five felony arrests (three of those for sexual assault) and when authorities finally were able to begin sorting out his horrific crime spree, he was found to have committed four rapes and some burglaries in the community near the university in the weeks leading up to his sudden departure from life early on the morning of November 16, 1998.

This despicable, dangerous human garbage was the subject of essays by writers Robert Waters ("Another Thug Done Gone"), author of *The Best Defense: True Stories of Intended Victims Who Defended Themselves with a Firearm* and F. Paul Valone, at the time president of Grass Roots North Carolina, and now its executive director. Valone wrote about the Cathey case in an Op-Ed piece that appeared in the Charlotte *Observer* on October 6, 1999. Neither of these gentlemen pulled any punches in discussing Cathey, and why should they? He was the epitome of evil.

The Charlotte *Observer*, in reporting the abrupt conclusion of Cathey's crime spree, noted that the "unsolved burglaries and a subsequent string of sexual assaults near the University of North Carolina's Charlotte campus had female residents there fearing for their safety. It was that heightened sense of awareness, and an armed woman, that helped prevent yet another attack."

According to the Charlotte *Observer*, Cathey was responsible for a rape on January 8, 1998 when he broke into a home by "jimmying" the lock. About seven weeks later, on the night of February 20, he was the knife-wielding rapist who broke into a condominium and assaulted two female roommates after gaining entry through a sliding glass door. On October 19, he got into another apartment through a sliding glass door and raped the female occupant at knife-point.

But then came his misadventure of November 16. Evidently, Cathey didn't read newspapers or listen to the television, because his rape spree had the community terrified and it was no secret that many women in the community were taking precautions, including obtaining firearms.

It was at about 3 a.m. when he once again gained entry to an off-campus apartment at the Lake Point Apartments near the university, moving through the house to find a co-ed that he had, according to Waters' account, been stalking. He apparently figured to find the woman asleep.

But Cathey's luck had run out. As he attempted to rape the young woman, she reached into a nightstand, pulled out a handgun and pulled the trigger. Adrian Rodricka Cathey managed to stagger all the way out into the parking lot of the apartment complex before he hit the ground. That's where his corpse was found by the police a short time later.

The shooting was ruled a justifiable homicide, and local authorities – to say nothing of the college community at large – heaved a sigh of relief that one more bacteria had been removed from gene pool.

In retrospect, author Waters asked some questions that remain valid today after any dangerous predator's life is cut short:

Would the UNCC co-ed who killed the serial rapist have been better off without firearm?

Would society have benefited had she not had a weapon with which to defend herself?

Should she have waited on the police to come to her aid, as most anti-gunners claim is the proper procedure when threatened?

Would she have been able to defend herself if she'd been required to keep a trigger lock on her gun?

How many future victims were saved by the armed co-ed?

How would you answer? Perhaps the best answers might come from the 72-year-old woman whom the Colorado Springs, Colorado *Gazette* described in its February 7, 2001 edition as having "the presence of mind and just plain pluck" to have used a gun to shoot a man who had broken into her house the previous November.

Colorado Fights Back

Anthony Peralez, 40, was someone that people in the Colorado Springs area really wanted to meet, especially if they were police officers. Standing 5 feet, 8 inches tall and weighing 145 pounds, Peralez had terrorized the community since September 12, 1999 when a 51-year-old woman was attacked, kidnapped and raped.

On August 6, 2000 he was back at it again, raping and brutally beating a 74-year-old woman and that crime was followed less than a month later with a vicious September 2 attack on a 56-year-old woman, according to accounts in the *Gazette*.

But on November 18, Peralez' string of crimes came to an end when he discovered about a nano-second too late that his final intended victim had plans of her own that did not include being brutalized. To his surprise, this "plucky" 72-year-old pulled a .38-caliber revolver and shot him twice.

Peralez managed to get to his car and speed away as well as anyone gushing blood from two bullet wounds might manage. He was eventually stopped and arrested by the police, and thanks to DNA analysis, his involvement in the earlier crimes was well established by the time he went on trial in front of a less-than-sympathetic judge.

Charged with 54 counts, Peralez was convicted on 51 of the charges and he will never get out of prison. The judge sentenced him to an astonishing 868 years behind bars.

One might think that this kind of harsh justice would send a message to the criminal element, but apparently Nathan Victor Melikidse wasn't listening. On the morning of December 30, 2001, the drunken Melikidse broke into the Boulder, Colorado home of a family, tying up the parents and then raping their teenage daughter.

Whatever else Melikidse, originally from California, happens to be, he is one incredibly lucky individual; "lucky" in the sense that the father of the young woman he had just raped did not realize, at the time that he was able to turn the tables on this animal, what had just happened to his daughter.

Gripping newspaper accounts in the Boulder *Daily Camera* revealed how Melikidse awakened his victims at 5:30 a.m. and then pulled a gun when the father answered the door. The gunman tied both the husband and wife with tape and left them in the living room, then after disabling some, but not all, of the telephones, he sexually assaulted the 18-year-old daughter in another room.

Accounts of the incident differ in separate newspaper reports, but the *Daily Camera* ultimately reported, during its coverage of Melikidse's trial, that the father managed to scoot his chair to where he retrieved his cell phone and was able to call the sheriff. Subsequently, the father got free, apparently by asking for some water, and he grabbed a loaded shotgun and turned it on Melikidse, holding him until lawmen arrived.

At trial, a psychiatrist testified that Melikidse, according to the newspaper account, suffered "from attention-deficit hyperactivity disorder and post-traumatic stress disorder from an abusive childhood" and he was also "drug dependant." The psychiatrist also testified, the newspaper said, that Melikidse had "poor self-esteem and a sense of failure."

There is ample reason to shed tears in this case, but not for Melikidse, who was sentenced to 38 years in prison. He will not get out until he is 57 years old. Instead shed a tear for the family he terrorized and especially weep for the young woman he viciously attacked. This traumatic incident will haunt that family for the rest of their lives.

In a letter to the court, the father wrote, "Had I known at the last moment, when I held the defendant at gunpoint, that my daughter had been assaulted, I would also be a murderer – because I would not have let him live."

The attack caused a strain in the marriage, the newspaper mentioned.

But it was the mother's letter to the court that truly explained the evil that this miserable wretch had done.

"The defendant wanted to know the most valuable thing we had in the house," the mother recalled in her note. "He found it – one of our daughters. He stole her innocence and dignity in a most repugnant fashion."

Yet it is remarkable that with cases like these, there are still critics of a statute passed in the Centennial State that allows homeowners to shoot intruders. Sneeringly called the Colorado "Make My Day" law – capitalizing on a line in one of the "Dirty Harry" movies – this statute was hailed by law-abiding citizens who still believe that their home is their castle, and that they should not be expected to meekly surrender their possessions, or their lives, in the interest of political correctness.

The anti-gun Denver *Post* editorialized against expanding the scope of the "castle doctrine" law to include being able to act in self-defense while in their cars or businesses. The newspaper attempted to portray this law as potentially providing legal cover for gang-bangers and other miscreants who commit drive-by shootings and other violent crimes. The rhetoric was strikingly similar to the doomsday predictions tossed around the political landscape by opponents of concealed carry laws, and it is already well-established how accurate such predictions have been.

Striking Back at Abusers

Women in America have more to fear than rape at the hands of a stranger. Far more common are sexual assault at the hands of an abusive mate or ex-mate. Abusive relationships have no real winners, but some people lose a lot more than others. For many female victims of abusive relationships – and lest anyone think this is just a one-sided type of crime, many men have found themselves victimized by abusive mates as well – when it comes time to fight back, an increasing number of women have decided that their lives, and the lives of their children, are valuable enough to protect with whatever force necessary.

There is nothing dramatic about it. You do not hear a victorious musical background to the scenes of mayhem. And for the victims who defend themselves, there may be far less a sense of victory than simple survival.

In late December 2006, a Pembroke, North Carolina woman identified in press accounts as Dixie Oxendine was so terrified of her ex-boyfriend, Ertle Ray Bell Jr., that she had purchased a handgun just before Christmas.

According to the *Robesonian* newspaper in Lumberton, for which Oxendine worked as a newspaper delivery driver, the three-month relationship between Oxendine, 38, and the much-younger 24-year-old Bell had soured months before. In April, he reportedly tried to run her off the road.

Then, just days before Christmas, Bell called Oxendine's home and threatened to kill her. Oxendine did what many women in such circumstances do. She purchased a handgun for protection and made plans to file for a protection order after the holidays. Bell did not give her that much time.

On Christmas day, as Oxendine was delivering newspapers with her nephew, identified as Michael Brandon Dial, Bell showed up and blocked her truck with his car.

Walking up to the truck, Bell told Oxendine to step out and talk. He evidently meant it to be a heated discussion, because he was armed with a rifle. He wanted Oxendine to leave with him, and she refused. That kind of trip far too often winds up being one-way.

Instead, obviously fearing for her life, she got out of her truck and closed her eyes, and according to the newspaper account, raised the handgun in Bell's direction and started shooting. Bell took a round in the head and four more in the upper torso. He died at the scene.

If Bell is roasting in Hell, he has company in the form of Ricky Tillman, who never lived to enjoy his 32nd birthday. His miserable existence ended on Monday, May 28, 2001.

Having stalked his ex-girlfriend for some eight months, according to accounts carried in the Atlanta *Journal-Constitution* and by the Associated Press, Tillman set in motion a series of events that would end with him lying dead at a Dalton, Georgia truck stop several hours after kidnapping 38-year-old Alisha Cox from the Nashville, Tennessee home of her mother, whom he shot to death on the front porch.

Tillman and Cox had dated for some two years prior to their breakup in September 2000.

On May 28 at about 7 a.m., Cox was visiting her mother, Sylvia Butts. She saw Tillman's tractor trailer truck cab pull into her mother's driveway and asked her mom to tell Tillman that she was not there. Mrs. Butts went outside to speak with Tillman, and he shot her four times at point blank range with a 9mm handgun. One of the bullets went through her shoulder and punctured her heart, and she fell dead.

Hearing the shots that killed her mother, Cox reportedly leaped out of an upstairs window, fracturing her back when she landed hard on the concrete driveway. Severely injured, she could not outrun Tillman, who forced Cox to his truck cab, tied her up and headed south to Georgia's Whitefield County, a drive that took about four hours. It was when he pulled into the Pilot Travel Center truck stop, because Cox had been vomiting, that the incident played out to its grim finale.

When Tillman went inside to get something to control the vomiting, published accounts said, Cox managed to get free and leave the truck. Tillman came out of the store, spotted Cox and made some sort of aggressive moves, and that's when Cox, using the gun that had hours before been used to murder her mother, shot and killed Tillman.

The first of three rounds slammed into his chest and through his heart, a wound ironically similar to the one that killed Mrs. Butts hours before. The second and third rounds hit him in the lower leg and in the foot.

Georgia law enforcement authorities declined to press charges, instead calling the demise of Ricky Tillman a justifiable homicide.

Paper Protection

A story that appeared in the Sunday, January 21, 2007 edition of the Kennebec *Journal* detailed some of the problems of domestic violence and noted that protection orders "do not guarantee safety."

Under federal law and statutes in many states, individuals served with protection orders may not purchase or possess firearms. The story in the Kennebec *Journal* noted that Kate Faragher Houton, a community educator with the Family Violence Project, an arm of the Maine Coalition to End Domestic Violence, acknowledged that protection orders "don't always work to enhance safety…sometimes they can escalate the abuse of the offender."

The story, again quoting Faragher Houghton, also noted that "national studies show that about 50 percent of offenders abide by the terms of a protection order."

So, what about the other 50 percent, the offenders who do not abide a protection order and come after their victims?

From that realm emerge people like William Franklin Lewis, 46, an Alabama man who evidently did not get the message when his wife divorced him in November 1999, and after months of harassment took out a protective court order, according to an account in the May 30, 2001 edition of the Mobile *Register*.

In a story headlined "Woman Defends Herself after Courts and EPO's (sic) Fail," the tale of William Lewis and his former wife, Lori, grimly underscore just how ineffective a piece of paper can be against someone determined to break the rules.

On the night of May 28, following what the newspaper described as "months of escalating conflict," Lewis showed up at his former wife's home. It was the last in a series of remarkably stupid moves, having pushed her into filing three separate harassment complaints the previous March, and being arrested and charged with stalking in April. Now, out on $5,000 bail, Lewis showed up on his wife's back porch and attacked her, and tried to shoot her. He missed. She didn't.

There was, according to the newspaper, quite a scuffle during which Lori Lewis suffered "cuts and bruises" before managing to break away to her bedroom, where she grabbed her handgun. With her ex-husband in pursuit, she turned and fired. At 1:07 a.m. the following morning, William Lewis was pronounced dead. The ordeal was over.

Out of this tragedy came a wry and understated observation from a Foley police lieutenant identified as Richard Springsteen.

"She was trying to calm him down," he was quoted as stating. "I don't think it was working too well."

Many states have provisions in their concealed carry statutes that allow for the emergency issuance of a carry permit or license in cases where someone is in fear of immediate danger. Though they are not often utilized, the mechanism does exist so that in addition to having a firearm in the home for protection, someone in genuine fear for her or his safety can obtain a carry license to be armed outside the home.

While social agencies, and social "do-gooders" will almost uniformly argue against arming one's self against what appears to be a serious threat of grave bodily harm or even death, many Americans, and particularly women, are increasingly taking such advice with the proverbial grain of salt.

They need only look at cases like those involving Lisa Pelland in Santa Fe and Lori Lewis in Mobile, or think about the likes of Adrian Cathey, Anthony Peralez, Nathan Victor Melikidse, Gary Ridgway or Theodore Bundy showing up in their neighborhoods to clarify the issue of self-defense, and put concerns about "more guns in the community" in their proper perspective.

CHAPTER 4

'Arm Yourselves'

Something remarkable happened in a political and social sense on January 24, 2001 in South Carolina. It was remarkable not only for the occurrence, but that it happened at all in a country wherein politics seems steeped in political correctness.

That was the day that then-South Carolina Attorney General Charlie Condon essentially declared an open season on home invaders. In what amounted to a legal milestone that might have given prosecutors in a state like New York or New Jersey a sudden onset of heartburn, Mr. Condon advised all solicitors, sheriffs and police chiefs in the state that citizens who used force to defend their homes would not be arrested or prosecuted.

On his website at the time, Condon announced that he had sent a memorandum to all of those law enforcement chiefs and prosecutors explaining bluntly, "As Chief Prosecutor of South Carolina, I am today declaring open season on home invaders. That season is year-round. Citizens protecting their homes who use force even deadly force will be fully safeguarded under the law of this State and subject to no arrest, charge or prosecution. In South Carolina, would-be intruders should now hear this: invade a home and invite a bullet."

Condon said the reason behind his announcement was a rash of home invasions that had been carried out by gang members "and other criminals." In one of those crimes, the homeowner had defended himself with a sword.

The highly unusual, and politically explosive move stunned some people, and made others happy. In his message, Condon noted that South Carolina case law "gives iron-clad protection to the citizen in safeguarding his or her home. Inside the citizen's home, there are no legal technicalities for the criminal to rely on."

While American citizens have begun fighting back, pushing their lawmakers to overturn laws that force them to retreat while adopting statutes that either create or strengthen concealed carry and self-defense statutes, it is rare that a public official, and especially the chief law enforcement officer of a state, would make such a declaration.

Three months later, Condon announced that he would "re-think" his position, based on reaction to a case in which a woman identified as Lisa Gant fatally stabbed her 39-year-old boyfriend after he had smashed through her front door. Gant had been released on February 26 under the Condon policy, but it created more than a few raised eyebrows.

Not that the dead man was a martyr. According to published reports at the time, Gant and Brock had been lovers, and Gant had born a child fathered by Brock, while he was married to a woman living in Texas. The account of what happened fits the definition of domestic violence.

According to the April 2, 2001 edition of the *Daily Gamecock*, the University of South Carolina newspaper, the fatal February 17 incident began in an argument over money for the child. Brock reportedly slapped Gant and put her in a headlock before she managed to break free and push Brock, who reportedly weighed 300 pounds, out of her apartment in Waterloo.

Brock forced his way back inside, and Gant grabbed a kitchen knife. She stabbed Brock in the chest, and then called 911 twice to report "an unconscious man" lying outside her apartment, apparently without mentioning that he had a knife wound. After authorities arrived, Brock was taken to a local hospital, where he was pronounced dead.

Condon subsequently promised to consult with local police officials before simply refusing to prosecute someone.

But the point had been made, not only in Condon's home state, but across the country as word of his brash January declaration spread over the Internet on chat lists and various public forums. Here was a public official saying what a lot of frustrated citizens had been wanting to hear for many years.

Even though he fell under criticism from civil rights advocates for his declaration, the *New York Times* reported in a personality piece on Condon published on Jan 13, 1998 that the head of the ACLU in

South Carolina admired Condon.

Quoting ACLU State Director Steven Bates, the *Times* reported that Bates said, "He is not afraid to take a bold stand, usually on the popular side of an issue. But that may be because he is of the people rather than a panderer to the people."

Condon, now in private practice, has not been forgotten for what he said or did, and to the delight of many self-defense advocates, he may have set an example that a few other public officials are following.

Take, for example, the remarks of Montgomery, Alabama Mayor Bobby Bright in mid-September 2005, about two weeks after Hurricane Katrina had devastated three states and left tens of thousands of people homeless. That storm also left an environment in some areas of chaos and anarchy, and Alabama residents were not immune.

In the midst of this, Mayor Bright addressed a civic meeting, offering his personal solution to crime. It was not the first, or the last time that he offered this advice. Directing his remarks at the police chief, who was also present, the mayor said, "Get a gun and teach our folks how to use them and shoot 'em."

According to press accounts that were carried over the wire services at the time, Bright continued: "That's the only thing that we can really tell our folks to do at this point in time."

The local NBC affiliate quoted police Lt. Huey Thornton, who concurred with Mayor Bright: "The mayor made some good points. If a person chooses to own a handgun, then we think it is important they know how to use that handgun and they know when the law allows them to use it."

Bright later discussed his remarks with one of the authors for an article in the national firearms newspaper *Gun Week*.

After telling the *Montgomery Advertiser* that "In my opinion, people need to buy a weapon, buy a gun, educate themselves on how to use that gun and they need to use that weapon to protect themselves from the criminal element out there," he told the newspaper *Gun Week* that he was not about to change his message.

"I'm not your typical politician," Bright said in a telephone interview. "I don't tell people what is politically correct, I tell them what I think they need to know. . . . A lot of mayors are going to tell people 'don't get a gun, don't use a gun, keep away from a gun'."

When public officials like Condon and Bright make such statements, it sends shivers up the backs of gun rights opponents and criminal rights advocates who view this attitude as nothing short of calling out the vigilantes. However, the counter argument to that position is that people who defend themselves are acting within existing law, and that they have an inherent moral right as well as a legal right to defend themselves from grave bodily harm or death.

Should anyone wish to debate that concept, they might contact Tracey Roberts, an Iowa mother who shot and killed a home invader in December 2001, and sent a second man fleeing.

According to the December 15, 2001 edition of the *Des Moines Register*, Roberts was alone at home with her three children, ages 1, 3 and 11 at the time. Her husband, Mike, was out of town on business.

Two thugs broke into the home and assaulted Roberts before she managed to get her hands on a gun and open fire, fatally wounding a man identified as Dustin Wehde, 20, of Early, Iowa.

Roberts was taken to a local hospital where she was treated and released. The crime shocked the small town, where many were thankful that Tracy Roberts' act of self-defense protected them as well.

Refuting the Rhetoric

While attorneys general like Charlie Condon and mayors like Bobby Bright are rare, perhaps even more rare are municipal police chiefs willing to stand up for a citizen's right to self-defense, and a major city newspaper not only supporting concealed carry but criticizing news colleagues for essentially spinning the facts, or simply ignoring them.

Early in 2007 in Colorado, state lawmakers began debating whether to expand the state's infamous "Make My Day" law to include a person's place of business, and even their automobile. As the bill made its way through committee hearings, it was roundly condemned by the *Denver Post* and other newspapers, and anti-gun activists – sounding as if they were reading old scripts from opposition to the state's concealed carry law from years past – once again predicted that passage of an expanded law would lead to "Wild West" gunfights and more violence.

Into this controversy stepped Montrose Police Chief Tom Chinn, who might run against the grain of typical police chiefs who owe their jobs, and their loyalties, to mayors and city councils, many of whom are vehemently anti-gun. Chinn's observations were worthy enough to merit the attention of the Montrose *Daily Press*.

Chinn told that newspaper that he did not believe passage of the legislation would lead to more violence.

Matter-of-factly, Chief Chinn told the newspaper, "I think it (the law) needs to be extended. That may not be a popular stand as far as law enforcement and the district attorneys are concerned; I know it makes it tougher. But I think people need to be allowed to protect themselves a little more. I think it's a good thing."

Likewise, Colorado State Rep. Ray Rose (R-Montrose) backed up what his police chief said.

"We heard a great deal of conversation when we passed the original (law) how Colorado was going to be a bloodbath and that has not taken place," Rep. Rose told a reporter. "If anything, it's gone the other direction. We're hearing the same rhetoric now. I beg to differ."

Let us consider this just for a moment. Here is a police chief encouraging the passage of a state statute that would broaden self-defense rights, including the use of lethal force, to cover someone's place of business. That may seem like common sense to many people who have had a steady diet of reality videos from convenience store robberies where some clerk has shot back or fought back, but in the real world of legal jeopardy, the typical reaction from police officials is that they "encourage citizens to call us and not take the law into their own hands."

This is essentially what District Attorney Myrl Serra suggested in reaction to Chinn's remarks. Serra told the newspaper that he feared expanding the self-defense statute would "promote vigilantism."

"That's bad," he said. "That's what law enforcement's for. I'm all for gun rights, but I think this is something that could go bad."

A growing number of frustrated American citizens might disagree. They have seen too many criminals twirl through the revolving door of the judicial system, and too many prosecutors plea bargain away serious crimes to get a conviction on a lesser charge.

So Chief Chinn's remarks were something of a blast of fresh air.

How many times have you read or heard some official say what Chinn said on television? It seems an almost obligatory statement when a police spokesperson is interviewed following a self-defense shooting, or an incident in which an armed citizen comes to the aid of a person being attacked, that they discourage armed citizen intervention almost out of habit.

There are exceptions to this rule, and the case of Rory Vertigan of Phoenix, Arizona is such an example.

March 26, 1999

Vertigan, described in the April 1999 Gottlieb-Tartaro report authored by Alan Gottlieb and Joseph Tartaro, as "as burly 27-year-old man (who) drives a late-model Kia with a National Rifle Association decal on the front window and 'Keep Honking, I'm Reloading' license-plate holder," has just dropped his boss off at home after finishing a shift as a security guard, when he finds himself following a white Lincoln Town Car.

Unbeknownst to him, the Lincoln has been observed and followed by Phoenix Police Officer Marc Atkinson. According to chilling accounts in the June 28, 1999 issue of TIME ("Death on the Beat") and *Thank God I Had A Gun* by Chris Bird (published by Privateer Publications), Atkinson has just run the Lincoln's license plate and found it to be suspended.

At that moment, the Lincoln comes to a stop with Vertigan's Kia about 50 feet to the rear, and all hell breaks loose. Three illegal aliens, all Mexican nationals who are carrying illegal drugs and firearms, are in the Lincoln. Two bail out but a third, later identified as Felipe Petrona-Cabanas, hangs back in the car and as Atkinson rolls up beside the Lincoln, Petrona-Cabanas opens fire with a .357 Magnum. Atkinson, fatally wounded, slumps in his patrol car that rolls across the pavement and strikes a utility pole.

The gunman is out of the car and he swings the revolver toward Vertigan's car. Vertigan, thinking he is about to be shot at, has by now drawn his licensed Glock pistol chambered for the .357 SIG cartridge, and shifts the gun from his right to left hand, according to the accounts, thrusts his left hand out the car window and opens fire with a devastating fusillade. He came up out of the Kia to take a solid rest on his open door as the gunman ducked back inside the Lincoln to reload. A moment later, Petrona-Cabanas rams the Lincoln into the smaller car. It would later be determined that every round he fired slammed into the Lincoln, and one bullet hit Petrona-Cabanas in the shoulder.

Out of ammunition, Vertigan charges the gunman and wrestles the revolver away from him. An unidentified man runs to help, and Vertigan hands the gun to him and tells him to cover the downed thug and then rushes to Atkinson's car.

By now, other Phoenix police officers are arriving, and Vertigan has gone back to where the other man is guarding the gunman. He retrieves the handgun, and surprisingly, the Samaritan disappears. But sadly, Atkinson is dead, having suffered fatal head wounds.

Now for a departure from the norm: With his own pistol seized as evidence, the Phoenix Law Enforcement Association gave him a check for $500 and honored him as a hero four days after the shooting. Another $250 check came from the officers' association of the Arizona Department of Public Safety, all presumably to help Vertigan replace his pistol. The Phoenix police also, according to author Chris Bird, arranged counseling for Vertigan, as they would for a fellow officer who had just been through such a horrific experience.

Vertigan's life had some ups and downs over the next several months, but he is on record stating that he would do the same thing again.

In addition to the gunman, the other two criminals were captured, tried and found guilty. They are all in prison and that's where they will be staying.

'A Time and a Place'

Returning for a moment to Montrose, Colorado Police Chief Tom Chinn and something else he said about the proposal to expand the state's self-defense statute, his logic applies – or should apply – to every state in the country.

"I don't believe anyone rational wants to hurt, or kill or harm anyone," he said early in 2007, "but I think there is a time and a place to protect yourself. Whether it's self-defense or Make My Day, I think people should be allowed to protect themselves and this is just one more element to allow that to occur."

There may be no better time or place than when your life, or the life of a neighbor, is in immediate jeopardy.

A 25-year-old South Kitsap, Washington woman was awakened from sleep early on the morning of December 17, 2000 to find an armed man in her bedroom, threatening her with rape, robbery and death before beating her severely to evidently prove he meant it.

But according to an account in the *Bremerton Sun* newspaper the following day, an armed neighbor came to the rescue, firing shots over the man's head as he fled after the woman screamed, causing his dogs to bark. The intended female victim and her courageous neighbor lived at opposite ends of the same duplex, the newspaper account said.

The scenario is all-too-familiar to anyone who understands how rapes unfold into nightmares. The unidentified attacker demanded that the woman undress, but she stalled by asking to go to the bathroom and get a drink of water. The man threatened to hurt her young daughter if she did not cooperate by allowing the rape, the newspaper detailed, and then when she attempted to dial 911, he struck her in the face and hit her on the head with his pistol before kicking her in the head and stomach.

Then the would-be rapist demanded to know where she kept her money, and when she denied having any cash, instead telling him to take her television and VCR, he left and told her to stay put for several minutes, the newspaper reported.

But her screams while being beaten got the attention of neighbor Richard Sample, who responded with a .22-caliber pistol. He saw the attacker running from the woman's house and fired three shots over his head because he did not know what Washington State law allows when dealing with intruders, he told the newspaper.

They also have home invasions in Kentucky, and citizens there also fight back.

Take the case of 79-year-old Gayle Martin of Dry Ridge, who opened fire in self-defense in July 2005 when two men identified as Paul McGraw, 25 and Justin Moore, 19, broke into his house.

According to accounts carried on WLWT in Cincinnati, Ohio, Martin was at home at 5 a.m. on July 9 when the two suspects kicked in his back door. Martin opened fire with a .357 Magnum revolver, and hit both younger men. One of them was found a short time later lying in the driveway, and the other was found by Grand County sheriff's deputies after they followed a blood trail.

One of Martin's neighbors, identified as Everett Musgrave, told the television station, "At that time in the morning, if I was in that situation, I might try to do the same thing."

Another neighbor, identified as Lisa Garner, added, "My grandfather would have done the same thing."

Both suspects were subsequently charged with second-degree burglary, and a county grand jury quickly convened to determine that Martin had acted in self-defense.

Common Sense Prevails

In any number of cases of self-defense that have been increasingly reported around the nation in recent years, county prosecutors have been increasingly guided by not only well-crafted statutory self-defense reforms, but by common sense.

This admittedly is not always the case, but more and more, especially where homeowners defend themselves against home invasion robberies or assaults, and where shopkeepers or their employees defend themselves against violent robbers, the right of people to defend themselves is gaining considerable traction.

So-called "Stand Your Ground" and "Castle Doctrine" laws are being supported by members of both political parties in state legislatures around the country, despite protests and alarmist rhetoric from gun control groups that steadfastly oppose such laws. There are any number of theories about why this is the pattern, but there is a suspicion in gun rights circles that gun control proponents simply do not want people to realize, understand and become comfortable with the concept of defending themselves with firearms because that makes it more difficult to convince the American public that guns have no place in society.

But increasingly, it is becoming evident that guns still do have such a purpose, perhaps even moreso now than in past generations when gun ownership was not merely acceptable, but expected. And as noted above, the pendulum seems to have swung back in favor of citizens who defend themselves so that they are not hounded by headline-seeking district attorneys. Quite the opposite appears to be happening in many jurisdictions.

In King County, Washington, for example, gun rights expert Joe Waldron, executive director of the Citizens Committee for the Right to Keep and Bear Arms – one of the nation's premier grassroots firearms rights organizations – told the authors that he cannot recall a single instance in the past several years where that county's Prosecutor's Office has made the wrong call on a self-defense case.

Under the so-called "Reasonable Man Doctrine," seasoned prosecutors will place themselves in the position of the person who defended himself or herself. Then, understanding the situation, and "knowing what they knew at the time," these attorneys will make a judgment call on whether the private citizen acted within the law. If so, no charges are ever filed, and in jurisdictions where grand juries make such determinations, a prosecutor who believes in serving justice over racking up a conviction rate may encourage the grand jury to "no bill" the case, meaning that no indictment will be issued against the citizen.

It is horrible for any rational person to take the life of another, no matter how justified such a killing would be portrayed in the media, or ruled by the prosecutor or a coroner's inquest. The taking of a human life is an "unnatural act."

Except, perhaps, in a growing number of cases involving recidivist offenders; people who have been in and out of the courts and jails repeatedly, and whose violent habits will land them there again. One can debate the condition of the judicial system today, with its "turnstile justice" that seems to turn loose even the most violent repeat offenders time after time, until they either kill, or are killed.

But even in America, where citizens are fighting back, we ask ourselves why it needs to go that far before such an animal is forever removed from society.

And this brings us around to Robby Bailey, a man with at least eight aliases and a criminal record that went all the way back to 1987, when he was still a teenager. Even a brief glance at his most recent criminal history underscores what is wrong with the justice system.

Convicted of aggravated assault for a crime committed in February 1994, he drew a five-year prison sentence in Georgia. He escaped on September 20, 1996, and was sentenced to five years for that, plus five years for a theft that occurred on the same day he escaped, according to his rap sheet. That record included convictions for assaulting a peace officer, possession of narcotics, burglary, shoplifting and obstructing a police officer.

Incarcerated in March 1990, he was out in March 1993. Incarcerated in April 1994, he was out that September. Incarcerated in June 1995, he was out in January 2001. Incarcerated in July 2002, he was out in

September 2003. In all, Bailey spent more than ten of his 37 years behind bars.

Shortly after midnight on January 21, 2007, the 37-year-old Bailey – standing 5 feet, 6 inches tall and weighing 155 pounds – showed up at the Gainesville, Georgia home of Doug Magnus, president of a company called Conditioned Air Systems. Bailey was wearing a ski mask and was armed with a handgun. He had parked a red Jeep Cherokee about a half-mile away, and walked to the house.

According to accounts in the Gainesville *Times* that detailed the events, Magnus – at home with his wife, Diane – heard a loud noise outside his home and, after prudently arming himself, went to investigate. Just outside the door, the masked Bailey confronted Magnus and opened fire, shooting at him several times, but fortunately missing his intended victim.

Doug Magnus, according to published reports, fired once. The bullet struck Robby Bailey in the head, fatally wounding him. He died at the Northeast Georgia Medical Center. After reviewing the case with sheriff's investigators, District Attorney Lee Darragh declared that Magnus had acted in self-defense.

Often times, it takes weeks, if not months, for all the facts of a case to be sorted out and a determination made, but for Magnus, justice took a swift and proper course.

A family friend and attorney, Eddie Hartness, was quoted by the newspaper explaining the situation profoundly: "Doug and Diane Magnus were twice victims of a crime Saturday night. Not only were they the victims of an attempted home invasion, but Mr. Magnus was forced to take a human life when the perpetrator attacked him, firing a weapon. Needless to say, the experience was very traumatic and unsettling."

There is something to consider, of course. To feel unsettled and traumatized, one must be alive. And yet, as many a battlefield veteran might explain, after having survived a life-or-death struggle in which you were forced by circumstances to take a human life, you may carry a strange sense of guilt for the rest of your days.

CHAPTER 5

Defending Your Livelihood

Shopkeepers and small business owners work hard for every penny they take home in profit, and often, that's not very much. They will be damned if they'll happily turn over the contents of their cash registers to career criminals like Tyrone Ingram.

A growing number of these shop keepers who have previously had guns thrust into their faces, are fighting back. They have become all too familiar with accounts of other small business operators or their employees being brutally, senselessly and casually assaulted or murdered by thugs who are too strung out on drugs, or simply too lazy to work.

The 32-year-old Ingram was apparently just such a miscreant; a man who had, according to an account in the April 13, 2001 edition of the Chicago *Tribune*, a record that included armed robbery attempts, assault, attempted aggravated battery, and "mob action." It appears that in his effort to be a criminal, he may not have been very good at it. For the two months prior to this fateful spring day, he had been staying with different relatives in the Chicago area. Hardly someone an average person would invite home to dinner, for shopkeepers like Anselmo Nieves, Ingram was not even the kind of person you'd want as a customer.

But Ingram was not in Nieves' South Side grocery that Thursday morning to buy anything. He was in there to take something, and in the process, he struck the 57-year-old Nieves over the head and knocked him to the floor.

It was not the first time Anselmo Nieves had been victimized by an armed thug. In 2000, a robber had entered the store and put a gun to his head, actually pulling the trigger. Fortunately, the bullet only nicked the shopkeeper's ear, the newspaper account recalled.

That this present crime was going down at 10 o'clock in the morning is hardly unusual for a metropolis like Chicago, where criminals don't take time off, and something bad can happen 24 hours a day. Chicago, of course, is a city in which it virtually impossible for a law-abiding citizen to carry a handgun for personal protection, or even have one in his place of business unless he or she has been licensed and has had a permit for more than a generation. Years ago, Chicago stopped issuing permits and without one, you cannot have a handgun.

This prohibition naturally did not prevent Ingram from strolling into the Cidras Super Market that morning with a gun in his hand. It was a gun that, because of his criminal background, he legally could not have. He aimed it at a female cashier, prompting Nieves to hand over the cash drawer and some cigarettes before he unceremoniously battered the shopkeeper to the ground.

And then a female customer walked in, and Ingram turned his attention, and the gun muzzle, toward that woman.

In that instant, according to the newspaper account, Nieves didn't reach for a handgun, he grabbed a shotgun and cut loose. At what amounted to point blank range, the shot charge slammed into the left side of Ingram's face, ripping a gaping wound and killing him instantly.

Chicago police declined to seek charges against Nieves, about whom one neighbor observed, "We need more people like him in this neighborhood. He must have been scared. I know he wouldn't want to hurt anybody."

Another neighbor added, "He's been robbed so many times. He had to defend himself."

Of course, one Ingram's relatives, identified as a cousin by the *Tribune*, contended that the shooting of Ingram was wrong, regardless what he was doing at the store.

"It's too much to take somebody's life for money," the relative told the newspaper.

One might reasonably snap right back at this relative: "Well, that's what your scumbag cousin was threatening to do when he struck Mr. Nieves over the head and aimed a gun at his customer."

To understand Tyrone Ingram, you would also have to understand 26-year-old Charles F. Harmon, 26, of Lexington, Kentucky. Another criminal with his eye on an easy dollar in broad daylight, Harmon walked into the SubCity Market at the corner of Lexington's East Seventh Street and Shropshire Avenue on the morning of June 11, 2006. For Mr. Harmon, it would be a one-way trip.

Once inside the market, he approached the check-out and implied to the clerk that he had a gun, another one of those "fatal errors in the victim selection process."

According to an account in the *Lexington Herald-Leader* of June 11, a female clerk in the store had her own gun when Harmon demanded money at 9:30 a.m. She drew her handgun and shot Harmon, at point blank range, and the much-surprised and mortally-wounded thug "stumbled outside the store and collapsed," the newspaper reported.

Police not only had a verbal account of what occurred from the female clerk, they had the entire incident on video, courtesy of the store's security camera. There was not much room for error, and the clerk's account accurately described what the detectives saw on the video.

By no small coincidence, the newspaper account explained, this market had been robbed several times in the past, and had only a week before this incident been burglarized. In the past, clerks have complied with robbers' demands. This time, a female clerk fought back, and the Lexington police, after reviewing all the evidence, told the newspaper that they had no intention of filing any charges against her.

Sometimes criminals don't wait for business hours to strike, but occasionally that strategy doesn't work, either in an America where people are fighting back to protect what they work so hard to earn.

At approximately 4:30 a.m. on Friday, June 30, 2006, an 18-year-old carryout employee at the Columbus, Ohio Express Market Drive-Thru was asleep inside the establishment, having worked all night re-stocking shelves, according to accounts on WCMH/NBC4 in Columbus, and printed in the *Columbus Dispatch* newspaper.

Two men identified in press accounts as Eric M. Ford, 28 and Lawrence A. Ford, 38, broke into the business. They were hardly collecting for the local food bank.

According to a homicide detective identified as Jay Fulton in the newspaper account, the teen employee came out of the office where he had been sleeping, armed with a handgun. He was confronted by a man armed with a crowbar, behind the store's counter. The unidentified teen fired in self-defense, killing Eric Ford with a shot to the torso. Lawrence Ford was apprehended about two blocks from the store, and he was charged with aggravated burglary and murder. In many states, a criminal perpetrator can be charged with homicide if a death results from the criminal act, even if he or she was not the one who pulled the trigger.

What this case demonstrates is that a criminal does not have to be armed with a gun in order to be stopped in his tracks by some intended victim who does have a gun. A crowbar, knife, razor, broken bottle, chain, baseball bat, hammer; any number of ordinary or unusual objects can be used as deadly weapons, and when that happens, the person using them can, in a self-defense encounter, be shot dead by the intended victim.

There are times when criminals have all kinds of advanced warning that they might face lethal resistance, and many times in that kind of environment, you will find that the incidence of crime will drop.

Fair Warning

Early in 2007, store owners in the Burlington, Vermont area made it pretty clear they had had enough with robberies. But instead of going on some sort of a "vigilante crusade," as it would have been doubtless portrayed in the local press, these shopkeepers went through an important "first step" in their campaign against crime.

They met with police, and it was highly publicized in the *Burlington Free Press* newspaper and on WCAX-TV. The television report clearly noted that "Some small store owners say they are armed, waiting, and willing to shoot if they are targeted by a gun-toting robber."

Frequently, gun-packing employees can be spotted in gun shops all over America. Where else would it be more proper and perhaps expected to see armed staff than in a store selling firearms? It is a clear signal that gun dealers – cognizant of the fact that their product line is a prime target for robbers – are sending a visual signal to would-be bandits that they will be committing a crime in peril of their very lives.

Now, when was the last time you ever heard of someone robbing a gun shop?

It has happened only once that the authors could find, on February 3, 1990 in the "highlands" area of Renton, Washington, a suburb of Seattle. At about 4:40 p.m., a man identified as David Zaback walked past a clearly marked King County Police patrol vehicle and through the door of H&J Leather & Firearms, Ltd.

There were several people in the shop, including uniformed King County Officer Timothy Lally, clerk Danny Morris and some other customers. Zaback drew a .38-caliber pistol and declared a robbery was in progress, and that he would kill anyone who moved. Lally was in the rear of the shop with the store's owner, Wendell Woodall when Zaback saw him. Published reports at the time left it unclear who fired first, and a subsequent detailed account on "Snopes.com" – the website that debunks urban legends, but holds this account to be true under the heading "Dead Stupid" (it was, author Workman actually worked the story as part of a news roundup in *Fishing & Hunting News*) – is equally undecided on the issue.

What is known is that Zaback, Lally and Morris exchanged gunfire. Lally was armed with a 9mm semiautomatic pistol and Morris was armed with a 10mm Colt Delta Elite. The 10mm cartridge has been held by various firearms experts to be the semi-auto equivalent to the .41 Magnum and at close range it has devastating knock-down power.

Other customers in the store also drew their legally-concealed handguns, but could not get clear shots. Zaback was hit by four rounds, one in the arm and three dead center in the chest. He was dead when he hit the ground outside.

And *that* is why people do *not* attempt to rob gun stores!

But for small shopkeepers whose businesses have nothing at all to do with firearms or sporting goods to be arming themselves and doing it publicly is something of a rarity in a politically correct society. But not always.

Vermont has a long and proud heritage of carrying firearms, both openly or concealed and with no permit or license required, for the purpose of personal safety. Handguns may be carried inside or out in Vermont, thanks to a state Supreme Court ruling that dates back more than a century. So long as there is no intent to harm another person, the practice is perfectly legal. Granted, for the many transplants moving up from neighboring Massachusetts, where gun laws are considerably more restrictive, seeing armed citizens going about their business is something of a culture shock.

A string of armed robberies in the Burlington area, mostly unrelated to one another, brought the guns out of the closets and drawers. Burlington's small business owners are like other small businessmen and women all over the country. They work hard for their money.

In the WCAX report of February 9, 2007, reporter Brian Joyce told viewers, "None of the armed store owners were willing to speak on camera, but they stressed they want any would-be armed robber to know that they will not hesitate to shoot."

Almost as if on cue, the reporter noted that Vermont State Police, while acknowledging that the use of lethal force in self-defense is legal in the Green Mountain State, "it is not the right response." The police advised in this case, as police will do all over the country that "it would be far wiser and safer to simply hand over the money, and let the cops catch the bad guys."

In a perfect world, maybe that's how it works. This is not a perfect world, and as one can find in case after case of armed robbery, far too many criminals have no remorse whatsoever about murdering their victims so they cannot testify in court.

Take the news report that ran on Cleveland's News Net 5 on May 14, 2002 about a gas station bandit who met with a sudden demise at the hands of his intended victim. The report acknowledged, "Many times, an innocent convenience store clerk gets gunned down, but… this time, the alleged robber paid the price."

Burlington's string of armed robberies was suspected to be largely the work of drug addicts in need of quick cash for a drug purchase. But drug addicts armed with guns and desperate for a fix can be just as deadly as any other armed robber. When Burlington police met with businessmen and women at a public meeting Monday, February 12, they revealed that there had been 19 "incidents," which is a sanitized way of saying "armed robberies."

While several arrests were eventually made, that did not entirely erase the concerns of store operators who did not care for the idea of having the next person coming through their door end up sticking a gun in their faces. Yet the *Free Press* did report that, following a public meeting with the police chief of nearby Richmond, local business people did feel that Richmond police were being responsive, and willing to cooperate in efforts to alert them about criminal activity.

Armed robbers don't care to tangle with the police under normal circumstances, and they are loathe to deliberately confront intended victims when they know in advance that their selected victim may be armed and ready to fight back. When it is publicized that the "victim pool" is working closely with local law enforcement to fight back, that's bad news for bad guys.

It is highly-publicized actions like this that often result in a decline in the local crime rate across the board, and not just commercial armed robberies. If there actually is a shooting that results in the death of the would-be perpetrator, it certainly removes at least one criminal from the landscape, and it can send a powerful message to others that warnings from shopkeepers that they will defend themselves is more than idle conversation.

Perhaps this philosophy can be summed up in the story of Miami, Florida liquor store owner Pedro Agudelo that appeared in the *Miami Herald* on January 9, 2007 after Agudelo had fatally shot a would-be robber in a late-evening confrontation.

Said the shopkeeper: "I'm just a working guy, a victim of a crime, and I fought back, and that's all."

Evidently, the fact that Agudelo was "just a working guy" made no difference to 22-year-old Dusviel Hernandez, a native of Cuba. He entered Agudelo's LeJuene Liquors at 930 SW 42nd Avenue in West Gables about an hour before closing time, pulled a handgun and demanded that Agudelo hand over his cash. Instead, the store owner came up with his own handgun from behind the counter and opened fire. Hernandez fell dead.

This was not a first for the 63-year-old Agudelo. In 2001, according to the newspaper, he opened fire on another would-be bandit, but that time the perpetrator survived. Agudelo never faced any charges then, and thanks to the passage in 2005 of Florida's strengthened "Stand Your Ground" statute, he would face no charges again, and justifiably so.

'Not Worth Your Life'

The Second Amendment Foundation, one of the nation's leading gun rights organizations, based in Bellevue, Washington in a small office complex called Liberty Park, has for years produced a small window sticker that notifies one and all: "The owner of this property is armed. There is nothing inside worth risking your life for."

At gun shows, in gun shops and at gun rights gatherings like the annual Gun Rights Policy Conference, that small square sticker sells by the bundle to people who take them home and hand them out to friends. This decal is hardly a novelty item meant for eliciting a few giggles. It is a deadly serious warning to criminals that they should take their trouble elsewhere.

It is, perhaps, wasted ink where armed robbers are concerned, because in case after case, thugs will ignore such warnings and the fact that there are security cameras operating in the convenience stores and gas stations they target for a quick heist. In many cases, the faces of these dangerous people are captured on video, and on occasion, their final moments of life are also captured as they meet with an armed store owner or clerk who has determined to not be robbed and beaten or murdered by these malefactors.

In late November 2001, two masked men marched into a pawn shop in East Hartford, Connecticut and announced they were robbing the place. According to the *Hartford Courant's* November 21 edition, store employee Bill Kane warned the man heading toward him with a pipe that he had a handgun, but the determined robber evidently either did not believe there was a gun, or didn't think Kane would use it. He was fatally wrong on both counts.

In the detailed newspaper account, the robbery occurred at about 5:30 p.m. when Kane was working in the rear of the shop. Up front was Ralph Lane, another employee, who was working at a jewelry repair workbench. The shop is located on East Hartford's Main Street.

Both masked men burst into the store carrying metal pipes, demanding that Lane open the safe. They began hitting jewelry cases and everything else in the shop with their pipes, and finally one of the robbers hit Lane, who triggered a burglar alarm to summon East Hartford Police.

But police response time always seems like an eternity, and a violent act can occur in a heartbeat. While one robber held his attention on Lane, the other advanced to the rear of the shop, where he confronted Kane. It would be the biggest, and last, mistake he ever made in life.

Armed with what the newspaper described as a .380-caliber semiautomatic pistol, Kane – who was licensed to carry the gun –

warned the advancing thug that he was armed. When the robber kept coming, Kane raised his pistol and fired seven quick shots. Two of those rounds slammed into the masked man. His accomplice fled, and responding officers, even with the aid of a police dog, could not apprehend him.

The mortally-wounded robber was pronounced dead at a nearby hospital.

One week before this robbery in Connecticut, and several states to the west, a man identified as Perry Pinkelton, 36, of Elsmere, Kentucky wandered into the Deli Mart Express in nearby Covington. Like so many others who try their hand at crime, he was not in the store for food or drink, but easy cash. Pinkelton, the father of two sons, the son of Vivien Pinkelton of Cincinnati, brother to Yolanda Pinkelton of San Antonio, Texas and Andre and Guy Pinkelton of Oregon, according to a news brief in the November 17 on-line edition of the *Kentucky Post*, would not be successful. Instead, he stopped several bullets after exchanging gunfire with the shop owner, later identified by the *Cincinnati Enquirer* as Khader Sbeih, who had only been in business at this spot for a year. He ran the store with a nephew, the newspaper said.

When Pinkelton came in, he fired three shots at the nephew. Sbeih, who was licensed to carry a handgun, fired back. At the time, this was getting to be something of an issue because he had been victimized at least twice before during the previous 14 days.

Pinkelton was hit several times, but neither Sbeih or his nephew suffered a scratch. Pinkelton died at the scene. While some might argue that cases like this may not prevent future armed robberies, it is guaranteed that Pinkelton won't be pulling any of them.

In the previous encounter, a gunman had aimed a handgun right at Sbeih's face and gotten away.

In the aftermath of the Pinkelton shooting, Covington police said almost immediately that they did not plan to file charges against the shopkeeper.

It is rare that an armed robbery that ends in a fatality brings any kind of amusement, but there are a handful of occasions when it appears there has been divine intervention of the most macabre variety, and such was the case on January 19, 2001 when a suspect later identified as David Id-Deen walked into an Akron, Ohio mini-mart and tried his hand at armed robbery.

According to a report found on writer Robert A. Waters' "The Self Defense Files" dated February 1, this may have been one of the shortest criminal careers on record.

Id-Deen confronted store owner Saleh Husein, ordering him to "freeze." No doubt remembering his brother, who had been murdered the previous year by a robber, Saleh pulled his own handgun and fired four times at Id-Deen. One bullet grazed his head, and the robber dropped his handgun and ran out the door.

But he didn't run very far. Proving himself to be as inept at fleeing as he was at robbing, Id-Deen actually ran into the street, and into the path of an oncoming car. The impact of the car slamming into Id-Deen sent him flying, and it also broke his neck. Scratch one robber.

Stop the Revolving Door

It is not unusual to discover that armed robbers involved in convenience store stick-ups have criminal records, and if this teaches the American public anything, it is that there really is a "revolving door" at the courthouse, and that it is no longer a "justice" system but a "judicial" system that is broken, perhaps beyond repair.

Critics of such a conclusion dot the landscape of the talk show and lecture circuit. They exist mainly on grant funding for this or that research organization, or perhaps have a good job on the public payroll. Rarely do any of these people have much background in the private sector, from whence come the victims upon whom recidivist criminals prey.

To the social engineers, and especially those who are anti-gun in their philosophy, these victims are nothing more than statistics to be tossed around when they contend that the way to reduce crime is to restrict ever increasingly the public's access to firearms, and thus strangle the public's exercise of a constitutional civil right, the right to keep and bear arms.

It is when armed citizens fight back, and help remove one of these repeat offenders from the streets – temporarily or permanently – that the opponents of lawful self-defense seem to cringe. If it were really true that gun control proponents, who consistently oppose concealed carry statutes and "Stand Your Ground" legislation, do support the right of self-defense, then why aren't representatives from the Brady Campaign to Prevent Gun Violence and all of the state-level "CeaseFire" organizations cheering loudly anytime an armed citizen brings down a thug, and especially one with a criminal track record?

All of this brings us around to Willie Brown, Kinney Bethea and Clifford Hall; two of the three were still breathing as this book was written, but the third had his career permanently interrupted a few years ago.

According to the April 5, 2002 edition of the Muncie, Indiana *Star Press*, Brown has a "history of crime." Briefly, in 1982, Brown drew a six-year prison sentence following his conviction for burglary in a Muncie apartment building. Now pay attention: He drew that sentence from Delaware Circuit Judge Steven Caldemeyer.

Nine years later, in September 1991, Brown — at the time on probation for a burglary conviction in Missouri — was back in Muncie, and standing before the same Judge Caldemeyer to earn a 20-year prison sentence after being convicted of robbing a Pizza King restaurant.

Now, do the math. Brown was sent to the penitentiary for 20 years in 1991. So, what was he doing in a southside Muncie convenience store on March 15, 2002, attempting to rob the place? Well, whatever else he was doing there, he was stopping a bullet.

Released from prison in May 2001, Brown evidently had grown so fond of prison food he wanted back in line. Or maybe he is one of those individuals who are simply beyond rehabilitation, and crime is the only profession he knows.

The now-44-year-old Brown has entered the Zipp's Deli claiming to have a gun in his jacket, the *Star Press* report detailed. He wanted the money from the cash register. As he turned to leave the convenience store, the clerk grabbed a gun and opened fire. Five rounds left the barrel, and at least one of them struck Brown, who was apprehended a short time later at a nearby home. He still had the holdup money.

This time around, Brown was nailed for armed robbery, a Class B felony in Indiana that carries a ten-year prison term.

Two months later, in Rockledge, Florida, Clifford Hall is keeping a date...with a judge. According to the May 21, 2002 edition of *Florida Today*, Hall has a criminal record that stretches back more than 13 years, starting with his arrest and conviction in 1988 for burglary and grand theft.

But instead of occupying a prison cell a year later, Hall is back in business, although not for long. In 1989, he is sacked for grand theft, forgery and "multiple counts of burglary," and on one of those counts, the newspaper said, "he should have received a life sentence."

So how does one explain Hall's freedom six years later, long enough for him to have been arrested by the Cocoa police in 1995 on charges of aggravated battery with great bodily harm? Those charges were eventually dropped, the newspaper explained, but he apparently did not take any of this as a warning to stay out of trouble.

In 1996, Hall was pinched by a traffic cop for a violation, and two years later, in 1998, he was charged with battery and three years after that, in 2001, Hall racked up a charge of domestic violence. In September 2001, he was arrested for forging a drug prescription.

Hall is a felony-level repeat offender who is, according to the newspaper account, also an armed robbery suspect, so in May 2002, it was probably no big surprise to Cocoa police that the man they apprehended following an 18-mile high speed chase turned out to be Clifford Hall, now 37 years old. He is wanted this time for several armed robberies in the Rockledge and Cocoa area, culminating in the holdup of a convenience store, a liquor store and a hotel.

But when he bailed out of his car, he made the mistake of running to the Canaveral Groves neighborhood and breaking into a home, only to find himself staring at the gun barrels trained on him by the homeowners. When Americans fight back, they don't always pull the trigger, but somebody goes down.

The door stopped revolving in November 2004 for Kinney Bethea, according to the Wilmington, North Carolina *Star News* on-line. A suspect in several armed robberies in North Carolina's Columbus County including an October 31 stickup at an IGA supermarket in Tabor City and a second robbery near Fair Bluff, Bethea is a resident of Bennettsville, South Carolina when he enters Hill's Grocery at Lake Waccamaw on a Sunday evening 25 minutes before the 10 p.m. closing time.

The published account of what happened next seems all-too-familiar to people who study this kind of crime.

Bethea entered the store and walked directly down an aisle to confront store manager Richard Wilson, telling him bluntly, "You come with me." This was not a debate, as Bethea was holding a 9mm handgun and he meant business. When Wilson asked where they were going, Bethea told him "To the office," published reports explained.

The gunman also motioned to a 17-year-old employee to accompany them, and when they reached the office at the rear of the store, Bethea apparently spotted a female cashier and ordered her to the back of the store, too. She didn't move, and Bethea walked up to her and grabbed her, and began dragging her to the store office.

In far too many such cases like this, it's not just a robbery that is going down, but a prelude to execution so there are no witnesses. That evidently crossed Wilson's mind, and when Bethea went to grab the cashier, Wilson – who had worked at the store since November 2003 and who was licensed to carry a concealed handgun – made his move.

Newspaper accounts said Wilson had worked in the grocery business in New York before retiring and heading south to warmer and more gun-friendly environs. But he came out of retirement to take the job at the market, which was part of a chain, whose president was State Representative Dewey Hill. Hill would later tell a reporter that it is "not a general policy" to keep firearms in his stores, but on this particular evening, the fact Wilson was armed may have prevented a mass murder. Fortunately, nobody will ever know whether that would have been the case.

When Bethea came back, dragging the frightened teenage cashier, Wilson took him by surprise and shot him four times, hitting him in the head and chest. Kinney Bethea hit the floor stone dead. He would rob and terrorize no more grocery clerks.

In the aftermath, Rep. Hill said this about Richard Wilson: "(He) is a fine gentleman, a good Christian guy and I think he would have thought very carefully before he did something like that."

No rational person wants to take a human life. However, no sane person would allow himself to be sacrificed on the altar of political correctness, or allow someone else's life to be snuffed out as well. Those who advocate complete compliance with someone who is violent and appears kill-crazed have never been faced with a life-or-death decision to act. Those who argue that people should not be allowed to carry concealed handguns for personal protection have never met the likes of a Tyrone Ingram, Perry Pinkelton or Kinney Bethea.

They should pray hard that they never do, and they should also pray for the safety of their fellow citizens who have met these monsters, and other criminals like them. And they should thank all the gods in heaven that, on their behalf, there are Americans who are fighting back.

CHAPTER 6

Fighting Media Bias

Wednesday, January 16, 2002 was a typical winter day on the campus of the small, private Appalachian School of Law at Grundy, Virginia. While the school had thrived in relative anonymity in the arena of law schools – its reported enrollment was a mere 170 students – today it would become a part of history, but hardly the kind of notoriety the school, its faculty or administration could ever be happy about.

Peter Odighizuwa was something of a hard-luck student who had actually flunked out of the school in 2001 but had been permitted to come back and try to change his academic course. He had just been dismissed a second time, the day before, again due to poor grades. It would later be said that the Dean of the school had "bent over backwards" to give Odighizuwa every chance to succeed.

Nigerian by birth and naturalized as a U.S. citizen, the 42-year-old Odighizuwa had scheduled a meeting with L. Anthony Sutin, dean of the school, to talk about his grades. Presumably, Sutin was one of the school officials who was aware that Odighizuwa had a history of mental instability that was disclosed in a report by the Newport News *Daily Press* the following day.

The Associated Press and other biographical information described Sutin as a 1984 graduate of Harvard Law School, who in addition to being the dean was also an associated professor. He had been a judicial law clerk for the United States District Court, Northern District of Texas, and a partner in the Washington, D.C. law firm of Hogan & Hartson, L.L.P., according to one biography. He had worked on Bill Clinton's successful 1992 presidential campaign and for the Democratic National Committee before going to work at the Justice Department as an assistant attorney general. He left that post to "go back to school" by helping to found the Appalachian School in a renovated former junior high school building in 1997. He and his wife, Margaret, had two children, according to published biographical accounts.

Known around campus as "Peter O." because of the difficulty pronouncing his name, Odighizuwa first met with Professor Dale Rubin when he arrived at the school that Wednesday morning. According to published reports in various newspapers, and by the Associated Press, Odighizuwa chatted with Rubin about his poor grades, and then, as he was leaving, he reportedly asked Rubin to pray for him. It may have seemed an odd remark, but in actuality, it was an ominous prelude to what would happen moments later.

Odighizuwa then went to the offices of Sutin and Professor Thomas Blackwell.

Born in 1961, Blackwell was a highly-respected man in his field. He taught classes in contract writing, and Odighizuwa had been one of his students. According to a brief biography, he had been a visiting assistant professor of law at Chicago-Kent College of Law from August 1997 through May 1999. He had been an associate with Jenkins & Gilchrist, in Dallas, Texas and the managing partner of Blackwell & Bruning, L.L.P., also in Dallas. He taught Legal Writing at Texas Wesleyan School of Law, and had published a book of Texas business legal forms on disk for West Publishing Co. He and his wife, Lisa, had a daughter and two sons.

When Odighizuwa arrived at their offices, he drew a .380-caliber semiautomatic pistol and shot Sutin and Blackwell to death. He went downstairs and opened fire into what one news account described as "a common area." One of his bullets hit a student, Angela Denice Dales, killing her.

Described in a memorial service pamphlet as a "life-long resident of Buchanan County," Dales was treasurer of Phi Alpha Delta and was on the Dean's List at the school. She was a 1992 graduate of Virginia Intermont College, where she earned a B.A. in History/Political Science and Creative Writing. The author of the campus newsletter *The Chronicle and Today*, she was also an editor for the *Moore Street Review*. Ms. Dales had a daughter, Rebecca.

Odighizuwa fired three more shots, wounding students Stacy Beans, 22, of Berea, Kentucky; Rebecca Brown, 38, of Roanoke, and

Martha Madeline Short, 37, of Grundy.

And then he stopped shooting. Odighizuwa went outside, as students were diving out windows and running for cover. What happened then became rather murky if one were to rely solely on, and believe, various press accounts. Those reports, it turns out, were deliberately murky and lacking in specific detail.

For the record, a student named Tracy Bridges raced to his parked car and grabbed a handgun he had locked inside, and then rushed to the scene of the shooting. At the same time, and proving that smart minds think alike, student Mikael Gross dashed about a hundred yards to his parked car, and retrieved his handgun. Gross and Bridges were acting independently of one another. Neither knew the other had a firearm. But most Americans didn't hear about the fact that these two students instinctively armed themselves. Most news accounts reported that students "tackled" the gunman to the ground.

It was hardly that simple. Bridges and Gross drew down on Odighizuwa, who quickly dropped his pistol, and a third student, Ted Besen ran up to him and Odighizuwa promptly socked him on the jaw. Besen struck back and then there was a pile-on. Within moments, Odighizuwa was subdued and in handcuffs.

There are various definitions for the kind of news coverage that followed in the wake of the Appalachian School of Law shooting, the most polite of which might be "organic fertilizer of male bovine origin." Whatever else they might have been, the news reports were deliberately and undeniably factually misleading by omission.

It is the same kind of factual exclusion that followed in the wake of a high school shooting in Pearl, Mississippi on Wednesday, October 1, 1997. In that incident, an angry 16-year-old student named Luke Woodham, who had murdered his mother earlier that morning by slitting her throat, showed up at Pearl High School and opened fire. Armed with a .30-30 caliber rifle, Woodham targeted his first victims, former girlfriend Christina Menefee and her friend Lydia Dew and killed them on the spot. He then swung the rifle around and fired into a crowd of students before dashing to a parking lot and climbing into his dead mother's car, apparently to drive to a nearby junior high school and kill some more youngsters.

But Woodham hadn't counted on Assistant Principal Joel Myrick. When the shooting started Myrick ran to his car, where he retrieved a

.45-caliber handgun, loaded it and rushed to intercept Woodham, who was by then behind the wheel. Woodham tried to drive around another car but ran his vehicle into a tree. Myrick aimed his gun at Woodham, made him get out of the vehicle, got Woodham on the ground and pressed the muzzle to the teen's neck until police arrived.

Myrick's gun was in his car in violation of the federal Gun Free School Zones Act, a piece of legislation that, the authors wrote in October 2006 in an opinion column entitled "The Dirty Little Secret of Gun Free School Zones," has created free-fire zones on school campuses all over the nation. That column was published in several newspapers following a shooting at an Amish school in Pennsylvania, and hit a raw nerve with readers wherever it ran. In generations past, school kids used to bring their .22 rifles to school to participate in the school rifle team, or they might – in most rural areas of the country – simply have it to shoot a rabbit for the dinner table on the way home. In those days, nobody suffered so much as a hurt feeling from any of those students with guns.

That Norman Rockwell image of America has been changed to one where students who even play cops and robbers in the school yard, substituting their fingers for guns, can be severely punished for simply being children. Zero-tolerance laws that have ostensibly removed firearms from school campuses – they haven't stopped killers from coming to school – have accomplished what the authors suggest is less than nothing.

Zero tolerance statutes have become a substitute for common sense, and they strip teachers and administrators of perhaps the most important lesson of all they can hope to pass to another generation: the exercise of good judgment.

Wrote the authors: "We can no longer afford the empty-headed Utopian illusion that such statutes keep anyone safe, because they don't. Like other restrictive gun control measures, this one has been a monumental failure, and it is literally killing our children."

The late gun rights activist and author Neal Knox wrote in October 1997 that he had spoken to Pearl High School Principal Roy Balantine about the incident. Balantine made it clear that Myrick had been out to his parents' home the previous weekend and had actually forgotten that he had the pistol in his car. The sound of gunshots fortunately jarred Myrick's memory, and thanks to what amounted to a violation of what many believe is an insane federal law, Myrick was able to act under the older natural law of self preservation, and he intervened to prevent even greater bloodshed.

For the longest time, news reports overlooked the fact that Myrick had taken Woodham at gunpoint without firing a shot. That is the way it happens in the overwhelming majority of cases where a legally armed private citizen intervenes in a violent situation, or merely defends himself, his family and/or his property. No shots are fired, but the would-be perpetrator either finds himself held at gunpoint or breaks off the attack to run like the coward he is.

Media Bias against Guns

The mainstream press, what some gun rights activists sarcastically call the "Lamestream Media," doesn't like guns. Reporters frequently mischaracterize firearms because they know virtually nothing about them. Reporters are largely ignorant of firearms because they choose to be; they believe guns are "bad," and the only people who have them are criminals or ignorant rednecks. Many also believe that only police and the military should have guns, and if they cut any slack at all for firearms rights, it is only to the extent that they think, mistakenly of course, that the Second Amendment protects hunting rifles and shotguns with a demonstrable "sporting purpose."

When it comes to talking about firearms used in self-defense, it is far from common to see stories about private citizens defending themselves successfully with a gun, unless there is some obligatory quote from a police official sternly advising the public that they really ought to leave that sort of thing "to the professionals."

Unfortunately, it is rare that "the professionals" are around when a violent crime is actually committed.

In the aftermath of the Appalachian School of Law shooting, researcher John Lott among others took a hard, analytical look at press coverage of that event. He came to a startling conclusion that the mainstream press was loathe to hear: The media is biased against guns, and furthermore, he could prove it.

Writing in the *New York Post* on January 25, 2002 – one week after the Appalachian School of Law outrage – Lott noted that the most remarkable thing about press coverage of that crime was that "out of

280 separate news stories (from a computerized Nexis-Lexis search) in the week after the event, just four stories mentioned that the students who stopped the attack had guns. Only two local newspapers (the Richmond *Times-Dispatch* and the Charlotte *Observer*) mentioned that the students actually pointed their guns at the attacker. Much more typical was the scenario described by the Washington *Post*, where the heroes had simply 'helped subdue' the killer."

"The *New York Times*," Lott continued, "noted only that the attacker was 'tackled by fellow students.' Most in the media who discussed how the attack was stopped said: 'students overpowered a gunman,' 'students ended the rampage by tackling him,' 'the gunman was tackled by four male students before being arrested,' or 'Students ended the rampage by confronting and then tackling the gunman, who dropped his weapon.' In all, 72, stories described how the attacker was stopped without mentioning that the student heroes had guns."

Sadly, Lott lamented, this kind of selective news coverage "was not unusual." The press does it all the time.

When was the last time, for example, that you read anywhere outside of a letter to the editor that researchers have determined there are approximately 2 million defensive uses of firearms every year? When have you ever read that the overwhelming majority of defensive firearms uses never involve a single shot being fired?

How many stories have you read, or heard on television or radio, that mentioned the fact that in the United States today, there are between 4 and 5 million legally-armed private citizens who have been licensed by their states to carry concealed firearms in public?

How often have you been reminded by the mainstream press that legally-armed, licensed private citizens are statistically far less likely than the average citizen to ever get in trouble with the law, for anything?

When did you ever hear about peaceful citizens who carry their handguns openly in Arizona, Vermont, Idaho, Wyoming, Washington and Virginia, and who have harmed nobody you know?

"This misreporting actually endangers people's lives," Lott suggested in his *New York Times* essay. "By selectively reporting the news and turning a defensive gun use story into one where students merely 'overpowered a gunman' the media gives misleading impressions of what works when people are confronted by violence. Research consistently shows that having a gun is the safest way to respond to any type of criminal attack, especially these multiple victim shootings."

In the Fall 2003 edition of the *Claremont Review of Books*, media coverage of the Appalachian School of Law shooting, and John Lott's research of the aftermath, was discussed. The *Review* noted that "When Lott called the *Washington Post* to find out why its story hadn't mentioned the guns, the reporter, who had written only of the students 'pouncing' on the offender, confirmed that both the armed students had told her the same story but that she didn't focus on the 'details' of the incident; also, 'space constraints' were a factor. Even more striking, the Associated Press media relations manager, while denying any intention to downplay the defensive use of guns, expressed his shock at the students' actions. As he told the *Kansas City Star,* 'I thought, my God, they're putting into jeopardy even more people by bringing out these guns'."

One might reasonably lean back and demand of the nearest newspaper editor, "What the hell is going on here? A reporter can skip important details like the fact that two armed students stopped a nutty law school gunman? 'Space constraints' prevented you from adding a single word – *armed* – to your description of responding students?"

Systematically omitting this kind of detail runs counter to what every professor of journalism teaches, or should be teaching, to every journalism major in every college and university on the map. "Detail, detail, detail"; it is the mantra of good newsmen and women who still believe the public has a right to know.

The *Claremont Review of Books* was reviewing Lott's book, *The Bias Against Guns* (Why Almost Everything You've Heard About Gun Control is Wrong). The entire second chapter is devoted to the media bias against firearms, and it is a searing indictment of the way newspaper reporters and editors systematically weed out positive uses of firearms in such news coverage.

Lott actually went to the trouble to count the number of words some newspapers – such as the New York *Times,* Washington *Post* and *USA Today* – devoted to coverage about crimes involving guns as opposed to coverage of stories in which there was a positive gun use. The results of his sampling were not simply startling, they were damning.

He discovered that the *New York Times* during 2001 devoted 104 stories to gun crimes involving 50,745 words and a single story on the defensive use of a gun, which ran 163 words. *USA Today*, he revealed, expended 5,660 words on gun crimes, and not a single word on the defensive use of a firearm. The *Washington Post* published 44,884 words on crimes committed with firearms, but generously expended a whopping 953 words on self-defense stories where a gun was used.

It's not just Lott who is critical of news coverage, or lack of it, when the defensive use of a firearm is left out of a story.

Celebrated former CBS reporter Bernard Goldberg, author of *Bias* and *Arrogance*, his two blistering books about the press, was interviewed by a blog called Ratherbiased.com, the transcript of which is available on-line. Goldberg details how he first read and heard about Lott's findings, and then – as any seasoned reporter will do out of curiosity and a quest for the facts – he did some personal research.

"So I looked at this (issue) simply as a reporter," he explains, "a reporter who doesn't like guns even! And I said, 'This takes it to a new level. This goes beyond groupthink, this goes to group lying.' This is one of those things where you have to say, 'Wait a second, wait a second! How could you have left this stuff out'?"

Beyond School Grounds

Press bias against the responsible use of defensive firearms certainly extends beyond school shootings and how at least some of them were resolved. It does appear to be improving somewhat, in that there are more stories appearing in local newspapers, though they are more often than not smaller daily newspapers and not the big city newspapers.

But these stories are appearing more frequently on gun rights forums such as KeepAndBearArms.com (KABA), a site owned jointly by the Second Amendment Foundation and the Citizens Committee for the Right to Keep and Bear Arms. Rarely does a day go by when there are not one or two, and sometimes more, brief stories about armed self-defense.

The most consistent and disappointing pattern to these stories is that they *are* typically very brief, and there is rarely any follow-up by the same news agency. For example, one day there might be a three-paragraph story gleaned from some newspaper or a local television station about a foiled armed robbery or attempted home invasion in which sometimes suspects are named, sometimes they are not. Sometimes victims are named, frequently they are not.

Yet one can go to the same news agencies or newspapers for follow-up details and they are nowhere to be found. In the television news business, there is an unwritten rule about news coverage that goes beyond the legendary "If it bleeds, it leads" philosophy. This is the rule that says "If it's not happening today, it's not happening."

But sometimes, newspapers can be not only remarkably responsive to the interests of their readers, and the public at large, by doing a bit of research on some gun-related issue, they can be brutally honest.

Such was the case with the New York *Sun*, which editorialized in its February 2, 2007 edition against coverage that had appeared in the rival New York *Times* about the status of concealed carry in the state of Florida. Why the *Times* was focusing on Florida's concealed carry law is, in itself, an issue of media bias against guns.

The *Florida Sun-Sentinel* had done an "expose" on concealed carry, revealing that under the concealed carry statute that went into effect 20 years ago, the state had issued some concealed carry permits to felons. When a series of stories appeared about this, it was cause for anti-gun newspaper editors to join the lynch mob in an attempt to portray such laws as the media has so often portrayed gun shows: sources of guns for criminals.

But the New York *Sun* was having none of it. In a show of remarkable fortitude for a New York newspaper, this one berated the *Times* for its invective that included accusations about the Florida Legislature's "gruesome handiwork" at having passed the concealed carry statute in the first place.

And then the *Sun* did something even more remarkable: It published details about how Florida's violent crime rate had plummeted since passage of the concealed carry law, called the Jack Hagler Self Defense Act.

Said the *Sun* editorial: "Since the Jack Hagler Self Defense Act went into effect in 1987, crime in Florida has gone down by almost every measure there is. According to statistics provided by the Florida Department of Law Enforcement, firearm murders in Florida between 1987 and 2005 dropped in real terms to 521 from 697. Expressed as the number of firearm murders per 100,000 persons, the drop is even more dramatic, to 2.9 from 5.8. That's a change of 50%. The drop in violent crime overall is less precipitous but equally steady, including drops in the rates of murder, aggravated assault, robbery, and sexual assault."

While the newspaper acknowledged that it would be presumptuous to credit the crime drop entirely to the concealed carry statute, the *Sun* did say that it is difficult "to argue that legalizing the carry of concealed weapons has increased crime. Or that it has had some terrible adverse consequence."

Recall earlier references to dire predictions by anti-gun newspapers that passage of such laws would invariably lead to blood in the streets and gunfights at traffic accidents.

The *Sun* put it bluntly: "Predictions of wild-West style shootouts and lawlessness have proven false. That's not what happened. Not in Florida or in any of the other 37 states with legalized concealed carry. There is nothing 'lethal' or 'gruesome' about permitting law-abiding citizens to defend themselves by carrying a weapon — or simply to carry a weapon without defending themselves."

And the New York *Sun* didn't stop there. It went for what one might consider the Times' jugular, when it concluded its editorial by observing, "The truth is that if there is a lesson to be drawn from the *Sun-Sentinel's* reporting, it's not, as the *Times* suggests, that there is something wrong with existing laws. Rather it is that judges should start treating criminals as the law prescribes.

"In Florida," the *Sun* concluded, "the law on concealed carry allows persons who have committed serious crimes and have reached plea agreements with judges to have their records scrubbed, to become eligible once more to receive a concealed carry license. An ordinary person might expect an editorial writer opining on all this, particularly in a city where the mayor is trying to make an issue out of 'illegal' guns, to look into the statistics on crime and include these facts in an editorial, if only to deal with them. But at the *Times*, they're not fit to print."

Pandering Gun Control

When Americans fight back, they should not have to worry about the media coverage that follows. All too often, when reports are printed or air about the defensive use of a firearm, reporters will frequently say that the suspect was "gunned down" by the person using a firearm in self-defense.

This has happened many times when police officers are forced to shoot a suspect, but this term also finds its way into news coverage of self-defense.

One might honestly wonder if there might be some correlation between a newspaper's editorial position on gun control, and the way its news staff covers self-defense stories. The same can be asked of television news agencies, particularly those that are network affiliates.

In a piece titled "Outgunned: How the Network News Media Are Spinning the Gun Control Debate" (available on-line at www. mediaresearch.org/specialreports/2000/rep01052000.asp) that appeared January 2, 2000, Geoffrey Dickens, senior analyst at the Media Research Center, blasted the major networks for their bias toward gun control.

"ABC's *World News Tonight* was the most biased in favor of gun control," he wrote, "airing 43 anti-gun stories to only three pro-gun segments, with 24 neutral reports. Within that sample, the talking head ratio matched the overall average of 2-to-1, with 125 gun control sound bites, 62 for gun rights, and 120 neutral clips.

"CNN's *The World Today* slanted in the direction of gun-control arguments in 50 stories," Dickens continued, "compared to only seven with substantially more arguments in favor of gun rights. (Thirty-four reports were neutral.) CNN's selection of talking heads advocating more gun control was the most disproportionate (98 to 40, with 79 neutral clips).

"*CBS Evening News* stories promoted gun control 28 times and favored gun rights on just three occasions (22 were neutral)," he said. "CBS had the closest ratio of talking heads with 59 for gun control, 35 opposed, and 74 neutral.

"*NBC Nightly News* was the least imbalanced," Dickens noted, "albeit with a tilt of five to one: 43 anti-gun rights stories versus eight pro-gun rights stories, with 36 neutral pieces. But three of the pro-gun stories came on one night (April 30, 1999). By a ratio of almost 2 to 1, NBC aired gun control exponents with a count of 130 advocates to 72 opponents (and 24 neutral voices)."

He also had some observations about morning network news programs.

"Out of 353 gun policy segments," he wrote, "anti-gun stories outnumbered pro-gun stories by 193 to 15, or a ratio of more than 13 to 1 (145 were neutral or balanced). Analysts counted both morning news reports and interviews."

This bias cannot be explained away by the press simply pleading ignorance. There is substantial data available to show what the true facts are about armed private citizens using firearms in legal self-defense situations.

Writing in the September 22, 2003 issue of *The American Conservative*, author and conservative commentator Pat Buchanan alluded to research that was published in the Northwestern Law School's *Journal of Criminal Law and Criminology* by Florida State University Prof. Gary Kleck, one of the nation's foremost authorities on the effect of firearms laws.

Buchanan pointed at Kleck's paper, "Armed Resistance to Crime: The Prevalence and Nature of Self-Defense with a Gun." In that paper, Kleck noted that "law abiding citizens use guns to defend themselves against criminals 2.5 million times a year or about 6,850 times every day," Buchanan wrote. He also noted that about 200,000 of those defensive gun uses are by women defending themselves against sexual assault.

Buchanan also noted that citizens shoot and kill about twice as many criminals as do police officers during an average year.

Here, again, the press seems to ignore this unless someone like Buchanan writes about it.

Whether the issue is self-defense with firearms, or closing some mythical "gun show loophole," the mainstream press has consistently been at odds with the lawful ownership of firearms to one degree or another. It may be an editorial calling for tougher gun laws after some shooting, overlooking the fact that the hundreds, if not thousands, of gun laws already on the books did nothing to prevent the crime that led to the editorial.

It might be one-sided news coverage of a gun control effort, in which a reporter may contend that they could neither find someone from the other side to interview, or that their calls for a reaction were not returned…even if the call was placed ten minutes before press time or air time.

And it may just be the pattern of omission that surfaced in the news coverage following the Appalachian School of Law shooting in 2002.

Perhaps the problem was best summed up in the final paragraph of the Claremont Institute's October 13, 2003 review of John Lott's book.

"Unfortunately," the review observed, "*The Bias Against Guns* has not yet received the attention it deserves, with almost no reviews in the nation's leading newspapers and journals of opinion. By rights, Lott's new book ought to have a powerful effect on the gun control debate in the country. One fears, though, that the bias is so strong that it is impervious to facts. As Lott convincingly shows, the stakes in this debate are unusually high."

CHAPTER 7

Gun Free Folly

Violent acts happen from time to time in places where one should theoretically least expect them, and as previously explained, the murderous people who commit those crimes do not make appointments.

Yet in the aftermath of the February 2007 killing spree by a teenage gunman at Salt Lake City's Trolley Square shopping mall, gun control activist Gary Sackett, a board member of Utah's Gun Violence Prevention Center, insisted, "I'm not comfortable arming our entire country for protection. That's a paranoid notion."

Quoted by the *Salt Lake Tribune* on February 14, Sackett added, "You can't protect against every madman with a firearm or a hand grenade. That sort of thing is going to happen from time to time."

But instead of acknowledging that maybe, just *maybe*, an armed citizen might be able to intervene against some "madman with a firearm," Sackett and his group steadfastly oppose the notion of concealed carry, or being prepared to confront a violent attack. Instead, he seemed quite resigned to accepting the possibility that innocent citizens occasionally are murdered.

The following day, the same newspaper carried yet another gem from the mouth of Mr. Sackett: "If we arm everybody, we are a lost society. And most western countries have figured that out."

Sackett's remarks seemed as lame as those uttered by Paul Helmke, president of the Brady Campaign to Prevent Gun Violence in the wake of a school shooting at an Amish school in Pennsylvania in 2006. Helmke's reaction was that "we need to do something about that." He suggested a national dialogue on the subject of such violence, as if more talk will stop suicidal maniacs like Amish school gunman Charles

Roberts from carrying out their cowardly, despicable deeds.

Presumably for people like Sackett and Helmke, in order for us to prove we have achieved some higher moral ground, we must occasionally accept a few "sacrifices" on the altar of political correctness. Cut through all the rhetoric about lost societies and national dialogues and what you have left is the preposterous notion that some people must die in order that others be prevented from killing in self-defense.

Salt Lake City's Trolley Square shares one thing in common with all-too-many crime scenes around the country where multiple-victim shootings occur. There's a sign posted at the entrance that says firearms are not allowed on the premises. You will find such signs in many locations in many states; Minnesota and Ohio statutes, for example, have provisions allowing private property owners to post their businesses off limits to individuals licensed to carry concealed handguns.

Such places are what most firearms and self-defense experts agree are risk-free working environments for criminals and homicidal lunatics.

What occurred at Trolley Square, when 18-year-old Sulejman Talovic, armed with a shotgun and a handgun, the latter obtained illegally, is proof positive that armed intervention is a justifiable reaction to a mass killing in progress; hand-wringing and arm waving about how wrong it is to meet violence with violence be damned.

Talovic's bloody rampage came to an abrupt end in a fusillade of gunfire from Salt Lake City police officers and another man, an off-duty police officer out of his jurisdiction. Ogden Officer Kenneth Hammond was dining with his pregnant wife, Sarina, at a restaurant in the shopping mall when Talovic opened fire. Armed with a .45-caliber semiautomatic pistol, Hammond heroically rushed to the sound of the gunfire, and engaged the gunman.

At the time it could be reasonably and substantially argued that Hammond was merely an armed private citizen with a concealed carry permit. Miles away from his city, dressed casually like any other citizen, it might be also argued that Hammond had no business packing a pistol inside the Square. But don't expect there to be much debate about that because of his heroism, and the fact that he was instrumental in stopping a murderous rampage.

Salt Lake Police Chief Chris Burbank explained it best when he told the *Tribune* that Talovic wanted to "kill a large number of people" and that he probably would have been successful, had not Hammond intervened, cornered Talovic and traded shots with him, keeping him busy until uniformed officers arrived.

In a rather insightful essay titled "How to Stop Shooting Sprees," published by the Heartland Institute in the January/February 2001 edition of *Intellectual Ammunition*, author Morgan Reynolds unknowingly at the time established a rock-solid rebuttal to the arguments of people like Utah's Gary Sackett.

Quoting research done by William Landes of the University of Chicago and John Lott, then of Yale University, Reynolds noted that the two researchers found an average of 21 multiple-victim shootings per year from 1977 to 1995. He said they were "rare events" compared to other offenses.

Lott has gone on to write a couple of milestone books mentioned in earlier chapters, and he is a recognized authority on the effects of firearms laws on crime.

Reynolds wrote, "After every one of these aberrant events, leftists demand 'more gun control': longer waiting periods, more restrictions on purchases. Nearly any gun control will do. A lack of evidence that such regulations actually reduce public shootings fails to dampen the enthusiasm. One suspects the real agenda is not to solve a problem, but to reduce private gun ownership and expand the power of government.

"There is, however, one law highly correlated with a sharp drop in multiple killings: a 'shall issue' or 'right-to-carry,' concealed handgun law," Reynolds continued. "This kind of law mandates that if a citizen meets certain objective criteria like age and no criminal history, then he or she shall be issued a permit to carry a concealed handgun upon request.

"Landes and Lott," Reynolds revealed, "find that the number of mass public shootings plummeted by 85 percent, mass murders dropped 89 percent, and injuries plunged 82 percent in the 14 states that... adopted shall-issue carry laws between 1977 and 1995. (Lott's book, *More Guns=Less Crime*, gives more detail.) Most of the decline comes in the first year of the law, leaving little doubt about the cause."

So, how does one explain a shooting like the one at Trolley Square, in a state with a fairly liberal concealed carry law? It happened in a place where law-abiding citizens were functionally disarmed by a gun prohibition. Such a prohibition, it is becoming all too clear, is only obeyed by someone who would not break the law. Gun prohibitions, as Talovic and so many others have proven over the course of the last several years, have no effect at all on people bent on mayhem and murder.

Firearms are not permitted at the Tacoma, Washington shopping mall, either, though that mall really had not been posted off limits to licensed concealed carry when accused gunman Dominick Sergio Maldonado opened fire in November 2005. Incredibly, the person who suffered the most serious injury was an armed store employee identified as Brendan "Dan" McKown who, according to differing accounts, lowered his gun and tried to talk the teenager into surrendering, only to be wounded in a burst of gunfire, and left permanently disabled.

It has been speculated that his actions forced the gunman to retreat into one of the stores, at which point the shooting stopped and police were able to later corner him and talk him into surrendering. What is clear is that the accused gunman never expected to be confronted by an armed citizen, and McKown's intervention, regardless its personal consequences, resulted in a greater good by possibly saving other lives.

On a website operated by the Buckeye Firearms Association, an Ohio-based grassroots gun rights group, one member posted the notation that "Criminals respond well to force. It's one of the things they understand. You can always decide not to respond with a gun you are carrying, but if you ever want the option to respond with a gun, you need to plan ahead."

The author of that piece left out one important consideration: If you ever want the option to respond with a gun...*you need to have a gun with you.* Under social and even media pressure from anti-gun politicians or activist groups, or perhaps even their own insurance companies and attorneys, business owners can hardly be blamed for buckling.

Financial and social pressures are powerful tools used by gun control proponents.

On the other side, however, there are efforts to hold such business establishments liable for any injuries that occur on their premises if someone could have acted in self-defense, had he or she been armed.

Noted Gerard Valentino in a commentary on CNSNews.com

December 16, 2004: "At first it sounds like good public policy to ban firearms in establishments that serve liquor. Further scrutiny however reveals that any gun free zone, including schools, restaurants, bars and government buildings offer criminals the freedom to kill with impunity."

'Victim Disarmament Zones'

They are called "Gun Free Zones" by their proponents, but among gun rights and self-defense activists, they are known sarcastically as "Victim Disarmament Zones."

This issue is particularly sensitive in Ohio, where concealed carry is a relatively new freedom being enjoyed by a growing number of Buckeye State residents. But many places are off-limits, including places of worship. But the Buckeye Firearms Association reported that historically, not only did people bring their guns to church, they were encouraged to do so.

Doing a bit of historical research, the BFA revealed that in 1788, a law was passed to establish and regulate a militia in Marietta. This law required all men between the ages of 16 and 50 to turn out for drill every Sunday and they had to appear with a musket and bayonet, cartridge box, powder horn, one pound of powder and four pounds of lead.

In 1791, according to this report, the law changed to require drills on Saturday. Those who attended Saturday drills did not have to attend Sunday church services. However, if those armed men showed up at church with their guns on Sunday, they were exempt from the Saturday drill.

How times have changed in Ohio, and evidently not for the better.

On Sunday, January 28, 2007 in Columbus, a man and woman robbery team decided to pull a holdup in the one place where they did not expect to face any resistance: Christ the King Catholic Church.

Wendell K. Hollingsworth, 43, had a criminal history dating back to 1981. Between then and 1992, Hollingsworth was, according to an account in the *Columbus Dispatch* of January 29, arrested a dozen times on various serious charges including kidnapping, robbery, aggravated burglary and safecracking. His companion, Celeste M. Smith, had pleaded guilty in 2004 to theft, forgery and receiving stolen property.

Once in side the church, Hollingsworth waited as Smith went through the pews, grabbing purses. When one of the parishioners ran to grab Smith, Hollingsworth pulled a handgun and declared that a robbery was in progress.

But the 67-year-old worshipper was not about to let go of Smith, and Hollingsworth struck the older man on the head several times with the handgun. When the robber aimed his pistol at the man's chest, the parishioner raised his hands and gave up.

But that was the moment when four other church goers came charging through the doors and tackled the gunman. Those four men, reportedly aged from their late 50s to their early 70s, piled on top of Hollingsworth, knowing he had a gun.

Moments later, summoned by other parishioners using cell phones, the police arrived and carted Hollingsworth and Smith off to jail.

In that brief moment, five Americans fought back and prevailed, despite the fact that none were armed. So far as the BFA is concerned, they ought to have had the option.

In the aftermath, the BFA website posted a commentary that noted, "These two criminals couldn't have cared less about state legislators establishing this private property as a victim disarmament zone. A gun control law which prohibits felons from even possessing firearms didn't stop Hollingsworth either – nor did the justice system" which had paroled the gunman only four months earlier, in August 2006, after having spent 14 years behind bars of a sentence originally set to run between 18 and 53 years.

Quoting firearms researcher David Kopel of the Colorado-based Independence Institute, the BFA noted that powerful church organizations – evidently ignoring the "separation of church and state" tradition that they often wave when there is talk of such things as taxing churches – lobbied hard against reforming the Gun Control Act of 1968.

One gun control lobbying group, the National Coalition to Ban Handguns, later re-named the Coalition to Stop Gun Violence, according to the commentary and Kopel, was founded by yet another powerful church organization.

Of course, churches are not the only places established as victim disarmament zones. Hospitals, restaurants, sports stadiums and, of course, the workplace, have all been posted off-limits to defensive handguns by various states' concealed carry statutes.

Take a look at Timothy Baker, Jr. who appeared on Monday, May 22, 2006 at the Cleveland, Ohio office where his estranged girlfriend was employed, despite the fact that not only did the girlfriend have a restraining order against him, but there was also a "no guns" sign posted at the entrance of the Euclid Office & Medical Plaza where she worked.

According to the *Cleveland Plain Dealer*, Baker, 28, took five people hostage and held a gun to the head of a chiropractor, but then ordered all of the hostages out of the office. Police negotiators tried to talk Baker into surrendering, but instead, he shot himself in the head. Fortunately, nobody else was hurt.

It doesn't always happen that way.

On December 26, 2000, a shaggy-haired man with a serious grudge against his employer, Edgewater Technologies in Wakefield, Massachusetts, opened fire with a semiautomatic rifle and killed seven co-workers. It was a brutal crime for which the killer, Michael "Mucko" McDermott, will rot in prison for the rest of his life.

Some gun rights activists think it could have gone another way, however, because one of McDermott's victims, Louis "Sandy" Javelle, a New Hampshire resident who worked at the Massachusetts firm, had been "legally disarmed" by Massachusetts gun laws.

In a gut-wrenching letter to the editor of the *Boston Herald* on Jan. 11, 2001, David Bergquist of Temple, New Hampshire – a friend of Javelle's – noted that "Sandy held both a federal firearms license and a permit to carry a handgun in New Hampshire. Ironically, the gun laws in Massachusetts prevented him from carrying a concealed handgun. But these same laws did not prevent Michael McDermott from obtaining illegal firearms.

"When the rampage started," Bergquist's letter continued, "Sandy told co-workers to lock the door behind him and barricade it. He then confronted McDermott and became the third victim. If Sandy had been permitted to carry a pistol, he could have stopped McDermott. That meant that five other people could possibly have survived this tragedy. But Sandy did not have that option."

A gun control law pandered to the public as one more tool against armed violent criminals instead disarmed the victims. Such laws, say gun rights activists who are trying hard to repeal or amend the statutes, only make it easier for monsters like McDermott to chalk up a body count.

The Luby's Massacre

There is, perhaps, no more vivid example of the results of a gun-free zone than the events that unfolded at Luby's Cafeteria in Killeen, Texas on October 16, 1991. This was the event that led to the passage of concealed carry in Texas in 1995, and contributed greatly to the downfall of the woman governor who had cavalierly vetoed concealed carry legislation, defeated by a man who promised to sign it. That man later became president of the United States, George W. Bush.

A madman named George Hennard, a Navy and Merchant Marine veteran who had been discharged two years earlier for reportedly possessing marijuana and making racist remarks, picked that October mid-day to drive his 1987 ford Ranger pickup truck through the front windows of the Luby's Cafeteria. He was heard to exclaim "This is what Bell County has done to me" before opening fire with a Ruger P89 and Glock 17, both semiautomatic pistols chambered in 9mm.

It was the day after his 35th birthday, and the last day of his life. But he did not go alone. By the time he had finished shooting, and taking his own life as police closed in, Hennard had murdered 22 people and fatally wounded two others, among them Alphonse "Al" Gratia, Jr, 71 and his wife, Ursula Edith Marie Gratia, 67. They were at the restaurant having lunch with their daughter, Dr. Suzanna Gratia Hupp.

It would later be discovered that some people in the restaurant had guns in their vehicles, including Dr. Gratia Hupp. But, due to there being no law in Texas at the time allowing concealed carry, nobody was armed, allowing Hennard a target-rich environment.

Dr. Gratia Hupp watched helplessly as her parents were murdered. On that day, she became a woman with a mission. Maintaining that had she been permitted by law to have had her handgun in the restaurant she would have been able to fight back, Gratia Hupp began campaigning for the passage of a concealed carry law. It would consume the next five years of her life.

Then-Governor Ann Richards, a Democrat and Texas' second woman governor (the first was Democrat Miriam Amanda Wallace

"Ma" Ferguson elected in 1924 for one term and again in 1932 for a second term), vetoed the legislation, arousing a tidal wave of anger among Texas conservatives. In 1994, she was defeated by George Bush in a race everyone expected her to win, but sentiment against her veto, along with a few other political missteps, irreparably damaged her campaign.

Meanwhile, Gratia Hupp was pushing concealed carry, and the measure was approved and signed into law by Bush. In 1996, Mrs. Hupp was elected to her first of five terms in the Texas Legislature, where she became an untiring supporter of self-defense rights.

The Luby's Massacre began a chain reaction that spread beyond the borders of Texas. Concealed carry statutes had been adopted in some states, but Americans tired of playing the victim and weary of being told to simply wait until police arrive had had enough.

What was happening in Texas was certainly part of a larger phenomenon. The Luby's case, and a strong tilt among the electorate to more conservative values after Congress during the first two years of Bill Clinton's presidency passed the Brady Law and the ban on 87 different types of semiautomatic rifles, shotguns and handguns, indicated Americans wanted a chance to defend themselves. What the Luby's incident taught the country is that there was, and still remains, what writer Gerard Valentino called "The False Hope of Gun-Free Zones" in his December 2004 CNSNews.com commentary.

"Once again," he wrote about Luby's, "the media never asked how many people were killed because the license holder was disarmed.

"Past instances of mass shootings," Valentino continued, "and common sense, teach us that when a victim resists with a firearm the violence ends quickly. Arguments claiming armed intervention by citizens leads to higher death tolls do not stand up to scrutiny. Death tolls are demonstrably higher when victims are unable to fight back as compared to cases where an armed victim resists."

Remember that Valentino wrote this in late 2004: "It's time to ask how many more people must needlessly die before gun control activists and legislators realize that disarming law-abiding citizens leaves them easy prey to criminals."

The argument never ceases to end, and not much seems to change. Or does it?

When Citizens Intervene

December 17, 1991 found citizens in Anniston, Alabama getting ready for Christmas, and the memory of the Luby's massacre three states away and two months earlier was fading.

A postal clerk named Thomas Glenn Terry was enjoying a late-evening dinner with his wife at a Shoney's Restaurant. There were about 20 customers and employees in the restaurant at the time, according to various published accounts. The most accurate of these accounts was written by J. Neil Schulman, author of *Stopping Power: Why 70 Million Americans Own Guns* and *Self Control, Not Gun Control*. The story was initially reported incorrectly, and Schulman, being the thorough journalist he is, corrected himself in an account that was just as chilling as the initial reports.

As the Terrys were finishing their meal, three thugs burst into the restaurant in a takeover holdup. The robbers rounded up everyone and after collecting wallets and jewelry, began herding them back to a walk-in cooler, but Terry managed to separate himself from the group.

He made his way to a rear door in an effort to get out and call police, but to his horror, he found the door chained shut. Some early accounts had Terry hiding under a table, but he told author Schulman that wasn't what happened.

Stuck at the back door, Terry is discovered by one of the robbers. What that thug didn't see, though, was the .45-caliber Government Model 1911 Colt pistol under his sweater. When the gunman aimed a pistol at Terry, he drew and fired, seriously wounding a man later identified as 25-year-old Levi Pace of Adamsville.

Terry then turned his attention to the second gunman, later identified as Reginald "Butch" Bean, 23, and a gunfight erupted. The third robber, later identified as Robert Earl "Rock" Franklin, 22, fled as soon as Terry shot Pace.

When the shooting stopped, Bean stumbled into the parking lot and died.

When Schulman and others wrote about this case, they compared it to the Luby's Massacre for one important reason: There was no massacre. Schulman actually wrote a piece titled "A Massacre We Didn't Hear About."

Terry became an overnight hero because it was widely believed that the gunmen were herding all the patrons and employees to the cooler to murder them.

Conservative commentator and author Ann Coulter summed it up in a 1999 column she wrote, noting why this case did not get the mainstream media attention that the Luby's killings did.

"A massacre is a story," Coulter observed. "Thwarting a massacre isn't. But once you know about Anniston, and similar averted tragedies, something will start to leap out at you as you read news accounts of gunmen shooting scores of innocents. Massacre stories always include a terrifying account of how the killers proceeded from victim to victim, pausing to reload, and shooting again. Mass murder requires that the victims be unarmed."

Schulman had this to say when he wrote about the case in the January 1, 1992 edition of the *Los Angeles Times*:

"Today's 'consensus reality' asserts that private firearms play no effective role in the civic defense, and that firearms must be restricted to reduce crime. The media repeat these assertions as a catechism, and treat those who challenge them as heretics…

"It's time to rid ourselves of the misbegotten idea that public safety can be achieved by unilateral disarmament of the honest citizen," he concluded, "and realize that the price of public safety is, like liberty, eternal vigilance. We can tire ourselves in futile debates on how to keep guns out of the wrong hands. Or we can decide that innocent lives deserve better than to be cut short, if only we, as a society, will take upon ourselves the civic responsibility of defending our fellow citizens, as Thomas Glenn Terry did in Alabama."

According to various studies, particularly one done by the National Institute of Justice and another done by Florida State University criminologist Gary Kleck, what Terry did at the Anniston Shoney's in 1991 is not that unusual in America, though the mainstream press seems loathe to report such incidents. Kleck has estimated that there may be as many as 2.5 million defensive firearms uses annually, and the NIJ study, though more conservative, suggested that up to 1.5 million Americans annually used firearms defensively.

Nobody will have to convince witnesses to an incident that unfolded on Thursday, August 25, 2005 at a Wal-Mart in Albuquerque, New Mexico, nor would a woman identified as Joyce Cordova (spelled Cordoba in some reports), 46, an employee at the store. There would be no argument from 72-year-old Due Moore, described in one report as "a cold case volunteer" for the Albuquerque Police Department.

Even Felix Vigil, 54, would attest to the critical importance of having an armed citizen present when a violent, deadly crime unfolds. That is, Vigil would attest to this if he was still around, but he's dead. By all accounts, he had it coming.

New Mexico's concealed carry statute took effect January 1, 2004. Thirteen days later, Due Moore was one of the first citizens in the state to get his concealed pistol permit, having taken a required certification course at Calibre's National Shooters Sports Center, according to the Associated Press account of August 30.

On the fateful day, Moore just happens to be part of the crowd at the Wal-Mart where Cordova works at the deli counter. According to Albuquerque's KRQE Channel 13 news, Vigil and Cordova have a "long history of domestic violence."

It is just after 5 p.m. when Vigil attacks Cordova and begins stabbing her repeatedly. Moore is about to make history. He will become the first licensed private citizen in New Mexico to use his legally concealed handgun to stop a vicious, potentially deadly crime. Witnessing the horror in front of him, he draws his gun and fires. According to witnesses – as reported by KRQE news – at least three shots are fired.

Vigil is mortally wounded. Cordova, stabbed several times, is transported to a nearby hospital, where she is treated and ultimately survives the attack.

Albuquerque Officer Trish Hoffman, who was quoted in Chapter One noting that the shooting of home invaders would hopefully "send a message to people who are breaking into homes. They're engaging in very dangerous behavior, not only to the people they're robbing, but to themselves," is quoted by local reporters in the aftermath of the Wal-Mart incident.

"It's probably a very good thing he (Moore) was there," Hoffman observed. "Ms. Cordova may not be here today if it had not been for him."

In a year-end wrap-up of killings in Albuquerque, a newspaper account said the death of Felix Vigil was a "justified homicide."

Lawful citizen intervention with a firearm does not always end with shots fired. More often than not, a crime is interrupted and stopped without gunfire.

In Indianapolis, Indiana on Thursday, August 17, 2006, a thug identified as William McMiller, Jr., 40, made the mistake of walking into a Kentucky Fried Chicken franchise at about 3:20 p.m., ordering a bucket of chicken and then demanding money from a cashier identified as Deanne Slaughter. According to the August 19 edition of the *Indianapolis Star* newspaper, he threatened to shoot Slaughter and had his hand in a pocket, as if he were holding a concealed handgun.

It was McMiller's bad luck that a customer, Paul Sherlock, actually did have a handgun, a 9mm Taurus, and when McMiller moved to jump over the counter, Sherlock stopped him. With the muzzle aimed squarely at McMiller's back, Sherlock held the would-be robber until police arrived.

Instead of a gun, they found a long screwdriver in his pocket.

This story underscores what researchers like Kleck and other authorities, including the National Rifle Association, have long reminded the public that in the overwhelming majority of defensive gun uses, a shot is never fired.

When he wrote about this phenomenon on September 3, 2005, columnist and radio commentator Larry Elder noted that in 2003, non-suicide firearms deaths totaled 12,548 people, and that number included homicides, accidents and "cases of undetermined intent."

Elder quoted UCLA professor emeritus James Q. Wilson, who noted, "We know from Census Bureau surveys that something beyond a hundred thousand uses of guns for self-defense occur every year. We know from smaller surveys of a commercial nature that the number may be as high as two-and-a-half or three million. We don't know what the right number is, but whatever the right number is, it's not a trivial number."

Elder also quoted firearms law expert David Kopel, who wrote, ". . . [W]hen a robbery victim does not defend himself, the robber succeeds 88 percent of the time, and the victim is injured 25 percent of the time. When a victim resists with a gun, the robbery success rate falls to 30 percent, and the victim injury rate falls to 17 percent. No other response to a robbery -- from drawing a knife to shouting for help to fleeing -- produces such low rates of victim injury and robbery success."

Gun control proponents will steadfastly argue that the risk of a homicide in the home is three times greater if there is a firearm in that home. This estimate, though, is based on a discredited study that did not take into account the potential that at least some criminals are deterred by the possibility of encountering an armed homeowner. It also did not take into account the fact that over 90 percent of these cases, the homeowner does not fire a shot, and in many cases holds the criminal at gunpoint until police arrive.

There has yet to be a definitive study that would debunk the value of having a defensive firearm in a place of business. There is no research that concludes that it is better to submit to a criminal attack, while there is ample evidence from Kleck, Kopel, Lott and others that fighting back can save your life, and perhaps many other lives.

As the authors observed in a 2006 opinion piece that was published in several newspapers, self-styled "liberal progressives" have championed this notion of "gun free zones" and the result – especially on school grounds around the nation – has been nothing short of disastrous. We wrote, on the subject of gun-free school zones, that such laws "leave our children and their teachers vulnerable to the whims of any nutball looking for 15 minutes of fame because of real or imagined problems or perversions."

Such laws, we wrote, "have defrauded American citizens, and especially our children, of genuine safety."

One need only ask those who survived the minutes of terror at Salt Lake City's Trolley Square about how safe they now feel in a "gun free zone." Or ask any of the survivors at Luby's Cafeteria.

Then balance that by chatting with the 22 people who walked out of the Anniston, Alabama Shoney's restaurant in December 1991, alive and unharmed, to enjoy Christmas with their families.

CHAPTER 8

'You're On Your Own'

According to an estimate by the National Shooting Sports Foundation (NSSF) – a Connecticut-based firearms industry group – there are more than 290 million privately-owned firearms in the United States today. The number of American households with at least one firearm has risen to an estimated 47.8 million.

Americans keep guns for various reasons, primarily for personal protection, followed by hunting, target shooting and competition and other recreational shooting, and, of course, collecting. There are between 80 and 90 million gun owners in the United States, but only about 15 to 17 million licensed hunters. Four million are members of the National Rifle Association, another 650,000 are members or supporters of the Second Amendment Foundation, 600,000 list themselves as members of the Citizens Committee for the Right to Keep and Bear Arms, and so on down the line, with smaller memberships for the Gun Owners of America and various regional gun rights organizations. For the sake of argument, say there are about 7 million gun owners in the country who belong to or are affiliated with one organization or the other and quite probably more than one group. That leaves tens of millions of unaffiliated firearms owners, which translates to the simple fact that these people do not have firearms because they are of a particular political or philosophical bent, but most probably because they feel the need for personal security. Since the terrorist attacks on September 11, 2001, the number of gun sales in this country has risen, and one of the fastest-growing markets is for semiautomatic firearms; handguns and rifles primarily, followed by shotguns that are not specifically designed for hunting or target shooting.

Perhaps most remarkable about these figures is something that gun control proponents have never been challenged by the dominant media to explain. While the number of firearms in the hands of private citizens has risen, the number of accidental firearms fatalities has actually declined, dramatically in some categories. This flies in the face of rhetoric from gun control organizations that have tossed about such claims that thousands of children die each year from gun violence. That is simply not true.

When it released its 2007 report on "Injury Facts," the National Safety Council revealed an impressive 40 percent decrease in the number of accidental gun-related fatalities over a ten-year period that ended in 2005, the most recent year for which data was available when this book was written.

That same report disclosed a whopping decline of 69 percent in the number of firearm-related accidents involving children ages 14 and under, between 1995 and 2003.

Most important of all revelations in the report, suggested the NSSF, *less than 1 percent* of the 109,277 accidental deaths recorded in 2005 involved a firearm.

"The most common deadly accidents involved motor vehicles, poisonings and falls, claiming 75 percent of all accidental deaths," the NSSF said in a press release detailing the report. It also said that the declining trends shown in the National Safety Council report were supported by "research available from the Centers for Disease Control and Prevention" in Georgia. It was the CDC that determined a dramatic decline in the number of accidental firearm-related deaths in all four sections of the United States.

Credit for this decline must go to various organizations, including the NSSF, which has created Project ChildSafe® in cooperation with the U.S. Department of Justice. Under this program, more than 35 million free gun safety information kits, including gun locks, have been distributed nationwide. NSSF has also distributed other safety literature and videos emphasizing outreach to public schools.

Add to that the firearm safety programs offered by the National Rifle Association – often called the "Red Cross of gun safety." The NRA is the country's premier gun safety organization, which can hardly be said of gun control groups masquerading as "gun safety" organizations. The next time someone from Americans for Gun Safety, the Brady Campaign to Prevent Gun Violence, Million Mom March or any of the state-based "CeaseFire" groups calls itself a "gun safety" organization, ask them how many certified firearms safety instructors they have.

The NRA has tens of thousands of volunteer firearm instructors, and it also helps train the nation's law enforcement instructors. NRA courses on home firearm safety, personal protection, basic pistol, rifle and shotgun shooting, and its renowned "Refuse to Be A Victim" course have trained hundreds of thousands, if not millions, of American citizens the safe use of firearms.

The award-winning Eddie Eagle safety course for children has been copied – usually without any credit at all to the NRA – by various organizations. It teaches youngsters a very simple lesson that has worked: "If you find a gun, Stop! Don't touch! Leave the Area! Tell an Adult."

The International Hunter Education Association, in cooperation with state fish and wildlife agencies, has been providing hunter safety education materials and model programs for the hunter education courses that are now mandated in all 50 states for youngsters and new hunters before they can obtain a hunting license. These courses are credited with raising awareness about firearms safety in the field, and reducing the number of hunting accidents and fatalities over the past half-century.

All of these safety efforts have contributed to a continued decline in accidental gun deaths. In 2005, there were 730 accidental firearm-related fatalities, down from the 750 that were reported in 2004. Accidental firearm-related injuries among teenagers between the ages of 15 and 19 declined 11 percent that year.

The rise of internet chat lists about firearms and shooting has also contributed to a growing awareness of gun safety and the role of firearms in personal protection. There are chat lists devoted to specific types of pistols and rifles, others that address concealed carry issues and even one that focuses on open carry, which is legal in more places than you might think including Ohio, Vermont, Virginia, Alaska, Arizona and Washington states, for example.

If one were to conclude that all of this interest in firearms was due in large part to a growing awareness among American citizens that they are ultimately responsible for their own safety, you would be correct. Indeed, various federal and state court rulings have consistently held that it is a "fundamental principle of American law that a government and its agents are under no general duty to provide public services, such as police protection, to any individual citizen."

Allow the authors to translate: The police are under no legal requirement to protect an individual citizen from harm. If you find yourself in danger, and the police do not come to the rescue in time, you are out of luck and on your own.

The legal language above is contained in a 1981 ruling from U.S. District Court of Appeals for the District of Columbia in the 1975 case of *Warren v. District of Columbia*. It is a ruling that many firearms instructors around the nation will often use to remind their students – especially women who come to learn about firearms and self-defense – of the need for every citizen to take responsibility for their personal safety, and the safety of family members and loved ones who may not be able to defend themselves

What is most important about *Warren v. District of Columbia's* language is that it bluntly refutes police chiefs or department spokespersons who habitually lecture the public that instead of taking direct action against criminal attack, they should call 911 and "let the police handle it." Police officials who tell people this know that there are always only two people at the scene of a violent crime: the perpetrator and the victim(s), and that the police arrive afterward, sometimes long afterward.

When police officials or gun control advocates insist that private citizens should depend upon the police department to come to their rescue, they should immediately and pointedly be reminded of Carolyn Warren, Joan Taliaferro and Miriam Douglas.

Who are these three women?

Nightmare on Lamont Street

It is the early morning of March 16, 1975. The city of Washington, D.C. never really sleeps because the government is always awake. But it is still dark as the clock approaches 6 a.m. outside of 1112 Lamont Street N.W., where Carolyn Warren, Joan Taliaferro and Miriam Douglas reside, along with Douglas' 4-year-old daughter, according to court documents. All are still asleep, though the eastern skyline will soon begin its slow rise toward daylight and start their day.

Warren and Taliaferro share a room on the third floor of this rooming house while Douglas and her daughter have a room on the second floor.

What awakens the women is the sound of the back door being smashed in. Downstairs, two men who represent the living image of evil have entered the modest building. Later identified as Marvin Kent and James Morse, these two monsters make their way to the second-floor room where Douglas is with her daughter, taking them hostage.

Kent forces Douglas into an act of sodomy, and Morse rapes her. This was not a quiet criminal act, and alerted by Douglas' screams, Warren calls the Metropolitan Police. The time of the call, according to court documents, is 6:23 a.m., and it is recorded as a "burglary in progress." Three minutes later, the call is dispatched to patrol officers as a "Code 2" despite the fact that this is a crime in progress, which is normally given a priority "Code 1" designation.

The police call receiver tells Warren to remain quiet and assures her that help is on the way.

Four police patrol units respond to the call and shortly three of them they arrive at the Lamont Street address. The fourth cruiser goes to another address, according to the court documents, to check on a possible suspect.

Warren and Taliaferro have by now crawled out of their room through a window to the roof, waiting for the police to arrive. They spy one police unit driving through the alley behind the house, but it did not stop, and instead pulls around to the front of the structure. He does not stop or even lean out the window for a better look, and he certainly does not check the back door.

At the same time, a second police officer approaches the front door of the residence and knocks. But there is no answer. Five minutes after they arrive, all three patrol officers depart the scene. It is 6:33 a.m.

Thinking that they have been rescued, Warren and Taliaferro, the court papers recount, crawl back inside their room. But they hear Douglas' screams again – which police apparently did not hear – and Warren calls the police a second time. It is 6:42 a.m. This time, she tells the call receiver that intruders have entered the residence, and she is once again told that police are on the way. This call is logged as "investigate the trouble." The call, according to court documents, was never dispatched to patrol units.

After waiting, Warren and Taliaferro become convinced that police have arrived and they are safe. They call down to Douglas to ascertain whether she is alright. But it is not police officers who hear their voices, and now Kent and Morse have two more victims.

The two criminals immediately force Warren and Taliaferro at knifepoint to accompany them downstairs to Douglas' apartment. There, over the course of the next 14 horrible hours, the three women are beaten, raped, robbed and, according to the court documents, "forced to commit sexual acts upon each other, and made to submit to the sexual demands of Kent and Morse."

Sometime after 9 p.m., the immediate ordeal is over, but a legal ordeal is about to begin. Warren, Taliaferro and Douglas are about to learn a cruel truth that will consume the next six years of their lives. This may come as a surprise to a public that has been lulled into a false sense of security by too many television dramas about heroic or maverick police coming to the rescue, but in reality, police departments have no legal obligation to "protect and serve" individual citizens, no matter what it says on the doors of their patrol cars.

This is not a manpower or budget issue, though it is true in just about every city and county in America, the police and sheriff's departments are often woefully under-manned, and sometimes criminally under-funded by local governments, which surprisingly never seem unable to find money to fund some pet project for some special interest group. That political reality, of course, is of little interest to Carolyn Warren, Joan Taliaferro and Miriam Douglas as they are being brutalized on the night of March 16, or for years afterward.

The victimized women sued the District of Columbia, contending that the city had failed to protect them. After all, this is what police departments and outspoken opponents of common sense concealed carry statutes, and even self-defense with a firearm in one's own home or business, have been preaching to the public for years: "Don't take any action yourself. Let the police handle it."

The District Court of Appeals ruling in this case destroyed that myth, or at least should have. But the myth lives on, and it is repeated time and again like a mantra. "The police will protect you." But the federal appeals court in the nation's capitol says they don't have to, and that court is not alone.

Incredibly, the following year, 1976, Washington D.C. enacted a ban on handguns and required that rifles and shotguns kept in private homes be disassembled so that they would be rendered useless, even for self-defense.

Three thousand miles to the west and 14 years after the horrendous incident on Lamont Street N.W., another case began unfolding that would lead to yet another federal court ruling that private citizens have no expectation of police protection.

It is a hot summer evening in the East Los Angeles, California suburban neighborhood where, on August 27, 1989, Maria Navarro is enjoying a birthday party at her home with relatives and friends. She is separated from her husband, Raymond, against whom she had obtained a restraining order in January of that year, but the restraining order has expired. Even if it were in effect, that piece of paper would have proven as worthless as the 911 call she was about to make.

At 10:30 p.m., according to court documents, Maria gets a call from Raymond's brother, warning her that the hot-headed Raymond is on his way to her house to kill her and anyone else he finds. Taking the threat seriously, Maria calls the Los Angeles County Sheriff's Department and tells the call receiver about the warning she had just received.

Incredibly, when she advises the sheriff's dispatcher that Raymond has not yet arrived but is definitely on his way, the dispatcher responds, "Okay, well, the only thing to do is just call us if he comes over there . . . I mean, what can we do? We can't have a unit sit there to wait and see if he comes over."

Maria Navarro hangs up in frustration. Moments later, Raymond arrives, enters through the rear of the house with a gun and starts shooting. Within minutes, Maria Navarro is dead, along with four other people. Two more are wounded in Raymond's shooting rampage.

Eleven months later, in July 1990, Maria's family filed a lawsuit in U.S. District Court for the Central District of California against Los Angeles County and the Sheriff's Department. The Navarros had a creative argument, in that the sheriff's department policy of not giving "emergency" classification to requests for assistance relating to domestic violence was a violation of the 14th Amendment to the U.S. Constitution.

The courts did not buy that argument, and for the next six years, the case wound its way through the system up to the Ninth Circuit Court of Appeals in San Francisco. A three-judge panel consisting of Circuit Judges Harry Pregerson, Cecil F. Poole and Dorothy W. Nelson heard oral arguments in the case on June 8, 1995 and the opinion came down in January 1996. Judge Pregerson wrote the opinion. Part of the case was remanded, but part of the lower court's ruling against the Navarro's claim was upheld.

The short version is that the Navarros lost. And so did you.

Taking Personal Responsibility

Each year around the country, tens of thousands of law-abiding American citizens enroll in firearms safety and personal protection courses. The bulk of those classes are taught by some 70,000 volunteers who are certified by the National Rifle Association as instructors, after completing an instructor's course in one or more disciplines that may include rifle, shotgun or handgun shooting, and there is also a Personal Protection course alluded to earlier in this chapter.

Not only do such courses contribute to an increased awareness about basic firearm safety, they have also provided millions of citizens with the fundamentals of marksmanship that may help keep them alive in an emergency.

But the NRA only provides what many consider to be a "basic" course; that is, the material is not of the level one might get by attending what has commonly become known as a "shooting school." These are the training camps of today's serious armed citizen.

Over the past three decades, a number of these schools have sprung up around the country. They include, but are not limited to, the famous American Pistol Institute/Gunsite Academy outside Paulden, Arizona; Thunder Ranch, which relocated from Texas to a new site outside Lakeview, Oregon; the Lethal Force Institute, headquartered in Concord, New Hampshire; the Chapman Academy at Hallsville, Missouri; the Firearms Academy of Seattle, which is not actually in Seattle, but about 90 miles to the south, outside the small community of Onalaska, Washington; and the Front Sight Firearms Training Institute located outside Las Vegas, Nevada.

The common thread among all of these schools is that

they teach "advanced weaponcraft" and skills far beyond the realm of merely being able to shoot bull's eyes at a static target. Students attending these courses learn to shoot from a draw, they shoot from sometimes awkward positions, and depending upon the course, can learn about shooting inside dark rooms, or how to move from room to room in order to "clear" their own residence of an intruder. They learn gunfighting skills and tactics that will theoretically help keep them alive in a lethal confrontation.

People attending such courses pay hundreds of dollars for a few days' worth of instruction. In the process, they may shoot up many hundreds of rounds of ammunition, learning the new shooting skills that might give them an edge in an emergency.

While it is true that the majority of students who attend these schools will likely never face a genuine lethal threat in their homes or on the street, they will almost unanimously explain that the reason they take such courses, often traveling several hundred miles to do so, is a matter of "insurance."

One does not purchase homeowner's insurance or a policy on their new car in hopes of ever having to use it, they say, but instead with the hope that they *never* have to. However, as with car or homeowner's insurance, the skills one learns at a shooting school will be "there if I need them."

Literally all of these shooting schools, and their various clones, have various course levels that allow a student to advance upward in terms of skill and tactics. Not surprisingly, a large number of law enforcement officers also attend these courses, and some schools have specific courses designed specifically for police. It is not unusual to find students returning to these schools to take the more advanced courses, depending upon their interest, available time and, of course, financial situation. These courses do no come cheap, but the logic in taking one or more courses comes when one asks the question "how much is my life worth?"

There is no accurate way of determining how many people who have attended these shooting schools have actually managed to save their own lives or the life of some other person thanks to what they learned, but the late Col. Jeff Cooper, who founded the American Pistol Institute, occasionally wrote about some member of his school's extended "family" who had survived a nasty encounter.

Massad Ayoob, founder of the Lethal Force Institute, maintains files on his students so that if one ever winds up in court following a shooting, his or her training file is available for use in a legal defense. Ayoob is also a recognized expert witness and has testified in countless self-defense cases.

The popularity of such advanced training has grown exponentially with the increase in the number of states that have passed concealed carry legislation. Graduates of these courses are often among the best pistol shots around. In 2007, for example, Front Sight actually filmed a "reality series" called the *Front Sight Challenge*, which pitted teams of private citizens against police officers, all of whom had trained at the Front Sight academy. In the majority of events, the teams of citizens outscored the police.

Though it could be considered an exercise in conjecture, one must ultimately ponder the genuine probability that a large number of murders, robberies and rapes might never have happened, had only the victims of those crimes possessed the skill levels of students who attend these training courses. Indeed, one could debate at length the difference it might have made in a particular situation if only the victim had been armed at all.

When Firearms Count

Unlike the late Maria Navarro, a South Carolina woman identified as Cynthia Franklin, did not put all of her faith in the ability of police to rescue her from peril, and as a result, she survived a confrontation with an abusive husband that left him dead. News accounts from WIS-News 10 in Columbia, South Carolina told the story of this incident in grim but matter-of-fact detail.

It is Friday evening, January 26, 2007. Dennis Alvin Franklin has been drinking again. In 1999, according to one report on the station, Franklin was arrested for having threatened his wife of 40 years, but attendance at an anger-management class allows him to escape jail and charges are dismissed. The couple has raised four daughters, but this is not one of those relationships one finds on a family-hour television program of the 1950s or 1960s like Father Knows Best.

Cynthia, 59, finds herself on the receiving end of a brutal, potentially fatal beating. Dennis, 63, has picked up a "big old stick" according to a transcript of the 911 call, and Cynthia has retreated into the bedroom where a firearm is kept for protection.

Anti-gunners will frequently argue that a gun kept in the home is more likely to be used on a family member than on an intruder. In many cases, such as this one, that use turns out to be entirely justified, leading to the question that gun control proponents are loathe to answer: "Would you rather that some domestic abuser beat his or her spouse to death than have the victim be able to defend herself or himself?"

When the 911 call is answered by the Newberry County Sheriff's Department dispatcher, Dennis Franklin is already dead, lying on the floor of the bedroom, shot twice. Cynthia insists in the conversation with the dispatcher that this is a case of self-defense, and the physical evidence supports her story.

When deputies arrive, they find Cynthia beaten severely with wounds to her face, head and upper body. The weapon is described as being "similar to the handle on a wooden tool" which would put it in the realm of a lethal blunt instrument. Cynthia, who suffers from heart problems – she has stayed with Dennis so long because her only hope of getting medicine to treat her ailment is through his insurance – is in pretty rough shape.

While on the telephone with the dispatcher, Cynthia has thoughtfully and dramatically stated, "If I don't make it, would you please tell my girls. I have four girls. I'm doing what I can. But will you tell them that I love them and I'm sorry this happened? I didn't know he was going to do this and he was set on killing me tonight."

But Dennis didn't kill his wife, and she is taken to the hospital where she is treated and she survives.

The television station interviewed a neighbor, identified as Talmadge Ellisor, who offered an observation one does not always hear in a case like this: "If it happened the way I have been told it happened, he needed what he got."

One month and a day later, on February 27, Newberry County Sheriff Lee Foster announced that the case had been closed, and that investigators from his agency had turned over their report to Eighth Circuit Solicitor Jerry Peace. Sheriff Foster released the contents of a letter he wrote to Peace that stated, "It is my legal opinion that Cynthia Franklin acted in self-defense. She was being beaten severely by her husband and took the appropriate action to protect her life. My recommendation is that charges not be pursued and that this investigation be closed."

Arming one's self out of concern over a genuine threat often proves to have been the difference between life and death. Many American citizens are reluctant to bring a firearm into their home, yet when faced with the threat of being seriously injured or killed, obtaining a gun seems the prudent thing to do.

Such is the reported case of Eric Cegon, a man whose story was told in detail in the pages of the Minneapolis *Star-Tribune*, the Rochester, Minnesota *Post-Bulletin* and other Minnesota newspapers.

In December 2006, Cegon fatally shot the ex-boyfriend of his girlfriend of three months, Samantha Simons. The dead man, Erik A. Richter, had broken into their home in Rockford, armed with a handgun, after months of threats. It is the culmination of a lengthy drama that played out to a fatal dénouement.

Things like this shouldn't happen in places like Rockford, a small community established in the mid-1850s that is located on the Wright-Hennepin county line at the confluence of the forks of the Crow River. With a population hovering around 3,500, Rockford lies about 34 miles west of Minneapolis. One website devoted to Rockford actually has a reference to this case, an indication of just how unusual something like this is to small-town America, or at least *should* be.

In 2006, Simons ended a long relationship with Richter that had produced a son, Jackson, who was 2 years old at the time of the shooting. According to the newspaper accounts, Richter's increasing use of methamphetamines, coupled with his increasingly violent behavior, was ample sign she needed to move on. Richter actually served time for meth possession.

Richter and Cegon had worked together on cars and had been friends. But when Simons and Cegon – who had never owned a firearm – began a relationship in September 2006, Richter threatened him several times, including once when he threatened to kill Cegon with a knife. He reportedly also showed Simons a shotgun that he threatened to use on Cegon.

These were no idle, blustering threats but the jealous rage of an ex-lover who, according to Wright County attorney Thomas Kelly, quoted by the *Star-Tribune*, "refused to let her go, and said that if he couldn't have her, nobody would."

On November 4, about two months after Simons and Cegon begin their relationship, Richter shows up at Cegon's residence, smashes all the windows in his car and tries to climb through his bedroom window, threatening to kill him. Two days later, on November 6, Richter is charged with making "terroristic threats" and for the property damage he did to the car.

Richter is ordered to have no contact with Cegon or Simons, and Simons also requests an additional restraining order. Under federal statute and many state laws, such no-contact orders require that the subject of the order must not possess firearms, but as history in such cases has graphically proven time and again, court orders are worthless pieces of paper when someone is determined to cause great physical harm, and all of the gun control laws in the world will not prevent someone with criminal intent from somehow acquiring a firearm. Gun control laws, unfortunately, all too often only disarm the victims.

But that is not the case in this Minnesota melodrama. Cegon, who has never owned a firearm, borrows a 12-gauge shotgun from a friend after the November incident, and according to the newspaper accounts, learns to use it. He has Simons' blessing, one newspaper account noted.

On December 6, Richter violates the court's no-contact order and threatens Simons with a knife. Wright County sheriff's deputies start looking for Richter on probable cause of felony assault, the newspaper account notes, and a court hearing on the no-contact order violation is scheduled for December 13.

But outside the sterile confines of a courtroom and a prosecutor's office, real criminals move about with impunity. Court orders and court dates mean nothing to them.

December 12 arrives and Cegon and Simons, and Simons' son, stay at her residence, counting down the hours until the court hearing the following morning. According to the *Star-Tribune* account, they take the precaution of barricading the door with a sofa, go upstairs to a bedroom and barricade themselves in that room with a dresser. Cegon has the borrowed shotgun, and a few hours later, it will be the tool that stands between him, Simons and her son, and the enraged monster his one-time friend had become.

Simons later tells a newspaper reporter that they could have gone someplace to hide, but realized that Richter would eventually come looking for them, so they decided to face the threat and place their trust in God.

It is 3:30 a.m. when the Devil arrives in the form of Erik Richter. In direct violation of the court order and federal law, he is armed with a .45-caliber Colt semi-automatic pistol. He reportedly also has brought with him pairs of handcuffs and leg irons, for what grisly purpose no one will fortunately ever know.

He smashes through the front door and charges up the stairs, pushing open the barricaded bedroom door and knocking over the dresser, a testament to the frequently-witnessed phenomenon of the almost super-human strength that can be induced by adrenalin-charged rage.

But Cegon has the shotgun and he fires at virtually point-blank range. The impact lifts the 6-foot Richter off his feet and throws him back. The pistol falls from Richter's hand, and he gasps – perhaps out of total shock as much as surprise that Cegon was armed and not simply cowering in fear, waiting to be murdered – "You killed me." Cegon fires again, and it is over. The county attorney determined that Richter's slaying was a case of self-defense.

But there is a post script to this story, as detailed by a heart-wrenching story in the *Star-Tribune* about the emotional roller-coaster ride Cegon and Simons have endured in the months since the shooting. Sleepless nights, nightmares, anxiety attacks; this is the natural human reaction to having committed an unnatural act, even in defense of one's own life.

There is always an "aftermath" to a fatal confrontation, and post traumatic stress disorder is frequently part of the experience. It is essentially what Elizabeth Greer, the woman from Mississippi whose story was told in Chapter One, went through in the months after she shot and killed predator Bobby Earl Hardy.

Different people react differently, and fortunately, there are counselors trained to help gunfight survivors deal with this disorder. They recognize that for long periods following a life-or-death encounter, the stress disorder can be triggered by a variety of factors. It is not unusual for someone to avoid the place where the incident happened, even if it means leaving one's home. Symptoms could include loss of appetite, stress-induced chest pains, high blood pressure and flashbacks.

Perhaps the most important thing for survivors of deadly encounters to remember – and help put things in their proper perspective – is that for someone to go through this stress, they must be alive and breathing. For all too many victims of violent attacks, who were unable to defend themselves, there is no aftermath because they do not survive.

For others, however, the pendulum has swung the other direction. They have made the decision that their lives are worth something, and they have decided to fight back.

CHAPTER 9

A Plague of Recidivism

By the time that Galen Patrick Sloan, 39, was shot and killed during a break-in at an apartment in Southeast Portland, Oregon on the night of October 7, 2006 he had a lengthy criminal history, according to a story about his demise that appeared two days later in the Portland *Oregonian* of October 9.

The newspaper account reads like so many other reports of people who are shot and wounded or killed during the commission of a crime, by armed private citizens or police officers. Sloan was shot by a tenant inside the apartment that he and an unidentified accomplice had broken into just before 9 p.m. It turns out, according to the newspaper, that the apartment owner knew Sloan and the other person, who got away.

Sloan's history, the newspaper account detailed, included burglary, assault, forgery, menacing and driving under the influence. While some bleeding heart liberals and opponents of self-defense might contend that Sloan's criminal record did not include offenses serious enough to warrant a lethal response, keep in perspective that he wasn't shot because of his poor track record, but because he and another individual had just broken into someone's residence, where they clearly had no right to be, and they were obviously involved in the commission of a crime.

In far too many cases of self-defense in which the perpetrator must be "later identified" by a coroner or medical examiner, it is turning out that a common denominator is the fact that the person on the cold metal autopsy table had a "long criminal history."

This is not a regional phenomenon. From the Pacific Northwest to the Midwest and East Coast, if one pays attention to newscasts and newspaper reports about robberies that go bad or burglaries that end with a dead burglar, somewhere in the report it may be mentioned that the suspect had been in trouble before.

It is not difficult to find such case reports. Indeed, there is something of a "clearing house" on the Internet for reports of armed citizens fighting back, maintained by historian Clayton Cramer and his colleague Pete Drum. Called the "Civilian Gun Defense Blog," accessible from Cramer's website at www.claytoncramer.com, this site keeps a remarkable, and in many ways disturbing, collection of reports from all over the country. The authors frequently relied on reports first posted on Cramer's blog for many of the anecdotal reports in this book, and used others to research more deeply into stories of self-defense.

Another place where such reports frequently show up is on KeepAndBearArms.com, a website and news forum owned and maintained by the Second Amendment Foundation and the Citizens Committee for the Right to Keep and Bear Arms.

Cramer, author of *Armed America* (Nelson Current, 2007) an historical look at firearms in America from past to the present, is a respected historian and scholar largely responsible for undoing the highly inaccurate book, *Arming America* by now-discredited author Michael Bellesiles. That book claimed that firearms were not commonly owned in frontier America and it essentially argued that the so-called "gun culture" of today's America was created by the firearms industry and the so-called "gun lobby."

In addition to pulling the cornerstone from that particular journalistic house of cards, Cramer's blog, which is now largely updated by Drum, is remarkably useful in refuting claims from the anti-self-defense crowd that incidents of armed self-defense occur rarely in this country. The truth is quite the reverse, and to their discredit gun control proponents know it but insist on projecting their own philosophy of denial onto society at large.

Knowing the truth certainly does not stop them from opposing "stand-your-ground" laws nor does it prevent them from campaigning to prevent passage of concealed carry statutes or "reform" amendments that would improve existing carry laws. Their actions, it might be argued, help create an environment in which recidivist offenders are able to come to someone's home and kick down doors in order to get their hands on someone else's property, or to commit more heinous crimes against the occupants.

However, when Americans fight back, it does not always turn out the way that the perpetrators anticipated, or the gun control lobby would like.

Examine the case of Jerry Allen Savino, also age 39 same as Sloan, who was killed on Super Bowl Sunday in 2007. The report of his demise was detailed on Tulsa, Oklahoma's KOTV News which noted that the Tulsa man was killed by multiple shots from a 16-gauge shotgun after he began beating on a homeowner's door for no apparent reason.

Pounding on someone's door is not a capital offense, but Savino's efforts didn't stop there. According to the station's account, Savino finally kicked in the door, and police said the evidence at the scene indicated he was attempting to burglarize the home. Instead, he took three shotgun blasts.

This happened, it should be noted, not long after Oklahoma had adopted a "stand-your-ground" law, which protects citizens legally and allows them to respond to a threat if they are in a place where they have a right to be. One's home is one's castle, and this so-called "castle doctrine" law is something of a novel concept sweeping through several states, though it is hardly new or unique. The theory that a person's home is their "castle" dates back centuries, but in more recent historical times, due to whatever faulty logic, many legislatures adopted statutes that essentially required crime victims to retreat, and that defense of life and property was the very last resort, after they had exhausted all other means to avoid a conflict.

After years of suffering with this kind of foolishness, the public demanded a sea change in statutory philosophy, leading to the adoption of "castle doctrine" or "stand-your-ground" laws.

This important statute protects from criminal and civil liability any private citizen who shoots in lawful self-defense, even if that person is outside the home.

Savino's criminal history, dating back to the 1980s according to the news station, included more than a dozen convictions for – *surprise!* – burglary and drug possession.

According to the Department of Justice, Bureau of Justice

Statistics (BJS), in a report on Criminal Offenders Statistics, "of the 272,111 persons released from prisons in 15 states in 1994, an estimated 67.5% were rearrested for a felony or serious misdemeanor within 3 years, 46.9% were reconvicted, and 25.4% re-sentenced to prison for a new crime."

These 272,111 criminals had racked up a phenomenal 4,877,000 arrest charges over their combined criminal careers, the report noted. This averages out roughly to more than 17 crimes and criminal charges per individual, and those are only the crimes for which they were charged. How many crimes did they commit without being apprehended or charged?

The report found that 53 percent of jail inmates were "on probation, parole or pretrial release at the time of arrest."

The BJS report further noted that, "Four in 10 jail inmates had a current or past sentence for a violent offense" and that "thirty-nine percent of jail inmates in 2002 had served 3 or more prior sentences to incarceration or probation, down from 44% in 1996."

This all translates to something police, prosecutors, public defenders and judges have known for years: There are a lot of repeat offenders wandering around on the streets of America, on the streets in your city, and perhaps in your neighborhood. They're just waiting for the right opportunity to come calling, at your home or perhaps the small business down on the corner.

It was just such a business, the Two Flags Deli and Grocery in Brooklyn, New York, where veteran thugs Jonathan Lynch and James Culbertson showed up for their last criminal act on Christmas Eve 2000.

According to accounts from the New York *Daily News*, Culbertson and Lynch were no strangers to the justice system in New York City.

At 6 feet and weighing a reported 170 pounds, Lynch, at 32, was the elder of the duo with a criminal record dating back to 1986. A Brooklyn resident, his package included arrests for armed robbery, assault and grand larceny, and at the time of the Two Flags Deli incident, he was on parole for a 1995 grocery store robbery at the time. Out of jail since the previous February, he's "back in business" for the holidays.

At 25 years of age, the 6-foot, 240-pound Culbertson was no saint. A resident of Queens, his criminal record goes back to his juvenile years. The newspaper duly noted that of his seven arrests, the records of six are sealed "apparently because he was a juvenile at the time." His most recent brush with the law was a November 1999 arrest in Queens for first-degree robbery and possession of stolen property. Not surprisingly in the turnstile New York criminal court system, he was allowed to enter a guilty plea on a reduced disorderly conduct charge, and was sentenced to a whopping *three days* of "community service," though it is not clear whether he actually performed any of this service.

And then came the fateful Christmas Eve robbery.

'Merry Christmas'

According to the *Daily News*, the local ABC affiliate and an interview from Michael Zeller that appeared in the December 26, 2000 edition of the New York *Post*, the Two Flag Deli Grocery is in Brooklyn's Greenpoint section. Think of a typical New York City bodega and this is one of those places. It is owned by Zeller's mother-in-law, Hilda Nieves.

It is just about closing time at the store and Mrs. Nieves has stepped out to go across the street to her apartment, where she is reportedly getting some bags and tucking in some of her grandchildren, who no doubt were thinking more about Santa Claus than the possibility that there were dangerous criminals on the loose on the streets outside.

But in the shop are Michael and Marie Zeller and their two children, 5-month-old Michael and 3-year-old Devin.

In comes Lynch, who asks Marie if he can get a sandwich made, and she says she will make him the sandwich. But Lynch then goes back outside, ostensibly to ask his friend if he also wants a sandwich. This makes both of the Zellers suspicious, according to one account, so Michael Zeller walks outside to get a closer look at the two men, who are now standing beside the open trunk of their car. It is a few hours from Christmas, and a few moments from Hell.

Suddenly, the men are back inside and Michael Zeller is staring into the muzzle of a .22-caliber revolver in Culbertson's hand. Lynch, meanwhile, is armed with a knife.

In the midst of this, 3-year-old Devin, seeing her father being ordered to the floor, courageously steps forward and tells the robbers,

"Don't hurt my daddy."

Unbeknownst to Lynch and Culbertson, "daddy" is an off-duty New York police detective, and he is about to terminate their robbery attempt with "extreme prejudice."

Unlike average citizens in New York City, where restrictive gun laws make it virtually impossible for most people to legally carry firearms for their personal protection, Michael Zeller's shield allows him to be armed. The gun laws that leave honest citizens unarmed and at the mercy of professional thugs like Culbertson and Lynch, who are armed with a handgun and knife, will not interfere with Michael Zeller this night.

Distracted by the child, Lynch and Culbertson get the biggest surprise of their lives when Zeller comes up with a drawn 9mm Glock semiautomatic handgun and opens fire while placing himself between these hulking criminals and his heroic daughter.

One published account of the shooting on the KeepAndBearArms. com Internet forum notes that the first two rounds out of Zeller's pistol properly rip into Culbertson. With the small-caliber handgun, he is the most dangerous threat, and the two 9mm slugs traveling across the short space of the bodega at more than 1,100 feet per second slam into Culbertson's chest, wounding him mortally.

Zeller's muzzle swings around and zeroes on Lynch and a bullet tears into his lungs, killing him almost immediately. Culbertson dies a short time later. It is over, and two more predators are removed from circulation. In all, Zeller has fired five rounds.

A 15-year veteran of the New York Police Department, Zeller is treated at the hospital for emotional trauma, but because of his quick action and deadly accuracy, neither he nor his loved ones physically suffer so much as a scratch. The television news report quotes then-Mayor Rudolph Giuliani, who suggests that the detective should be commended for his actions.

But Zeller's reaction is not so different from the actions of legally-armed private citizens in other parts of the nation not encumbered with the Draconian gun laws now on the books in New York City; laws that Giuliani and other politicians continue to support.

In a brief announcement on August 24, 2001 Kings County District Attorney Charles J. Hynes notes that the investigation into the Christmas Eve bodega shooting is closed. The case will not be turned over to a grand jury.

"An investigation by this office into the shooting by Detective Zeller has determined that his actions were justified in protecting himself and others in the store," Hynes says.

One might reasonably wonder just how it is that repeat offenders like Lynch and Culbertson, Savino or Sloan can be out on the streets committing crimes when they ought to be somewhere behind bars. The American legal system, from the courts to various corrections departments, is largely responsible.

This is not the "justice system" because if there were really any "justice," such violent recidivists would be removed from circulation long before some armed private citizen or a fortunately-armed off-duty police detective has to take care of them.

Perhaps a good example of how this sort of "revolving door" system works is found not in New York but 3,000 miles to the West in Washington State. In October 2006, an embarrassing, and revealing, incident occurred that left citizens outraged only months after a legally-armed private citizen who was being brutally attacked in public on a downtown Seattle street had to fatally shoot his attacker in front of scores of witnesses.

This incident involved a 25-year-old man named Daniel Culotti, whose history leaves any rational person to question just how someone like him could be roaming around in public.

Sentenced to prison in early 2002 for the July 2001 attack on his mother during which he assaulted her and burned down her home, Culotti reportedly complied with his therapy, according to the Seattle *Times*, and earned release from prison in October 2002 after serving only nine months behind bars.

Placed under supervision of the Department of Corrections and Seattle Mental Health, it would later be reported that Culotti was considered "one of 70 dangerously mentally ill people in King County." But instead of keeping him locked up, the state allocated $10,000 for his therapy, medications and housing for a period of five years.

But Culotti's actions on Saturday, October 7, 2006 would make it unnecessary for the state to spend all of that money. Almost exactly four years into his parole, Daniel Culotti shows up in Seattle's upscale Westlake Plaza, yelling at people and "randomly assaulting strangers near Boren Avenue and Pine Street," according to the Seattle *Times* and Seattle police who were interviewed by *Gun Week*, a nationally-circulated firearms newspaper published by the Second Amendment Foundation.

Incredibly, Culotti had been arrested three times during 2006 "for violating the conditions of his release into the community." Any of these arrests and charges should have landed Culotti back in prison, but they did not, and very shortly on this sunny Autumn Saturday morning, people will begin wondering why.

'Department of Chaos'

Washington is known as the "Evergreen State." A gem of the Pacific Northwest, it is – with the exception of Seattle and its surrounding suburbs – as far removed culturally and philosophically from New York City as one might get.

Unlike residents of New York, citizens in Washington are not simply "allowed" to carry firearms; the practice is strongly protected by the state constitution. Not only does Washington have one of the oldest and strongest concealed carry statutes of any state in the Union, it is also an "open carry state." That is, citizens can legally carry a handgun openly and even law enforcement academy training notes this, as do the training bulletins of many police agencies in the state.

But because Washington is among the top ten states per capita in the number of citizens who are legally licensed to carry concealed, the practice of open carry outside of wilderness areas and national forests is rare. And, as firearms enthusiasts in Washington like to remind people, it is also "surprising" to a number of miscreants who suddenly find themselves staring into the muzzle of a gun being held by an intended victim. Even in Seattle, the homicide rate for a city of its size is staggeringly small. In 2005, there were 25 homicides, and in 2006, there were 30, and Seattle police sources told one of the authors that this number is "skewed" due only to the infamous "Capitol Hill Massacre" in which six people died in March 2006. Without that crime, Seattle's murder rate would have actually gone down.

Seattle is the largest city in the state, and it lies on the waterfront of King County, where sources in the Sheriff's Department have observed to one of the authors that in the mid-2000s, law enforcement had started seeing a rise in criminal activity. This was due at least in part by the release from prison of criminals convicted back in the 1980s and 1990s for various serious crimes, who had finally completed their sentences. Once back on the streets, many of these individuals began re-establishing themselves in their old neighborhoods, and turf disputes erupted because while these thugs were behind bars, others had moved in to take their place, and weren't eager to surrender what they thought was theirs.

But gang crime is one thing. Crimes committed at random by people against others they don't even know is another problem manifested by so-called "turnstile justice."

It is 11:08 a.m. when a woman calls the Seattle Police Department to report a man acting "erratically" on a downtown street near the Westlake Plaza. Officers are dispatched to the scene and begin searching for this man amid a crowd of shoppers on the busiest shopping day of the week.

A 52-year-old African-American man, later reported to be homeless but still licensed to carry the .357 Magnum Ruger revolver he is packing this day, is among the crowd, minding his own business and enjoying the day. Suddenly, he is singled out by a ranting Daniel Culotti, screaming what may have been racial epithets. Culotti slams the man to the ground with several punches in an unprovoked attack and then begins stomping and kicking him.

Perhaps as a miserable testament to citizens of Seattle – the Evergreen State's liberal enclave and a city that one observer once jokingly referred to as being "only 20 minutes from the United States in any direction" – scores, perhaps hundreds of people looked on… and did nothing.

The Washington State Supreme Court has ruled more than once that in the Evergreen State, the law is "well-established" that "there is no duty to retreat" if a person is attacked in a place where he has a right to be. While Seattle is home to tens of thousands of transplants from other parts of the country who come from areas where gun ownership is not nearly as prevalent, they frequently get a lesson in geography, both socially and legally. On this day, watching Culotti beating his victim, that lesson is about to be dramatically delivered.

The city is in a state that is in "The West," and when faced with what could be a fatal beating, citizens there can fight back. The man on the ground did just that, drawing his revolver and firing one round upward into Daniel Culotti's abdomen at virtually point blank range. The bullet tore upward into Culotti's vital organs. Despite the presence in Seattle of the Harborview Trauma Center, arguably one of the finest emergency room setups in the world, the wound is fatal.

Police hear the shot and run to the scene. They question the older man and release him, keeping his handgun for evidence while the investigation runs its course over the next several months.

The case is just one of several that place not armed citizens or the state's gun and self-defense statutes, but the Department of Corrections, in the crosshairs of the traditionally anti-gun Seattle media.

Culotti is not the only nightmare story linked to the DOC in 2006. That year, two Seattle police officers were killed in traffic accidents in which the other driver was "under the supervision" of the Corrections department. A King County sheriff's deputy was shot and killed by a recidivist felon in another incident, and that man was also supposed to have been under DOC supervision. The common denominator among all three of these felons is that they had skipped mandatory reporting sessions with corrections officers. In one traffic accident, which claimed the life of Officer Beth Nowak, the driver of the stolen car that hit her also was killed. In the other crash, which killed officer Joselito Barber, that driver survived and was charged with vehicular homicide.

In February 2007, it was revealed that the DOC had ordered the release from jail of 83 convicted felons, all of whom were reportedly being held "because they had violated some terms of supervision." That is, while they were out of jail on parole or probation, they had committed other offenses.

Callers to Seattle-area radio talk shows began referring to the DOC as the "Department of Chaos." Governor Christine Gregoire, a former state Attorney General whose administration of that department suffered several political and legal black eyes, moved quickly to block any further such releases.

Early prison release due to overcrowded conditions in prisons or county jails is hardly a unique phenomenon in Washington State's most populous county. That happens all the time, all over the country. The result of such early releases has all-too-often come back to haunt not only the authorities, but the communities in which those convicted felons are released.

Yet with all the political posturing that follows such a disclosure about prisoners being released because there is no bed space for them, eventually the public's attention turns elsewhere and the press moves on to the next tabloid headline. Meanwhile, convicted felons, often violent, still keep moving back to the streets.

When Felons Kill

Washington isn't the only state where felons have been turned out of prison only to commit new crimes. An expose in the April 2, 2002 Sunday edition of the Detroit *News* told about how Michigan inmates had also committed murders, robberies and rapes after they had been released with little or no supervision, to relieve an overcrowding problem at the Wayne County jail.

The true crime here may be that the Wayne Circuit Court in 1971 had ordered that the jail population could not exceed the facility's 1,885 bed capacity. As a result, according to the newspaper, more than 60,000 felons had been set free over the course of seven years.

Out of that 60,000, according to the newspaper, "At least 1,085 people freed under the administrative release program in the last three years have been rearrested and charged with committing new crimes…" A dozen were convicted of murder, three more convicted of manslaughter, and another eight were, at the time, "awaiting trial on murder charges." Released suspects had also accounted for 46 armed robberies, 40 violent assaults, 11 rapes and 14 carjackings, the report detailed.

Wayne County Prosecutor Michael Duggan told the newspaper, "You can bet a lot of the others are still out there committing more crimes. If we could eliminate the jail release program, we could cut crime in this county by 20 to 30 percent."

Incredibly, Duggan was a fierce opponent of right-to-carry legislation in Michigan, yet he seems to understand that a large number of crimes in his jurisdiction are being committed by the same people.

The newspaper story profiled some of the people who seemed to go around and around in the jail turnstiles.

One of them was a 17-year-old thug identified as Anthony "Turk" Daniels who was released on an administrative leave from the Wayne County Jail. At the time he was awaiting trial on a cocaine trafficking charge, and he reportedly had a "history of assaults as a juvenile."

Two days before Thanksgiving 2000, Daniels is involved in a carjacking with two other men. They rob and murder a man named Gregory Flesner, getting a total of $39. But Daniels was finally caught and now he is serving a life sentence.

Then there was William Franz Koss, a 33-year-old escapee from a halfway house, where he was supposed to have been living after being arrested for eluding the police, the report explained. After his re-arrest – for drug charges and weapons possession – he was sent back to the halfway facility!

Authorities did not know it at the time, but between the time he was first sent to the halfway house on September 5 and the second time he was sent there on October 29, Koss had been a busy boy. On October 19, he reportedly told police, he met a man named William G. Cunningham, 49, in a gay bar and the two ended up in Cunningham's home in Romulus. Twelve days later, Cunningham's body was found by police at the home. His throat had been slit with a butcher knife, he had been stabbed twice with a steak knife and his skull had been crushed with a rock, the newspaper reported.

Incredibly, as Detroit *News* reporters Norman Sinclair and Ronald J. Hansen revealed, "Under the jail's guidelines for release, neither of Koss' prior convictions -- burglary and larceny from a person, for which he served prison time; and fleeing a police officer, for which he spent a year in jail -- would have disqualified him from the release program."

Koss is out of circulation now, in state prison, but how many other violent felons are still out there due to prison overcrowding and breakdowns in the system?

One of them is *not* 26-year-old Tony Lee Long of Gastonia, North Carolina. Scheduled to appear in court on April 5, 2005 on one of many break-in charges he had racked up over the years, he did not make that court date. Three days earlier, while attempting to burglarize Mac's M&M Auto Parts in Charlotte at about 6:40 a.m. on a Saturday morning, Long was shot and killed in a confrontation with the store owner.

According to the April 4, 2005 edition of the Charlotte *Observer*, Long had "a long criminal history."

Likewise described by the Jackson, Mississippi *Clarion Ledger* as having an "extensive criminal history dating to 1971" was 50-year-old Harold Mitchell, Jr. In the early morning hours of December 19, 2003, Mitchell was "pillaging" through a truck in Clinton when he was confronted by a homeowner armed with a 9mm pistol.

It went badly for Mitchell, who was shot twice in the leg after the homeowner had fired a warning shot, the newspaper reported. Mitchell's record included charges ranging downward from strong-arm robbery and cocaine possession to residential burglary.

Mitchell survived the shooting and was taken into custody.

Seventeen-year-old Melvin Dugger's criminal career did not last long enough for him to amass a lengthy record. Just two nights before Harold Mitchell's encounter with an armed homeowner in Clinton, Mississippi, Dugger tried to rob a convenience store in Macon, Georgia, according to the Macon *Telegraph*.

On a chilly Wednesday shortly before midnight, Dugger walked into Dani's Food Mart "waving a gun and demanding money," the newspaper reported. Store clerk Uzair Khan quickly sensed something was very wrong with this stick-up because even after he complied with the young gunman's demands, and handed over the cash, Dugger "refused to leave," the report said.

Khan's radar was up because he had been reading a newspaper account of another robbery that had resulted in a fatality. He was not about to become another statistic, yet Dugger continued glancing around, evidently looking to see if there were any witnesses. Khan surmised this was shaping up to be an execution, and he begged the teen not to shoot him.

Sensing he was running out of time, the 33-year-old Khan drew his own gun and opened fire. Dugger hit the floor fatally wounded. Thanks to the store's security video, Dugger's shooting was quickly determined to have been in self-defense.

Perhaps not surprisingly, these and similar accounts can all be found by checking author Clayton Cramer's website and the Civilian Gun Defense Blog.

There can be no doubt that Cramer's website will continue to expand, as people with "long criminal histories" increasingly encounter Americans willing to fight back.

CHAPTER 10

The Insanity of Public Disarmament

Following the bloody massacre of April 28, 1996 at Port Arthur in eastern Australia by gunman Martin Bryant, the Australian government imposed new, strict gun control laws that banned several types of firearms and led to a controversial turn-in that has been used – some say exploited – by the National Rifle Association in its efforts to prevent passage of strict gun laws in the United States.

But the real issue is not the gun ban itself, but what happened afterward in Australia. According to historian Benedict D. LaRosa, writing in the November 2002 issue of *Freedom Daily*, a publication of the Future of Freedom Foundation based in Fairfax, Virginia, "In 1997, just 12 months after a new gun law went into effect in Australia, homicides jumped 3.2 percent, armed robberies 44 percent, and assaults 8.6 percent. In the state of Victoria, homicides went up 300 percent."

Testifying before the U.S. House Committee on Government Reform on June 28, 2005, Prof. John Lott, then a resident scholar at the American Enterprise Institute in Washington, D.C., detailed his findings about the Australian gun control program: "Violent crime rates averaged 32 percent higher in the six years after the law was passed (from 1997 to 2002) than they did the year before the law went into effect. Armed robbery rates increased 74 percent. According to the International Crime Victimization Survey, Australia's violent crime rate is also now double that of the U.S."

The Sidney, Australia *Morning Herald* reported that two researchers in that country came to much the same conclusion after watching crime trends in the Island Continent for ten years following the ban and gun turn-ins. Here's what the newspaper reported:

"Half a billion dollars spent buying back hundreds of thousands of guns after the Port Arthur massacre had no effect on the homicide rate, says a study published in an influential British journal.

"The report by two Australian academics, published in the *British Journal of Criminology*, said statistics gathered in the decade since Port Arthur showed gun deaths had been declining well before 1996 and the buyback of more than 600,000 mainly semi-automatic rifles and pump-action shotguns had made no difference in the rate of decline. The only area where the package of Commonwealth and State laws, known as the National Firearms Agreement (NFA) may have had some impact was on the rate of suicide, but the study said the evidence was not clear and any reductions attributable to the new gun rules were slight.

"Homicide patterns (firearm and non-firearm) were not influenced by the NFA, the conclusion being that the gun buyback and restrictive legislative changes had no influence on firearm homicide in Australia,' the study says."

Yet, many in the gun control movement point to Australia as the "model" they wish the United States would follow. They would like to see sweeping bans on the ownership of handguns, semiautomatic rifles and shotguns, .50-caliber rifles and anything else they can get added to such legislation. They honestly believe, or at least want the American public to believe, that banning guns has some connection to reductions in the crime rate when nothing is farther from the truth.

Proof of that can be found in Great Britain, where handguns are essentially banned and long gun ownership is severely regulated. It used to be that anti-gunners pointed to the tranquility of England as their example of what America ought to be, but somewhere in the aftermath of the enactment of England's handgun ban, British criminals evidently discovered that victims can't fight back.

Self-defense in the United Kingdom is an act that often lands the victim in prison while the perpetrator goes free.

Consider what prize-winning journalist Ian Bell observed in a February 2007 commentary in the *Sunday Herald*: "Bans have utterly failed." There it is, terse and directly to the point; a hard admission from a man who was a vocal and dogmatic advocate of the gun ban a decade before.

Though Bell clings to the belief that banning handguns in the United Kingdom is still a good idea overall, he was compelled to admit that so far the ban – instituted following the shooting of several children at Dunblane, Scotland on Wednesday, March 13, 1996 by a lunatic named Thomas Hamilton just six weeks prior to the Port Arthur rampage – had accomplished any good. Quite the contrary, it seemed.

Bell had been one of the United Kingdom's foremost supporters of the British gun ban. He seems to have undergone some sort of moral epiphany, admitting that "guns have become commonplace, so commonplace that every would-be terrorist worth his salt must be armed to the teeth."

In a remarkable display of candor from someone who had condemned gun owners who disagreed with him years earlier, Bell admitted "that it is easy to impose laws on the law-abiding. Criminals, by definition, don't take much interest in well-meaning legislation. If they chose to arm themselves while the rest of society was, in effect, disarming, outraged newspaper commentators and their quick fixes might merely make matters worse."

Again, Prof. Lott has provided statistical data that would support and reinforce Bell's observations. Lott told the House committee fully two years before Bell wrote his piece in the *Sunday Herald* that, "The laws didn't do what was claimed. The British government recently reported that gun crime in England and Wales nearly doubled in the four years from 1998-99 to 2002-03. The serious violent crime rate soared by 64 percent, and overall violent crime by 118 percent.

"According to the International Crime Victimization Survey," Lott continued, "the violent crime rate in England and Wales now stands at twice the rate of that in the U.S. A figure published in the *Economist Magazine* last year (January 3, 2004) clearly illustrates how armed robberies were changing in Britain before and after their January 1997 handgun ban. Prior to the ban, armed robberies were falling dramatically. After the ban, armed robberies stopped falling and started rising."

This evidence is available for anyone to see on the Internet. Yet its availability is of no concern or interest to the gun control lobby. Their minds are made up and their beliefs are firmly entrenched. They have far less interest in preventing crime than they do in preventing gun ownership.

One can legitimately wonder why supposedly rational, intelligent and even intellectual American citizens would ever contemplate, much less rigorously campaign for, legislation that would strip their fellow citizens of their firearm rights, and their ability to defend themselves and their families, especially after seeing how ineffective such laws have been in other countries. Somewhere in the course of their maturation there has been something of a disconnect in the thought process.

In 1976, handguns were essentially banned in Washington, D.C. The ensuing years saw crime rates skyrocket, and that especially included violent crime.

That was confirmed by Lott during his June 2005 testimony about the ineffectiveness of the District's gun ban. The author of *More Guns = Less Crime* and *The Bias Against Guns*, Lott told the House committee, "if one looks at the data, it is clear that the law hasn't done anything to reduce violence."

"Over the last five years," Lott explained at the time, "the District, never far out of the running, had in three of those years the highest murder rate among cities over 500,000 people. The other two years the city ranked second and third. It seems clear that D.C. residents need more protection then they are receiving.

"Nor has there been any success in Chicago," he continued, "the only other major city to have roughly similar laws, and a city that has consistently had the highest murder rate of the U.S. ten largest cities."

Lott is a man who deals with statistics, a "numbers cruncher" as it were, and he sifts through data to arrive at some startling, and for gun ban supporters, devastating conclusions. He told the House Committee that "In D.C., crime has risen significantly since the gun ban went into effect. In the five years before the D.C. ban in late 1976, the murder rate was slightly declining: the rate fell from 37 to 27 per 100,000.

"But," he stressed, "in the five years after the ban went into effect, the murder rate rose back up to 35. In fact, while crime rates have fluctuated over time, the murder rate after 1976 has only once fallen below what it was in 1976. The preliminary estimate of a 35 per 100,000 people murder rate in 2004 is still well above what the murder rate was when the handgun ban went into effect."

In 2003, the Centers for Disease Control and Prevention released a study that actually surveyed dozens of previous studies on gun laws and their effectiveness, and came up with a conclusion that startled many people. The CDC revealed that gun control laws had been ineffective when it came to actually preventing violence.

The Washington *Times* was so struck by the CDC revelation that it wrote in an editorial, "There always has been substance to the cliché that guns don't kill people, people do. Correlative to that rule is that the criminals who use guns to kill usually possess their weapons illegally. These serial lawbreakers are not deterred by statutes prohibiting or regulating gun ownership. They will continue to use guns to commit violent crimes even if the rest of the population of sitting ducks are disarmed."

Here is another revelation that many people find astonishing, and gun control extremists deliberately ignore: "The task force also concluded that 'firearms-related injuries in the United States have declined since 1993' despite the fact that 'approximately 4.5 million new firearms are sold each year'."

More recently, according to the National Safety Council in its 2007 Injury Facts report, death from gunshot wounds in the United States remains at an all-time low even while gun ownership is increasing.

According to the NSC, there was a 40 percent decrease in accidental firearm-related fatalities from 1996 to 2005, the most recent year for which data was available.

That report also showed gun accidents involving children age 14 and under declined a whopping 69 percent between 1995 and 2003. The declines are supported by research available from the CDC, according to the March 20, 2007 edition of *Gun Week*.

"Yet over the past several years," *Gun Week* reported, "gun ownership has risen to more than 290 million firearms. It is estimated that there are now about 47.8 million American households with at least one firearm."

According to the NSC report, in 2005 there were 730 accidental firearm deaths, down from 750 reported in 2004. Childhood firearm deaths dropped 7 percent between 2004 and 2005, while accidental injuries involving firearms were down 11 percent amongst teens between ages 15 and 19.

Yet to hear gun control zealots, one would believe that children are dying at record rates from "gun violence" (which is never clearly defined). But truth is quite the opposite from what the anti-gun community says. It appears that children – and everyone else – enjoy a safer environment with increased gun ownership.

Everyone, that is, except criminals.

Wrong Victim Choice

If there is one thing a criminal tries to avoid, it would be an armed victim. Despite what anti-self-defense alarmists have been hysterically claiming for more than a generation, armed Americans who fight back are far less likely to be injured or killed than unarmed victims. Alas, too many people have been beguiled by rhetoric into throwing themselves on the mercy of a criminal who does not know the meaning of the word because it is not in his vocabulary, and he may not be able to spell it.

This is particularly true in the rising incidence of home invasion robberies. Perpetrators in these crimes are more likely to use violent tactics, and they are frequently brutal in nature. But on rare occasion – though not very often because home invasion robberies typically target specific victims – perpetrators kick in the wrong door and find themselves on the receiving end of a bullet.

Defense against being victimized in one's own home by criminals is at the root of a celebrated civil rights lawsuit in Washington, D.C. to overturn that city's ban on handguns, and it is why an increasing number of citizens who might otherwise not use a firearm are purchasing guns nowadays specifically for "home defense."

A reliable witness to this phenomenon would be 20-year-old Luke Irons of St. Petersburg, Florida. With a rather short, but busy criminal record dating back to 2004 that includes residential burglary, commercial burglary, cocaine possession, drug dealing and grand theft auto, Irons, 20, and Chrisanthe Apergis of Seminole launched a multi-county crime spree that came to an abrupt halt when Irons stopped a bullet.

Accounts of their mid-March 2007 crime spree were detailed in the March 13 issue of the Bradenton *Herald* and on the Fox News Channel 13 in Tampa.

Out of prison only a few months, Irons took his girlfriend Apergis on something of an unusual date when they staged a string of home invasion robberies that started March 10 and ended in gunfire the following evening.

Their first stop was at the El Rancho Mobile Home Park in Manatee County where they approached a 92-year-old man at 11 a.m., asked to use his bathroom and then dragged him inside his mobile home, sprayed pepper spray at him and severely beat him, the newspaper detailed.

Driving a car taken in Manatee County, Irons and Apergis showed up later at the home of Cora Canale, who was lying in bed with her oxygen hooked up. The 85-year-old Canale told the television news reporter that suddenly, there was a man standing over her bed, demanding money. The man was Irons, and he dragged the elderly woman into the living room, pushed her on the floor and covered her face with a pillow so she could not breathe.

The thug then began going through her belongings, and Canale took the opportunity to pull off her two diamond rings and hide them.

Irons and Apergia left the car he had taken in Manatee and took Canale's car. They showed up the following evening in Clewiston, a small Okeechobee lakeshore community, armed with a BB pistol and tire iron. At about 7 p.m., Irons and Apergis forced their way into the home of a 74-year-old man and 64-year-old woman, and a struggle broke out between all four.

Finally, the man broke free and retrieved his handgun, shooting Irons twice. The thug and his girlfriend got outside, but Irons only made it as far as the driveway. He was arrested and carted off to the hospital, and then to jail.

Years earlier, in January 2001, a string of home invasions in the Chattanooga, Tennessee area came to an end when a pair of masked gunmen picked the wrong address.

The story, detailed by Robert Waters, author of *The Best Defense: True Stories of Intended Victims Who Defended Themselves with a Firearm*, and the Chattanooga *Times Free Press*, noted that between October 2000 and the night of Jan. 12, 2001, the Chattanooga area had suffered 45 home invasions. Whether 27-year-old Mica Kaba Townsend was responsible for all of them perhaps doesn't matter so much as the fact that he was at the last one, and after that confrontation, home invasions in the area came to a sudden halt.

On the fateful night, Tiffany Bibbs, her 11-month-old child, her grandmother, Sarah Cousins and a friend identified as Gerald Lamar Beverly are in Bibbs' home when two masked and armed men burst in and order them to lie on the floor. They want money, and when Bibbs grabs a telephone, one of the intruders knocks it out of her hand, telling her "I know you're calling the police."

Bibbs finally tells the pair they have all the money in the house, and one of the thugs grabs her child and goes out the back door, only to put the toddler down on the steps. That's when things escalated quickly.

The newspaper reported that Cousins, the grandmother, handed a gun to Beverly, who followed the thug outside and started shooting.

When the police arrived, they found Beverly and a neighbor identified as Chip Bradford standing outside the house with guns. Lying dead in the driveway was Townsend. The second robber fled in a hail of bullets.

Then something unusual occurred, but was properly reported by the newspaper. Police spokesman Ed Buice – asked by a reporter about "vigilantism" – quickly fired back that "Protecting your home is not vigilantism. Check the definition."

Another neighbor, identified as Ray Young, was also quoted by the newspaper observing, "This should have happened a long time ago. If a man invades my home and I got the ups on him, I'd shoot him."

Perhaps that is the decision faced by 66-year-old James Wiggins of Fayetteville, North Carolina the night of March 9, 2007. Two men identified by WRAL TV news as Paul Euston Kent, Jr., 20, and Carlos Francisco Mozzo, both of Fayetteville, went to the Wiggins home wearing black ski masks, dark clothing and carrying a handgun.

When Wiggins' dog began barking, he looked outside and saw the two dark figures heading for his house. He raced to the bedroom, grabbed his own handgun and went to the back door as the two forced it open. Wiggins opened fire.

Kent was wounded in the right side of the face, just below the right eye. Mozzo was hit in the midsection and the leg.

Incredibly, both men reportedly worked for Wiggins in his roofing business. Well, not anymore.

Utopia Fantasy = False Security

The dream of one day living in a society free of crime and violence certainly motivates many people in the gun control movement – witness Ralph Fascitelli, president of the gun control organization Washington CeaseFire who is also a founding partner of something called "Utopian Marketing" – but their approach to the problem of criminal violence seeks to disarm the wrong people first. Instead of encouraging crackdowns on criminals, their solution is to make it difficult if not impossible for the law abiding element to own or even possess firearms for personal protection.

Though not universal, it is hardly unusual to find that those who oppose the use of firearms for self-defense are also opponents of capital punishment, and they are often more concerned with the civil rights of accused suspects than they are with the civil rights of law-abiding citizens.

In their Utopian fantasy world, there are no guns and everyone lives in harmony. There is no war, no hunger, no violence and no crime. When there is a problem, we all get together for a group hug and find a solution.

When a violent crime occurs in today's *real* world, their first predictable reaction is to demand stricter gun control laws to curb the flow of firearms into the hands of American citizens. They propose registration and licensing schemes, gun rationing that restricts purchases to one gun a month, repeal of concealed carry statutes and short of that, expanding the list of places where personal defense handguns are prohibited.

They also quietly support statutes that would add to the list of penalties both criminal and civil that might one day cause a person to be disqualified from owning or possessing a firearm.

In short, these "Utopians" equate armed citizens with criminals. Their rhetoric clearly reveals that they distrust average citizens with firearms, predicting the worst behavior. Some people have argued that their fears are based on their own self-doubts; that is, they think that they might behave poorly, and therefore suspect that everyone around them will equally misbehave.

In the Utopian world they are trying to create, gun turn-ins and confiscations would be a prelude. This is why they support registration laws; governments will find it easier to take firearms if they know where to look.

But as we have seen in Great Britain and Australia, for example, such schemes – traditionally pandered as the panacea to perhaps a single act of violence – have been total failures. In some cases, outlined by previously-mentioned historian Benedict D. LaRosa, gun confiscations have been the precursor to massive human rights violations and even genocide.

Gun rights proponents seem far more cognizant of this than gun control extremists, yet the same history is there for both sides to see. They have coined a term for this type of one-sided gun control: *victim disarmament.* LaRosa provided the ultimate potential of such confiscatory firearms policies it taken to the extreme in the second part of his two-part essay in the November 2002 *Freedom Daily*:

"But the record of strict gun regulations in other countries is quite dismal," he wrote. "In 1929, the Soviet Union established gun control. From 1929 to 1953, about 20 million dissidents were rounded up and exterminated. In 1911, Turkey established gun control. From 1915 to 1917, 1.5 million Armenians were exterminated.

"Germany established gun control in 1938, and from 1939 to 1945, 13 million Jews and others were exterminated," La Rosa noted.

"China established gun control in 1935; from 1948 to 1952, 20 million political dissidents were exterminated," he recalled.

"Guatemala established gun control in 1964, and from 1964 to 1981, 100,000 Mayan Indians were exterminated.

"Uganda established gun control in 1970 — from 1971 to 1979, 300,000 people were exterminated.

"Cambodia established gun control in 1956, and from 1975 to 1977 one million educated people were exterminated.

"In a more recent example," he wrote, "the British Broadcasting Company reported on May 10, 2000, that the United Nations convinced the people of Sierra Leone to turn in their private weapons for UN protection during the recent civil war. The result was disastrous. The people ended up defenseless when UN troops, unable to protect even themselves, were taken hostage by rebels moving on the capital of Freetown.

"Estimates run as high as 56 million people who have been exterminated in the 20th century because gun control left them defenseless," LaRosa reported.

While genocide may seem like a ridiculous concern here in the United States and be quickly dismissed as the doomsday fear of paranoid gun nuts, unilateral citizen disarmament has insidious ramifications that are genuine and provable, as demonstrated by the experiences in Australia and Great Britain.

Perhaps the knowledge of what can, and frequently does, happen in a community where authorities deprive citizens of their firearm civil rights is what swiftly led the Second Amendment Foundation and National Rifle Association of America to join forces in a landmark federal lawsuit to halt the confiscation of firearms from New Orleans residents in the wake of Hurricane Katrina in late August and early September of 2005.

It was a precedent-setting endeavor, and one that has never been given its full credit, for its partnership nature and for what it accomplished.

Incredibly, a large number of American citizens have been led to believe by press reports that one or the other organization had borne the burden of the New Orleans lawsuit entirely on its own. All too frequently, for example, published reports in various newspapers left the impression that the NRA had acted alone, which would not have been all that surprising, considering the outrage felt by its members when word of the gun confiscations began spreading across the airwaves and internet.

But in this case, SAF was a full partner in the legal action because its members and supporters were also furious about the gun confiscations. SAF was actually preparing to file a lawsuit on its own, but when it became clear the NRA was also going to act, the two organizations joined forces.

The joint lawsuit demonstrated to the entire country that firearms civil rights organizations *can and do* operate on the same page when it comes to defending the individual right to keep and bear arms. This partnership legal effort sent a signal to state and local officials that they, too could wind up on the receiving end of a federal civil rights lawsuit if they arbitrarily order the confiscation of privately-owned firearms in the wake of some new natural or man-made disaster or emergency.

New Orleans hurricane victims became victims of their own

government – which was supposed to be providing aid, not stripping them of their property without warrant or probable cause – when they were disarmed, sometimes at gunpoint, by roving patrols of police officers or National Guard units. This left them at the non-existent mercy of roving bands of looters and pillagers.

Myth versus Reality

During Prof. Lott's 2005 appearance before the House committee, he brought the issue of victim disarmament directly to Congress' front doorstep in terms committee members could more intimately appreciate: "In D.C., crime has risen significantly since the gun ban went into effect."

"In the five years before the D.C. ban in late 1976," Lott testified, "the murder "rate was slightly declining: the rate fell from 37 to 27 per 100,000. But in the five years after the ban went into effect, the murder rate rose back up to 35 (per 100,000). In fact, while crime rates have fluctuated over time, the murder rate after 1976 has only once fallen below what it was in 1976. The preliminary estimate of a 35 per 100,000 people murder rate in 2004 is still well above what the murder rate was when the handgun ban went into effect. (The explosion in murder during the late 1980s was likely due to the crack cocaine problem, which was a nationwide problem, particularly in urban areas such as D.C.)

"Robberies and overall violent crime changed just as dramatically," he continued. "Robberies in the five years before the ban fell from 1,514 to 1,003 per 100,000 and then rose by over 63 percent, up to 1,635 in the five years after it.

"These drops and subsequent increases were much larger than any changes in neighboring Maryland and Virginia," he said, showing the panel several charts. "For example, the District's murder rate fell from 3.5 to 3 times more than in the neighboring states and rose back to 3.8 times more within five years. After the ban was implemented the ratio of the murder rates between D.C. and neighboring Maryland and Virginia never fell below the rate seen in either 1975 or 1976. In other words, the relative gap between D.C.'s and Maryland and Virginia's murder rates are never reduced after the D.C. ban."

Writing in the October 2002 issue of *Freedom Daily*, historian La

Rosa noted, "After passage of the 1968 gun-control act, the number of robberies jumped from 138,000 in 1965 to 376,000 in 1972, while murders committed with guns increased from 5,015 to 10,379 in the same period. According to the Census Bureau, the proportion of cases in which the murder weapon was a firearm rose from 57.2 percent to 65.6 percent."

LaRosa had other revelations that are routinely ignored by gun control proponents who merely argue that the gun laws in place now aren't strong enough, so there need to be additional restrictions. New York Mayor Michael Bloomberg in 2006 launched a controversial campaign to use the civil courts to sue gun retailers in other states, blaming them for supplying firearms used in New York crimes. Eventually, the Department of Justice advised Bloomberg's office that it would not criminally prosecute any of the gun dealers targeted by a Bloomberg-inspired "sting" operation in which private investigators used illegal straw-man purchases to ensnare the dealers.

The Justice Department sent a strongly-worded letter to Bloomberg's office, advising the mayor to forsake any plans for future such sting efforts, because they could run afoul of the same federal gun laws that anti-gunners have been supporting for years.

LaRosa's embarrassing disclosures came almost four years prior to Bloomberg's rogue operation. The historian noted, "In New York City, long known for strict regulation of all types of weapons, only 19 percent of the 390 homicides in 1960 involved pistols. By 1972, this proportion had jumped to 49 percent of 1,691. In 1973, according to the *New York Times,* there were only 28,000 lawfully possessed handguns in the nation's largest city, but police estimated that there were as many as 1.3 million illegal handguns there."

Here, again, it would appear that the wrong people seem to be getting their hands on guns. Law-abiding citizens have a horrible time getting a permit to even own a gun in New York. Presumably, at least some of those 1.3 million "illegal guns" in the city are in the hands of frustrated citizens who simply want some personal protection in their homes and apartments.

Undoubtedly, however, many of those "illegal guns" are in the hands of criminals, who don't obey any other law so why would they be expected to obey a gun law?

Look at the state of Maryland. LaRosa did, and here's what he reported in his *Freedom Daily* essay: "In 1986, Maryland banned small, affordable handguns called 'Saturday night specials.' Within two years, Maryland's murder rate increased by 20 percent, surpassing the national murder rate by 33 percent. Then Maryland passed a one-gun-a-month law. Yet between 1997 and 1998, 600 firearms recovered from crime scenes were traced to Maryland gun stores. Virginia, one of only two other states with a similar law, ranked third as a source of guns used by criminals in other states."

Those who advocated tough gun laws in New York generations ago, and more recently in Maryland and Virginia, are the same people who believe that we can have a Utopian society someday, but first we need to be rid of the guns. And the first guns to go are those the social engineers can most easily target: Firearms owned by law-abiding citizens.

Ask privately of any of these social idealists how they personally suggest their fellow citizens deal with crime, and they invariably say "call 911 and wait for the police." Even some high ranking law enforcement officials will say that.

Jeff Snyder, an attorney who writes a very thought-provoking column in a magazine called *The American Handgunner*, has observed more than once the fallacy of such thinking. He summed up the Utopian mindset brilliantly in a September/October 2001 essay in that magazine with this observation: "We bear no responsibility for ourselves; we take nothing upon ourselves. Government must do something to protect us."

But a growing majority of Americans who still value the concepts of self-reliance, personal determination and individual liberty balk at Utopianism. Fervent gun rights activists have adopted the habit of calling such Utopia advocates "sheeple." It is a term of derision that compares such people to sheep, fearfully and blissfully flocked together, who depend upon shepherds and sheep dogs to protect them from wolves and other predators.

The good news is that in every corner of the nation, it is people, not "sheeple," who are taking responsibility for their own safety and that of their families. They have studied the landscape politically and socially, and have determined that in a nation of sheep, they are not part of the flock.

These Americans are fighting back.

CHAPTER 11

Lethal Self-Defense Is Moral

Expansion of state self-defense statutes is an effort that invariably gets debated in the comfort of a legislative hearing room, and later in the confines of a caucus, and quite frequently on the editorial pages of newspapers that are composed and printed in large buildings somewhat isolated from the real world.

These debates are conducted, and the editorials written, by people who – but for an incredibly unusual twist of fate and certainly by the grace of God – never have the intimate experience of knowing or confronting people who commit violent crimes; the kinds of crimes that inspire citizens to approach their lawmakers to adopt such legislation in the first place. Such debates do not occur in the course of the act of self-defense, as there is hardly time to have a discussion about the morality of self-defense when you are trying to prevent someone from murdering you so he can steal not only your life but all you possess, and perhaps rape and murder your wife and/or daughter or girlfriend in the process.

Meet 57-year-old James Slaughter. With a criminal record dating back to 1967 when he was about 18 years old – and drew his first prison sentence – Slaughter is a career criminal whose most serious brush with the law occurred in 1983, when he took a family hostage in Taft, Texas. According to accounts in the Corpus Christi *Caller-Times* and broadcast on KRIS-TV News, Slaughter had tied up the couple in that incident and then fled in their automobile after loading it with valuables and clothing. This was only hours after he had stolen a car, and the woman driver's purse, in Corpus Christi.

After a brief chase, San Patricio Sheriff's deputies finally force him to stop when they ram the stolen car. Slaughter emerged from the car and aimed a rifle at both lawmen, one of whom would later become the sheriff, Leroy Moody. But Moody and another deputy both shot Slaughter, who survived his wounds and ended up drawing a 45-year prison sentence.

Slaughter was paroled in 2000 after spending 27 years behind bars, and he spent the next few years in relative anonymity until a drug bust landed him back in jail, this time in Nueces County, in 2005. In June 2006, he was again reportedly arrested for a parole violation and sent to the Travis County jail.

Slaughter's story should be all that is necessary to demonstrate that people are put in prisons not to rehabilitate them, but to punish them and keep them away from the public.

It is the morning of Monday, October 11, 2006. Only three days before, on the previous Friday, Slaughter had been released from jail.

Rose Ann Kozlowski had been called to pick up her 14-year-old son, Michael, from the Incarnate Word Academy, where he is in ninth grade and is described in a published report as an avid soccer player. But today, Michael is ill.

After taking her son home, Mrs. Kozlowski goes to the grocery store. When she gets back, it is not an ill teen she meets, but James Slaughter. He is not there to comfort Michael.

Slaughter is armed with what the police and the newspaper describe as a folding lockback knife with a blade measuring about 4 to 5 inches long. Slaughter threatens to kill Kozlowski if she doesn't cooperate. He takes mother and son to the upstairs master bedroom, ties them up with her husband's neckties, and then begins systematically ransacking the house, the same thing he did to that other family in 1983 that put him behind prison bars for more than two decades. He begins loading valuables, including jewelry, into the Kozlowski's SUV.

Over the next 25 minutes, Kozlowski is able to free herself but Slaughter hears her wrestling with the ties, and comes back to re-bind her even more. After he goes back to looking for plunder, she finally manages to free herself a second time, and quickly unties her son. And then she does something that may draw shrieks from members of the Million Mom March, but that authorities will quickly condone as absolutely necessary under the circumstances: She opens a security box under the bed and retrieves a loaded revolver. She hands the gun to Michael and tells him to guard the door, which she has prudently locked, while she calls the police.

Slaughter has heard a commotion from the master bedroom and this time he is not happy. Returning to find the double doors locked shut, he slides the blade of his knife between the doors trying to unlock them. It is about 12:55 p.m. when the first call reaches the police dispatch, and Rose Ann Kozlowski anxiously reports that a man armed with a knife is in her home. Then the line is disconnected.

Hurriedly, the police dispatcher calls back, and in the short moments between the two telephone calls, facing the prospect that this vicious predator outside the doors is about to burst in, Michael has raised the revolver, aimed it carefully toward the widening crack between the two doors and fires a single shot. The bullet slams into James Slaughter's face, killing him instantly.

When the dispatcher gets through, Kozlowski reports that the man has been shot in the head and may be lying dead outside the bedroom. If the Corpus Christi police had been racing to the scene up to now, they floored it after that report with lights and sirens. The first officers reportedly arrived at the Kozlowski residence at 1 p.m. Five minutes is not an unusual response time to a life-threatening situation anywhere in the country, but for someone facing that threat, it can be an eternity.

The *Caller-Times* quoted Corpus Christ Police Capt. John Houston, who told a reporter, "There's a point in the tape where you can actually hear that they (Mrs. Kozlowski and her son) don't want to even leave the room, knowing that he's outside, because there's still that fear that something could happen."

In the Lone Star State there is a matter-of-fact saying that often crosses the lips of native Texans who have grown up knowing that life is hard, and sometimes people just turn bad. The observation goes like this: "He needed killin'."

That may or may not have been what was quietly agreed to by the grand jury that was called the following day, but a report on KRIS summed up their quick disposition of the case: "Yesterday, the grand jury ruled that there was no wrongdoing on (Michael's) part." Jurors ruled that the shooting was in self-defense.

There is a post script to the Slaughter incident. His ex-wife, Donna Olsen, tells the television station that the blame for Slaughter's death lies squarely with the Texas prison system. Insisting that "the system failed him," Olsen contends that had the system put Slaughter in a drug treatment program when he started going bad after what she described as nearly five years as a law-abiding citizen, the fatal encounter at the Kozlowski home might never have occurred.

Sheriff Moody had a slightly different take, telling the newspaper that Slaughter should never have been paroled in the first place, and that it was not the prison system's fault that his life ended on the upstairs floor of a home that he was terrorizing.

"He chose the lifestyle he lived," Sheriff Moody observed. "It's all about choices."

Barbarians at the Gate

Under the so-called "Castle Doctrine" that considers "a man's home to be his castle," so-called home invasion robberies are considered something of an act of war, and they merit a response of force. This notion dates to medieval times, and even earlier, perhaps to the very dawn of civilization, because the home/castle is a sanctuary and it must not be violated.

From ancient times to the present, such violations are considered to be criminal acts by the courts or whatever system of justice may have been in force at the time, and the perpetrators have traditionally been dealt with rather harshly, provided they survive.

In America, from the time of the early settlements and life on the Frontier as the line of civilization crept slowly across the continent, the castle doctrine has remained a cornerstone principle. Whether it was exercised against roving bands of Indians or wandering outlaws, the attempted invasion of a person's home could reasonably – and often sensibly – be met with a rifle ball, shot charge or a revolver bullet, and nobody would raise an eyebrow, much less a political or legal objection.

And then came modern America, with its myriad and often contradictory laws, its gun control statutes and "criminal rights" agenda. While it might be true that there have been crimes committed against people under the guise of self-defense, it is not a widespread phenomena and certainly no justification for the adoptions of rules and laws that restrict or eliminate the exercise of true self-defense.

After years of living with the jumble of laws that often find the victim of a crime become the victim of a seriously malfunctioning legal system, the public began demanding a return of the justice pendulum to its proper position. One result of this social and political movement has been the adoption of "castle doctrine" laws. Once again, police and prosecutors are looking at the invasion of one's home as an egregious crime that can be met with whatever force necessary to stop it.

Opponents of such statutes, which they mockingly refer to as "shoot first laws," fight bitterly to keep them off the books, invariably argue that human life is precious. Advocates of "castle doctrine" laws quickly counter, "Yes, human life is precious, and we must be allowed to defend our own against those who would take it from us."

Which brings us around to Paul Lee Bourff and Robert Wayne Evans of Campbell County, Tennessee; their case underscores the necessity of laws that protect victims of attack from unfair prosecution, or at least the value of common sense on the part of investigators and prosecutors.

On Tuesday, January 9, 2007, Bourff and Evans showed up at the LaFollette, Tennessee home of Sonya Dople. She is preparing dinner for herself and boyfriend Charles Green, according to accounts from WATE News in Knoxville and the Knoxville *News Sentinel*. There is a knock on the door, and when Dople opens up to see who is there, two masked men burst in, armed with what appears to be a handgun.

The gun subsequently turns out to be a BB pistol, and there was a time in America when it was pretty easy to tell the difference between an airgun and a real firearm. That is not the case today, and in more than one instance where a criminal has been unable to get his hands on a genuine firearm, they have picked up an airgun to commit a crime. So, in the quickly-unfolding series of events inside Dople's residence, it is not legally or even reasonably incumbent upon either victim to make a distinction.

On this particular occasion, the argument could easily be made that you should never take an airgun to a gunfight. Indeed, that's exactly what LaFollette Police Detective Jeff Allen told the *News Sentinel*. Unbeknownst to the two perpetrators, Green was armed with a real pistol.

Brought to the corner of the room by the commotion, what Green sees are two masked men, one of whom is aiming a gun at his girlfriend's forehead, while ordering her to get on the floor. In all too many cases, this is the prelude to an execution-style murder.

Green grabs his gun and opens fire, putting a round squarely into Bourff's chest. The two would-be home invaders flee, showing up a short time later at the home of a man identified as Ray Marlow, who apparently knows Bourff, but has no idea what has just occurred. Marlow takes him to the hospital.

The police take Evans into custody and Bourff is moved from one hospital to the University of Tennessee Medical Center.

When one is in fear for his or her own life, or the life of another innocent person, and the threat of deadly force appears genuine – but later turns out not to be – the parameters of castle doctrine legislation can come into play. In this case, there was a quick determination about who the good guys and bad guys were, and Ms. Dople put it succinctly in her comment to a reporter: "We have the right to protect ourselves. If we hadn't had the gun and he hadn't done that...it could've been us. We could've been dead today."

Yet, remarkable as it may seem in an America that is beginning to fight back, there remain strong sentiments in the offices of some state legislators against expanding such laws to allow the same kind of self-defense measures, and protections, to people outside the home and in their place of business.

In Colorado, for example, lawmakers arguing over the expansion of that state's so-called "Make My Day" self-defense statute passed several years ago amid emotional hand-wringing and cries from the Looney Liberal Left that the statute would lead to blood running in the streets, refused to retire their rhetoric.

The Denver *Post* reported that Rep. Dianne Primavera, a Broomfield Democrat, contended that passage of the legislation "could lead to business owners shooting people who made them uneasy based on stereotypes – young men of color, people wearing Middle Eastern dress or mental health patients."

And Colorado House Majority Leader Alice Madden reported predicted that Colorado residents would use the cover of an expanded law to commit "heinous murders."

"I don't want that blood on my hands," she was quoted as

stating.

Whatever their motivation, be they so-called "Nanny statists" who believe that citizens should trust their safety only to government and not practice anything remotely resembling self-reliance and self-defense, or whether this is yet another manifestation of the gun control mentality, the results are the same. They campaign vigorously against a citizen's right to self-preservation. As mentioned earlier, that comes rather easily when one is debating the issue in the safety of a legislative building.

It does not seem to occur to such advocates of non-violence that the scenario they protect is one of unilateral disarmament that leaves the law-abiding citizens incapable of warding off an attack. They do not seem to care, understand or acknowledge that the laws they protect and new laws they pass are routinely ignored by criminals.

'Reasonable Force'

Self-defense statutes vary from state to state, but if one were attempting to describe what such a law *ought* to be like, they would merely have to consult the statute in Washington State. This law, RCW (Revised Code of Washington) 9A.16.050, may read like something out of an attorney's lexicon, but it is actually rather simple to understand.

The statute clearly and plainly notes: *"Homicide (by a private citizen) is…justifiable when committed either:*

(1) *In the lawful defense of the slayer, or his or her husband, wife, parent, child, brother, or sister, or any other person in his presence or company, when there is reasonable ground to apprehend a design on the part of the person slain to commit a felony or to do some great personal injury to the slayer or to any such person, and there is imminent danger of such design being accomplished; or*

(2) *In the actual resistance of an attempt to commit a felony upon the slayer, in his presence or upon or in a dwelling, or other place of abode, in which he is.*

Translated to layman's terms, a person may act in self-defense, or the defense of a spouse, parent or child, sibling or another person in their presence (including a stranger) or company (including a friend) when it is reasonable to conclude that they are in imminent and unavoidable danger of great personal injury or death.

This statute has been on the books in its present form since 1975, and in Washington State, county prosecutors have rarely brought charges against a person who claimed self-defense when the evidence clearly supported such a claim.

The simple wording of the statute defines the "castle doctrine" pretty clearly, and also makes it abundantly certain that killing in self-defense has parameters, but that these parameters include defending one's self, loved-ones, and other persons who are either innocent bystanders or intended victims.

Such statutes do not excuse murder and never have, and the opponents of self-defense laws know it. Adoption of such statutes have never led to the kinds of massive bloodlettings hysterically predicted by gun control activists and gun ban extremists. Why they perennially distort the truth about self-defense is a question best left up to them to explain, provided they can.

Yet year after year, in state legislature after state legislature, where self-defense proponents pursue the adoption of such statutes, these arguments repeatedly are tossed out by the opposition, frequently without challenge by the press.

But what is "reasonable force" when an aggressor is not armed, or does not appear to be armed? Often times, the statutes are not very well defined, and only permit the use of force against another person "when the force is not more than is necessary." That can leave a door rather widely opened, but in actual practice, there have not been a great deal of excessive force complaints filed against law-abiding citizens who defend themselves from criminal attack.

As an example, one can strike back with a fist if one is punched with a fist, but one cannot under normal circumstances draw a gun and shoot someone who merely punched them with a closed fist, unless there is some great disparity of force, i.e. a larger attacker striking blows against a smaller and weaker victim.

One can respond with lethal force when circumstances and visual evidence lead one to conclude that lethal force is about to be used against one's self, or another person. And that brings us back to the Bourff shooting in Tennessee. The suspects in that crime charged into a private residence where they were not invited and had no right to be, and threatened the resident, Ms. Dople, with what appeared to be a real handgun, that is, a lethal weapon capable of causing death or great physical harm. In genuine fear for the life of his girlfriend, Mr. Green justifiably reached for his own handgun and opened fire.

The reasonableness of a lethal act is determined by considering what any reasonable and prudent person would have done, in the same situation, knowing what you knew at the time.

But all of this is academic debate that occurs after an event, and in a real life-or-death situation, one quite often has only a split second to make a decision that could save a life by ending another. And these are the kinds of situations that "castle doctrine" or "stand your ground" statutes are specifically written to address.

Why this concept escapes those on the Left remains a mystery. Perhaps the rationale really doesn't escape opponents of self-defense so much as it remains so foreign to them. Self-defense opponents frequently have no appreciation for the concept of self-reliance. The image of a "rugged individualist" is tantamount to that of a Neanderthal, or at least an unsophisticated lout.

But that philosophy of social bigotry is slowly giving way to the new, or perhaps resurrected, philosophy of self-determination and self-defense. Call it personal responsibility; a philosophy under which we are responsible for our own well-being.

To a growing number of Americans, this seems to be reasonable, sensible and logical.

Consider the Des Moines, Iowa case involving Shasta Bell, owner of an apartment building. It is March 17, 2007 at approximately 3 a.m. on a cold, dark, and snowy morning when Bell calls 911 for Des Moines police to report that she has just fired at someone coming through her second floor bedroom window.

Both KCCI NewsChannel 8 and the Des Moines *Register* cover the story, and a recording of Bell's call to police dispatchers is linked on the station's website. It is frightening yet somewhat funny, and Bell's own words do more to telegraph the urgency of the situation, and perhaps how easy it is for others, even a police dispatcher, to be detached – seemingly to the point of indifference – from a situation that, for the individual involved, is frightening.

The recording begins with Bell's voice telling the female dispatcher, "Someone's trying to break into my house."

Dispatcher: "What's your address?"

After Bell provides the address, the dispatcher asks, "Are they still at your window?"

Bell: "I don't know. I just fired at the (expletive)." And then she begs the dispatcher to "send somebody."

The dispatcher responds, "What do you mean, you just fired at them?"

Bell: "Am I supposed to just lay here and let somebody come in on me?"

Dispatcher: "Do you mean you just shot at them?"

Bell: "You're damn right! They're coming through my window!"

The dispatcher subsequently asks, "Where is the gun now? Where's the gun?"

Bell: "In my damn hands!"

Dispatcher: "I need you to put your gun down so when the cops get there they don't take you."

Bell: "When I hear the sirens. When they get here with their sirens on, I will put it down. Otherwise, you got to hell. You've lost your (expletive) mind."

Unbeknownst to Bell at the time is that outside on the platform of the fire escape outside her upstairs window lies the body of 45-year-old Terri Burgess, a woman with a history of arrests, including at least two for prostitution, in 1993 and 1998. According to one report in the *Register*, there was also a domestic assault arrest in 2002. She is reportedly an occasional visitor to one of Bell's tenants, a man identified as Brian Ashby, who is not at home at the time.

Another incident in her past involved a "fall" out of a moving tractor-trailer rig on Interstate 235. Burgess was found later smeared with blood and wandering along the freeway dazed, the newspaper reported.

Unbeknownst to Burgess, Bell has remained at home rather than take a planned trip, and Burgess' further ignorance about Bell proves fatal: the military veteran sleeps with a shotgun under her mattress. One newspaper account explains that Bell is a former Chicago resident, and is all-too familiar with crime.

Police discover that Burgess has a pair of scissors, presumably to be used to cut the screen of Bell's apartment window. She also is carrying a fire extinguisher, and investigators reportedly concluded this was to be used to break Bell's window, so it appears Burgess is definitely attempting to break into the apartment.

While police determine the shooting to be in self-defense, a spokesman tells the news station that this does not mean other Des Moines residents can break out their guns and start shooting people through windows.

The Moral of Self-Defense

Social moralists will be quick to point to the shooting of Terri Burgess as an unnecessary tragedy; a harsh punishment for what may have amounted to a minor crime.

They neglect to rationalize that Bell was at home, rather than somewhere else, and from her perspective, someone was attempting to invade her home. At that hour of the morning, home invasion robberies typically do not have pleasant outcomes.

But there is another moral involved, one that the liberal anti-self-defense zealots consistently and deliberately ignore. Burgess had no business trying to enter Bell's residence, whether she was home or not. Burgess was not a resident of Bell's apartment house. Even though she was an occasional guest of one of the tenants, she had no right to be there, on the upstairs fire escape, at 3 a.m. preparing to break into Bell's apartment.

The morality of self-defense has been the subject of considerable philosophical debate over the years, and there appears to be no meeting of the minds. Some oppose self-defense, particularly when it involves the defense of property, and others believe that using lethal force to protect yourself and your property is perfectly acceptable.

We live in a nation of laws, but criminals routinely ignore the law. That's why they are criminals. Whether these individuals suffer from some drug addiction, have some kind of mental problem, or merely steal from and hurt others because they are simply too lazy to find a steady job, the strongest proponents of self-defense argue that none of this should really matter to the individual who is suffering the immediate attack and injury or property loss. Their only concern should be to protect themselves and end the threat without harm to themselves or other innocents.

On the other hand, we have the compelling argument that human life is sacred, and we must not, as a society, allow life to be taken merely for the preservation of property, or even in defense of one's own life.

Pacifists insist that we should "turn the other cheek." Shooting through a door or window at a shadowy figure outside, they will argue, hardly has the same justification as one might *presume* to exist if someone has his hands tightly clenched around your throat.

Ultimately, we must fall back on the "reasonable man doctrine," what any reasonable person might do under the same set of circumstances, knowing what you knew at the time. To opponents of self-defense, using any kind of force is unreasonable. To self-defense proponents, resistance is a powerful deterrent to future such behavior, and if someone gets killed as the result of his own illegal actions, there is nobody to blame other than the decedent.

The most important perspectives on this debate do not come from academics or self-appointed moral arbiters, but from people like Michael Grant of Levy, Jasper County, South Carolina. His story can be found, like so many others, on Clayton Cramer's blog in the archives for 2004.

Early on the morning of August 23, Grant's home was invaded by two men, one of who was 32-year-old Michael Jenkins of Hardeeville, who happened to be holding a crowbar. This happened at about 12:30 a.m. and there is no reason for anyone to be entering a home that is not theirs at that hour. Grant was aroused from slumber by his home security alarm, according to one report published in the Beaufort *Gazette* of August 25.

Cramer's blog report, culled from WSAV in Savannah, Georgia on August 24, explained that Grant retrieved his 9mm semiautomatic pistol and opened fire. Jenkins was hit in the face and leg, and when the cops arrived, he was not in very good shape. Taken to Memorial Health University Medical Center in Savannah, Jenkins died at about four hours later.

Jasper County Sheriff's Chief Deputy Roy Hughes was quoted at the time stating that Grant "opened fire in fear for his life."

"The train of thought is," Hughes stated, "if you're in your home – especially at night and you're asleep in your home – and someone's breaking into your home, it's evident that they're going to try to do harm to you."

The report also quoted a spokesman for the South Carolina Attorney General's office, who explained the state statute as allowing people to "stand their ground and repel the attack with as much force as is reasonably necessary."

What happened to Michael Grant, and people like him, is not academic at all, but real life. When someone is coming through the door at you in the middle of the night, it is not to discuss the philosophy of life but quite likely to cause your death.

As San Patricio County Sheriff Moody noted, "It's all about choices." The choice we each have to make, typically in the fraction of a second, is whether we want to fight back and live, or are willing to surrender and die.

CHAPTER 12

Coming Soon to a Forest Near You

July 11, 2006 will be a date long-remembered by outdoor enthusiasts in Washington State, and particularly the hiking and backpacking community, even beyond that state's borders.

On one of the more popular hiking trails in eastern Snohomish County, about 40 miles northeast from Seattle, 56-year-old Mary Cooper and her daughter, 27-year-old Susanna Stodden made one of their many back country excursions on a day hike. This trek would be their last. Their bodies were found by a couple of other hikers only a few hours after they had all seen each other at the trailhead. Both women had been shot in the head for unknown reasons in what apparently was a sudden attack. They were killed at a spot in the trail that one source said was perfect for an ambush. As this book was written, the killer or killers had not been found, and there were no solid suspects. The crime scene is nothing more than a curved spot on the trail, no different in appearance than curves on any number of other wilderness trails anywhere in the United States. Depending upon whether there was any wind blowing through the area at the time of the killing, the sound of a gunshot might carry some distance through the evergreen forest, and then, again, it might not.

It is a mystery that one Snohomish County source suggested to one of the authors might take a long time to solve, and might never be solved unless someone comes forward and admits responsibility. The killer or killers left very little, if any, physical evidence.

Cooper and Stodden are not the only people to have ever been murdered in the wilds. Indeed, crime appears to be on the rise in the outdoors. While murders are still rare, other crimes including assault, rape, theft, vandalism and marijuana growing or the production of methamphetamine is becoming a problem in many state and national forests.

Too, in the particular area of northeastern Snohomish County where the crime occurred, there are a considerable number of so-called "blue tarp" people; hermit types who live solitary lives in the wilds, often in makeshift shelters, and do not care to interact with other people. It would be unfair to point fingers at any of these reclusive individuals, however, simply for their lifestyle.

But the Pinnacle Lake Trail incident that took the lives of Cooper and Stodden stands out because there is no indication that these women would have ever harmed another soul. It was their sad misfortune to have encountered someone else who would. There was no apparent motive for their murders.

Slightly more than ten years earlier, in late May 1996, Julianne Williams, 24, of St. Cloud, Minnesota and 26-year-old Laura "Lollie" Winans of Unity, Maine were murdered as they hiked the Appalachian Trail, which runs through several states from the South to the Northeast. Their bodies were found on June 1 by Shenandoah National Park rangers who had been sent to look for them when they became overdue. Both women's hands had been tied and their throats had been cut. The killer left a "witness," a golden retriever named "Taj" belonging to Winans.

In the November 1996 edition of *Out*, writer Barry Yoeman noted that the Winans-Williams killings had aroused concerns in the gay community because the dead women had been "sweethearts." It was wondered whether that had anything to do with their slayings, because one of the other nine murders along the popular Appalachian Trail between 1974 and 1996 had also been a lesbian who, according to Yoeman's account, had been fatally shot by someone who had seen her kissing her girlfriend.

For a time, there was someone under arrest and facing charges for that crime, but in 2004, charges were withdrawn against that individual. The man in question had been arrested and convicted in the attempted abduction of another woman in Shenandoah National Park.

On September 13, 1990 Appalachian Trail hikers Geoffrey Logan Hood, 26, of Signal Mountain, Tennessee and Molly LaRue,

25, of Shaker Heights, Ohio were murdered at their campsite in Pennsylvania.

Perhaps the most gruesome outdoors killings in recent memory were the murders in California's Yosemite National Park in 1999. Three of the victims died together. Carole Sund and Silvina Pelosso were found in a burned out rental car near Long Barn a month after they had last been seen alive at Yosemite's Cedar Lodge. The body of Sund's daughter, Juli, was found 30 miles away a week later.

Then, in July, a 26-year-old park worker named Joie Ruth Armstrong was decapitated near her park cabin. Ultimately, the man who killed all four women was apprehended, convicted and sentenced to death.

In all of these killings there has been but a single common denominator. None of the victims was armed. Indeed, firearms are prohibited along vast sections of the Appalachian Trail (by at least one estimate, 80 percent of the trail runs through areas that prohibit firearms), and hiking associations all over the country discourage the carrying of firearms in the back country. For example, the Appalachian Trail Conference's Hiker Security Task Force came up with some hiker guidelines for that trail in 1984, and chief among them was Item No. 8: "Carrying firearms is strongly discouraged. They are illegal if carried without a license or if concealed, and the odds are an innocent person will be hurt."

The Florida Trail Association had a similar proviso on its checklist, also Item No. 8: "Do not carry firearms. The FTA member code of ethics prohibits firearms when on the trail and it might end up being used against you or fellow hikers."

This is the same kind of "guns are bad" nonsense that one hears from police officials who recommend against defending one's self with a firearm in the home or business, instead advising that people call 9-1-1 and "let the professionals handle it." It is also the kind of foolishness all-too-often pandered by anti-gun activists who seem to have no limit to their efforts at victim disarmament.

There is but one small detail that the trail groups do not seem to grasp, but that a growing number of individual hikers do: When you are miles away from the nearest road, there is no such thing as 9-1-1. If something bad happens, you have to deal with it. The police aren't coming, ever, unless it is to retrieve a body and spray paint a black or white outline as part of an investigation. This applies equally whether you are attacked by a person or persons, or some wild animal, a likelihood not limited to Alaska.

In California, there have been a couple of incidents involving fatal mountain lion attacks, in which the victims were partly eaten. But the likelihood of being killed and eaten by a hungry predator is far lower than the possibility – also somewhat remote considering the number of people who use the wild lands for recreation – that you will become the victim of a violent wilderness crime.

However, as the incidents along the Appalachian Trail and in Washington State reveal, rare or not, when something of a criminal nature happens, it frequently has a very bad outcome.

Authorities in Snohomish County, Washington have been very tight-lipped about the Cooper-Stodden killings on the Pinnacle Lake Trail. They have declined even to discuss what kind of firearm was used to kill the two women, whether they were shot from a distance or at close range, or whether there were any shell casings or other evidence found at the scene that might one day lead to the arrest of the killer.

For weeks after the double homicide, it was a hot topic on Northwest chat lists, particularly one devoted specifically to hiking. And there was the inevitable disagreement – sometimes rather inflammatory – about carrying guns on the trail. Many hikers revealed they routinely go armed in the wild country, while others dismiss the practice as paranoid.

Armed on the Trail

The fact that hiking associations discourage the carrying of firearms on the trail, and even forbid their members from doing so, along the Appalachian Trail does have some solid foundation in the laws of that part of the United States. It might also be tainted somewhat with the social bigotry often found among "greens" (the slang term for nature lovers who tend to dislike firearms and hunting) who would rather never see a gun in the woods.

Author Workman has encountered such people on the trail. In the weeks following the Cooper-Stodden murder in Washington State, he ventured out on the trail on assignment for *Gun Week*, the nationally-circulated newspaper owned by the Second Amendment Foundation.

On more than one occasion, he encountered people who were visibly and verbally shaken at the sight of a firearm on the trail.

Conversely, he has also encountered other armed hikers, and discovered that among hikers and backpackers, there is considerable disagreement – usually quite polarized – about the value of firearms on the trail, and even their presence.

A small, but growing number of female hikers go armed. They carry their guns discreetly, often inside "fanny packs" that are worn with the actual pack on their abdomen, where the gun concealed inside is readily accessible. Depending upon the state, such carry may be perfectly legal or subject so some regulation.

In the West, where firearms laws are reasonable and where most state constitutions have so-called "right to bear arms" provisions and "right-to-carry" statutes, it is not unusual to find hikers outside of national parks with handguns on their belts or tucked close-at-hand in their backpacks. There is no consistent pattern to the type of firearm; some women carry smaller, lightweight pistols and revolvers, but one occasionally encounters women who have a .45-caliber or .357 Magnum. Likewise, male hikers who go armed may have a large-caliber handgun, such as a .41- or .44 Magnum.

In recent years, gun makers Smith & Wesson and Taurus, for example, have adapted strong, lightweight alloys in the production of their revolvers and pistols. These lightweight guns become popular with hikers, who are very cognizant of weight.

Smith & Wesson actually has produced a series of lightweight "Mountain Guns" in heavy calibers that pack well on the trail. The drawback to such firearms is that they exhibit nasty recoil because of their caliber, and one does not care to do much shooting with them.

In the bear country of Alaska, it is not surprising to find people in the back country who are armed with short-barreled 12-gauge shotguns, often fitted with some type of synthetic pistol grip. While legal, they are awesome in appearance, and at close range when loaded with slugs, they have been known to stop bears in their tracks when the need arose.

Check out the website for the Tongass National Forest in Alaska, where the following advice will be found under the heading of "Protection":

"Firearms should *never* be used as the alternative to common-sense approaches to bear encounters. If you are inexperienced with a firearm in emergency situations, you are more likely to be injured by a gun than a bear. It is illegal to carry firearms in some of Alaska's national parks, so check before you go.

"A .300-Magnum rifle or a 12-gauge shotgun with rifled slugs are appropriate weapons if you have to shoot a bear. Heavy handguns such as a .44-Magnum may be inadequate in emergency situations, especially in untrained hands.

"State law allows a bear to be shot in self-defense if you did not provoke the attack and if there is no alternative, but the hide and skull must be salvaged and turned over to the authorities.

"Defensive aerosol sprays which contain capsaicin (red pepper extract) have been used with some success for protection against bears. These sprays may be effective at a range of 6-8 yards. If discharged upwind or in a vehicle, they can disable the user. Take appropriate precautions. If you carry a spray can, keep it handy and know how to use it."

Likewise, a section on the San Juan National Forest "Frequently Asked Questions" website page notes: "Are you allowed a gun or rifle in a campground?"

And the answer follows: "Yes, but you cannot shoot it, unless in self-defense, such as if a bear was attacking."

It should be noted that the carrying of defensive firearms inside national parks is specifically forbidden. However, an organization called the Virginia Citizens Defense League (VCDL) has been pressing Congress to require the National Park Service and Department of Interior to change that regulation so that properly-licensed citizens would be allowed to carry their handguns.

This is another way Americans fight back: Through the grassroots lobbying process that can result in a change of policy, if not a statute.

The VCDL has been quietly, and on occasion not-so-quietly, lobbying for a change in the rules that would allow properly licensed private citizens to carry concealed within national parks, strictly for their personal protection. This is not an effort to legalize hunting, target shooting or any other form of recreation, but a specifically-targeted effort to allow citizens who may legally carry a concealed defensive handgun outside a national park to do the same inside the boundaries of that park.

Their timing might be crucial. According to the April 5, 2007 edition of the Washington *Times*, "The number of sworn officers in the U.S. Park Police has dropped to its lowest level in nearly 20 years."

The newspaper was quoting a group calling itself Public Employees for Environmental Responsibility. At the time, Park Police Chief Dwight E. Pettiford noted that there were 588 officers serving with the National Park Service. This 2007 total was down considerably from a similar tally of officers in 1988, when there were more than 200 additional officers in the NPS police. A 2001 study recommended a level of about 800 officers, the newspaper stated.

It should be noted that the Park Police provides marine, mounted and foot patrol officers in parks in Maryland, Washington, D.C. and Virginia. This would certainly explain the interest that the VCDL has in the issue, but what about in national parks across the country?

They're in the same financial fix that the U.S. Forest Service finds itself. In a 2006 report in the Seattle *Times*, the newspaper noted that 25 officers patrolled more than 1 million acres of national forest land in just the Mount Baker-Snoqualmie National Forest and Olympic National Forest. Between October 2005 and September 2006, Mount Baker-Snoqualmie officers handed out 709 citations for assorted crimes ranging from illegal dumping and vandalism to illegal off-road vehicle use, and wrote 2,197 incident reports.

Over in the Olympic National Forest, a total of 262 citations were issued, and another 875 incident reports were written, the newspaper said.

That is a lot of activity.

Inside Olympic National Park during 2005, the report added, there were 14 arrests and 523 citations issues. Most of the arrests were for drunken driving.

Rarely would you find any of these officers on patrol in the back country when a crime is being committed. They are hardly in a position to immediately respond to an emergency call that may be a half-day away by trail. By the time they arrive, the crime has already been committed and it might just be that the perpetrators are long gone.

So, it is not surprising why a growing number of hikers and back packers are quietly tucking guns in their gear.

The 'Oregon Rangers'

Fighting back can take more than one form. There are Neighborhood Watch programs endorsed by law enforcement that tend to concentrate on activities like "block watches" and gatherings to "take back the night." They occasionally get favorable publicity because they amount to politically-correct group efforts that visibly support the notion that the public should let the police handle things.

There is nothing inherently wrong with Neighborhood Watch programs. They've been proven to work, though they often lose momentum after an initial surge of activity and publicity.

Then there are the programs that do not get a robust endorsement from law enforcement or the dominant media, at least at the outset. The prime example of such a program is the Minuteman border watch project. While volunteers are carefully screened, and advised to take no action themselves but report illegal border activity to the authorities, they get a bad rap from liberal critics who accuse them of being founded on racism. Some in law enforcement dislike these volunteers because their mere existence suggests that police are not capable of handling a job, and the law enforcement culture disdains that impression.

There has been another strike against the Minuteman movement, and it is that many of these volunteers are armed. There is no evidence that any of these volunteers has ever used a firearm on someone illegally crossing the United States border. It's just that critics have this "gun thing" and the Minuteman volunteers represent the epitome of everything bad. That is, they represent self-reliance in an era when far too many people have become complacent about taking personal responsibility, even in the wake of the September 11, 2001 terrorist attacks.

While the Minuteman organization is specifically focused on reducing illegal border crossings, a small group of volunteers in Oregon came up with an idea for reducing illegal activity in the Pacific Northwest forests. They call themselves the Oregon Rangers, though this is hardly a descendant group from the original Oregon Rangers that were organized in early 1844 in the Oregon Territory. That group was essentially the local militia.

Today's Oregon Rangers are quite a bit different. According to their website the Oregon Rangers Association monitors 911 frequencies to "respond to logging accidents, auto accidents, and medical emergencies in Oregon parks and wilderness areas. The Oregon Rangers are E.M.T.'s with a full line of medical equipment on board our vehicles as well as high-powered radios and satellite phones."

These volunteers patrol the Beaver State's backcountry, to "locate and report trash dumps, meth dumps and illegal marijuana grows to the proper authorities."

"We are trained and equipped to help police and other emergency crews when needed," the website continues. "As such, we carry all state and federal licenses and certification needed to perform such tasks."

The Oregon Rangers Association is a registered volunteer group with the U.S. Forest Service, Bureau of Land Management and Oregon Department of Fish & Wildlife.

Do these people solve crimes? That's not their job, of course, but information they relay to the authorities can help put a dent in backcountry criminal activity. Too, their presence just might provide an additional layer of deterrence.

Writer Bill Berkowitz, in a story appearing in Z Magazine's October 2003 edition called "Patrolling the U.S. Back-Country," detailed the origin and activities of the Oregon Rangers. Noting that in late 2002, the Bush Administration began "privatizing" thousands of federal jobs, including jobs in the outdoors, Berkowitz led readers into the story of the Oregon Rangers, who were also profiled in June 2003 by the Eugene Register-Guard.

"At first glance," Berkowitz wrote, "the Oregon Rangers Association may appear to be another derivative militia group, but their sophisticated use of the language of volunteerism and public service sets them apart. The ORA's monthly newsletter reads like a Lion's Club digest of the group's productive activities."

The Register-Guard quoted ORA President Paul Ehrhardt, who noted, "I just get sick of our woods literally being taken over by the stuff…There's not enough cops out there and there's not going to be. The only way any of it's going to change is if the public gets involved. Most people won't do it and that's what makes the problem worse."

Ehrhardt stressed that ORA volunteers are not trying to be vigilantes. They are not simply looking for criminal activity, but to help the occasional stranded motorist or someone else in need. But he did acknowledge that finding small marijuana growing operations is part of their agenda.

Whether such organizations ultimately demonstrate any genuine value in the outdoors will perhaps take years to determine. But in an era when authorities like to promote public involvement there remains a certain bit of apprehension about what citizens "should" be doing to help put a crimp in crime. And that brings up the dilemma faced by many people who want to make a difference: On whose terms does one make that difference, yours or some bureaucrat's?

The dividing line comes with the presence of firearms, it would appear. Whether setting up a border watch or looking for trouble in the forests, one might almost be considered foolhardy to *not* be armed. And that brings us back around to the increasing number of hikers who prefer to arm themselves rather than to trust their luck to the goodwill of others who may not know the meaning of the term.

That nice person one encounters on the trail may be just as harmless as a butterfly. Then, again, he may be someone like Loran Cole, 27, and William Paul, 20. On February 18, 1994, these two men added a new dimension to the term "monster." Cole was an Orlando resident at the time, and Paul lived in Knoxville, Tennessee. People like this pair cause hikers and campers to *want* firearms, if not truckloads of volunteers like the Oregon Rangers providing security.

Conduct of Savages

Loran Cole had been out of prison less than eight months in mid-February 1994. Released in June 1993 after spending 18 months of a five and a half year sentence for grand theft behind bars, he was released from state prison due to overcrowding, according to the February 23, 1994 edition of the New York *Times*.

William Paul, then 20, had no criminal record and throwing in with Cole was to become the pivotal moment in his life.

According to court documents, John Edwards and his sister, Pam were headed into the Ocala National Forest for an overnight hike that would take them to Hopkins Prairie. At the time, Pam was a senior at Eckerd College in St. Petersburg and John was a freshman at Florida State University in Tallahassee. It was as they were setting up the camp that Cole appeared, introduced himself as "Kevin," and offered to help.

Later, after John and Pam had eaten dinner, Cole returned with Paul, who was carrying a walking stick and was introduced to the Edwards as Cole's brother.

The evening wore on as the four sat around the campfire, and then they decided to walk down to a nearby pond. However, the court documents said, they never found the pond. What they found, instead, was savagery.

Cole jumped on Pam, knocking her to the ground. She tried to get up and run, but Cole struck her on the back of the head, and then handcuffed her.

Meanwhile, Paul was getting the worse end of a fight with John Edwards, who had grabbed the walking stick from Paul's hands and started beating him with it. With Pam subdued, Cole joined that fight and the two attackers subdued John and moved him to a position where he was lying on the ground next to his sister. John thoughtfully apologized to his sister for having gotten them into this mess.

As they lay on the ground, Cole went through their pockets, taking car keys and anything of value. Paul took Pam up the trail while Cole stayed with her brother. The ex-con struck John at least three times on the head hard enough to fracture his skull, and then slashed his throat after demanding to know why John had struck "his brother."

"Cole then came to where Pam and Paul were sitting and told them that they were going to wait until John passed out," the court documents said. "Cole called back to John several times, and John responded by moaning. Eventually, Cole told Pam he was going to move John off the trail and tie him up. Pam then heard something that resembled a gagging sound."

The court documents then detail how Cole and Paul took their captive back to Cole's campsite, where she was forced to strip and then was raped. The following morning, after checking John's body, Cole returned to the campsite and lied to Pam Edwards that her brother was okay. Court papers say Cole left for a while to purchase marijuana, which he brought back and the three smoked, before Cole forced his captive to again have sex.

Before leaving Pam in the forest, she was gagged and tied to two trees. Cole and Paul then left in Pam's car and spent the night in a friend's trailer, where they foolishly left some of John Edwards' personal property.

Eventually, Cole and Paul went back to the Ocala National Forest and took John's car, leaving Pam's there. Pam finally freed herself and got help the following day, a Sunday. The next day, Monday February 21, police arrested Cole and Paul, and both were charged with first-degree murder, armed kidnapping, armed sexual battery and auto theft.

Paul pleaded *nolo contendre* to the charges and was sentenced to life in prison without possibility of parole for 25 years on the murder charge and concurrent terms on the remaining charges, court documents said.

Cole decided to fight the charges and pleaded not guilty. The jury didn't see it that way, and convicted him on all charges. The jury also unanimously voted to recommend that he be put to death.

After such heinous crimes, there is typically much discussion in the outdoors community, and by law enforcement authorities and national forest officials about steps that can be taken to reduce the odds of being attacked in the wilds. Typically they suggest hiking in groups, and never alone, and to leave a trip plan with someone who can notify authorities if a hiker is overdue. The trip plan will give searchers a place to start looking.

But after reading about the case of John and Pam Edwards, one feels compelled to ask the Florida Trail Association about its checklist notation against carrying firearms, mentioned earlier in this chapter. *"Do not carry firearms. The FTA member code of ethics prohibits firearms when on the trail and it might end up being used against you or fellow hikers."*

In September 2006, outdoorsmen and women in Indiana saw authorities in that state take what they considered a sensible step that might just make the Florida hikers association flush with shock. The Department of Natural Resources lifted a ban on handguns in Indiana state parks. While some news reports sneered that this constituted a "victory for the gun lobby" and the Indianapolis *Star* editorialized that it was not too keen for the idea, newspapers liberally quoted DNR Director Kyle Hupfer, who advocated the change.

He was remarkably to the point, noting, "If my life or my wife's life was at risk, I want to be in a position to protect her and myself."

Hupfer, described as a man who routinely carries a sidearm, explained to the *Star* that firearms can come in handy in the wilds, especially if one encounters an illegal meth lab.

Back in Virginia, VCDL activists continue advocating concealed or open carry, and pressing for a change in federal regulations for national parks. In an ideal situation, said VCDL President Philip Van Cleave, every state should honor the concealed pistol licenses issued by all other states. He would like to see national parks honor such permits and operate as national forests do, by simply operating under the laws of the state in which they are located.

But perhaps the best summation on the subject of firearms in the forests comes from Joe Waldron, executive director of the Citizens Committee for the Right to Keep and Bear Arms. CCRKBA is, coincidentally, headquartered in Washington State, where the Cooper/Stodden murder occurred in 2006.

While he acknowledged that homicide is a rare event in a national forest, that is not a reason for letting down one's guard. Violent crime can happen, and it does not occur by pre-appointed schedule.

"Parks have gotten less safe over the past 20 years," he said. "If they're just as safe, why do you see armed rangers when you never used to?"

And Vin Suprynowicz, the sharp-tongued columnist for the Las Vegas *Review Journal* noted in a December 6, 2006 column recalling the Cooper/Stodden murders in Washington State, "Some may argue that a gun on your hip won't save you against a determined assailant. I say it gives you a fighting chance, and more important it vastly improves the odds that any would-be assailant will pass you by, in the first place."

When Americans decide to fight back, it is best that they have something with which to fight. You have a couple of options. You can be practical and have a firearm for safety, or you can subscribe to a "code of ethics" like the one that the Florida Trails Association has adopted…and maybe wind up ethical but dead. It's your choice.

CHAPTER 13

Institutional Stupidity

Monday, April 16, 2007 is unseasonably chilly on the campus of Virginia Tech at Blacksburg, Virginia. There is even a very light snow falling; unusual for a state this far south at that time of year.

By the most remarkable of coincidences, it is the day after the National Rifle Association has held its 136th annual convention in St. Louis, Missouri, an event that has gone almost under the radar because gun control is not getting much attention as a national issue, either from the Democrat-controlled Congress, or the national press. All of that is going to change before noon.

Colder than the outside temperature in Blacksburg is apparently the blood running through the veins of Korean-born student Seung-Hui Cho. Over the course of two hours, in two different locations on the quiet 2,600-acre Virginia Tech campus, this monster would perpetrate the worst mass-shooting in U.S. history, murdering 32 students and instructors before taking his own life.

This was no "spur of the moment" crime, as authorities would quickly discover. Cho has prepared for his vile act of mass homicide methodically. He has purchased a 9mm Glock pistol in March and then just days before executing his murderous rampage, he took delivery of a second pistol, a .22-caliber Walther. The purchases were run through background checks and even timed to comply with Virginia's one-gun-a-month statute which, as this crime and previous crimes demonstrate, has had no effect in preventing a single criminal act with a gun.

Even more diabolical, Cho has prepared a rambling, hate-filled and occasionally expletive-laced video not unlike the video "testaments" that are prepared by Middle East homicide bombers before they strap on bomb vests to become "martyrs" for Islam. Two days after his rampage, this video shows up in an envelope to NBC News, which plays segments on its news broadcast.

There is no question that Cho is someone who does not "fit in" on the campus. His writings show a trend that alarmed some of his professors, and numerous press accounts have noted that in 2005, he was ordered by a Virginia special justice to get outpatient treatment for mental disorder. He was also investigated by university authorities for harassing and stalking female students, and it would soon become evident that Cho had a deep-seated hatred for his fellow classmates. Whether this was a symptom or the result of a mental illness may be debated for years by experts.

What is clear is that for whatever reason, Seung-Hui Cho was an angry young man, with the most evil of intentions, and he was in the most perfect environment of all to unleash his rage: A "gun free" campus zone.

Virginia is one of the most progressive states in the nation when it comes to personal protection and carrying firearms for self-defense. The state statute authorizing concealed carry enables legally-armed citizens to carry their firearms almost everywhere, including government buildings.

But what sets Virginia Tech and other institutions of higher learning apart is that they prohibit firearms on campus. Legislation that would have enabled college students and employees to carry licensed handguns on campus was derailed in 2006, with the full support of Virginia Tech administrators.

A story in the January 31, 2006 edition of the Roanoke *Times* noted that "Virginia Tech spokesman Larry Hincker was happy to hear the bill was defeated. 'I'm sure the university community is appreciative of the General Assembly's actions because this will help parents, students, faculty and visitors feel safe on our campus'."

As the authors detailed in Chapter Seven, these "gun free zones" tend to disarm everyone *except* killers and robbers. This has been a problem that has revealed itself far too many times in America. Every high school and college shooting, a shooting at a shopping mall in Tacoma, Washington and another in the Trolley Square retail mall in Salt Lake City, Utah all had one common denominator: They occurred in "gun free" zones.

Incredibly, and ironically, in the August 31, 2006 edition of the

Roanoke *Times*, an Op-Ed piece written by Virginia Tech graduate student Bradford B. Wiles focused on the issue of the campus gun ban. This was almost eight months before the tragic morning of April 16, and Wiles recalled an incident that had occurred on August 21 at Virginia Tech's Squires Student Center.

"We were interrupted in class and not informed of anything other than the following words: 'You need to get out of the building'," he wrote.

Once outside, he observed several heavily armed police officers "running down the street."

"It was at this time that I realized that I had no viable means of protecting myself," Wiles noted in his article.

Disclosing that he is licensed to carry a concealed handgun, he also explained that he is prohibited from carrying on the campus because of a school policy. Students caught with handguns, even legally-concealed guns, are subject to expulsion. Wiles notes that he would "never want to have my safety fully in the hands of anyone else, including the police."

He also says pointedly, "I am trained and able to carry a concealed handgun almost anywhere in Virginia and other states that have reciprocity with Virginia, but cannot carry where I spend more time than anywhere else because, somehow, I become a threat to others when I cross from the town of Blacksburg onto Virginia Tech's campus.

"Of all of the emotions and thoughts that were running through my head that morning, the most overwhelming one was of helplessness."

Almost comically, he tells that he revealed to a female professor that he is licensed and that he would feel safer if he had his gun, she responded, "I would feel safer if you had your gun."

"This incident makes it clear," Wiles concluded, "that it is time that Virginia Tech and the commonwealth of Virginia let me take responsibility for my safety."

It is all for naught. The college is inflexible, and wants its academic ivory tower community to be free of the weapons of violence. Unfortunately, that message seems to have either eluded, or been completely ignored, by Cho.

Classroom Carnage

According to various published accounts, Cho shows up at West Ambler Johnston Hall, a co-ed dormitory at approximately 7:15 a.m. This housing unit is home to 895 students including Emily J. Hilscher of Woodville, Virginia and a "resident assistant" (RA) named Ryan C. Clark, of Martinez, Georgia. Clark is something of a layman's counselor in the dorm.

Some early reports suggest that Hilscher and Cho had had a relationship, but friends of Hilscher deny that. It is possible that she had rejected advances by the misfit Korean native, but whatever their background, the two will become forever linked because of the crime Cho was about to commit.

Cho confronts Clark and Hilscher in Room 4040, where she is roommates with another student. The gunman kills both of them and then leaves the dormitory to vanish for almost two hours. Campus police are called to the scene and they erroneously begin investigating what appears at first glance to be a domestic dispute gone terribly bad.

While Cho is loose on campus, the police focus on another person, Karl Thornhill. Identified as Hilscher's boyfriend, he is a gun owner and various reports say that he had taken Hilscher and her roommate, identified as Heather Haugh, to a shooting range on a previous occasion. Thornhill is stopped by police as he is leaving the campus and detained for questioning. His apprehension erroneously gives police and campus authorities the impression that the trouble is over, so they did not shut down the school and begin a search for the real gunman.

News reports, many of which were boiled down for a report on the shooting on Wikipedia, note that as police are questioning Thornhill about two hours after the West Ambler Johnston Hall shooting, Cho strolls into Norris Hall. Showing once more his sinister planning, the first thing he does is chain the doors at the main entrance shut, perhaps to keep police out, and more likely to keep his victims in.

Not long before he appears at Norris Hall, Cho mails a package to NBC News that has his now-infamous video rant and some writings. The package is postmarked at 9:01 a.m.

Cho walks up to the second floor, and within moments, he begins shooting as he rushes from one classroom to another. In all, he will wound more than 60 people, killing 30 of them. Police believe he fired more than 170 rounds during the rampage. He has at least two 32-round after-market replacement magazines for the Glock pistol, and a considerable number of additional spare magazines, which accounts for his ability to fire that many shots in only nine minutes. Clearly, he spends little if any time pausing to reload magazines with loose ammunition during his shooting spree.

When word of the Norris Hall shootings reach police who are questioning Thornhill, it becomes obvious that the danger is far from over.

During the past two hours when Cho has been hiding out somewhere, he probably reloads the magazine for his pistol. But this is not the only magazine he carries for the pistol. There are more, and there is no doubt that he had planned mass murder.

When he is finished shooting his unarmed victims, Cho presses the gun to his head and squeezes off one last shot, killing himself instantly.

Among his victims are five college professors including Liviu Librescu, a Holocaust survivor who heroically blocked the door of his classroom with his own body, giving his students time to escape through the windows. Cho pumped five fatal rounds into Librescu.

There are 11 dead students in Room 211, where the gunman eventually took his own life. Another nine lie dead in Room 206. Four were killed in Room 207, and another died in Room 204. Many others are wounded.

In the aftermath, at least one prominent writer, Stephen Hunter of the Washington *Post*, notes that Cho's murderous rampage mimics elements in a couple of Chinese action movies, and speculates that Cho patterned some of his activities after scenes in the film "Oldboy." Hunter, a Pulitzer Prize-winning writer, also suggests that Cho followed scenes from another action film master, John Woo. Of particular interest to Hunter are films starring Chinese actor Chow Yun-Fat.

He describes those films as "gun-crazed ballets, full of whirling imagery, grace, masculine power and a strange but perhaps not irrelevant religiosity."

Hunter further observes, "Cho, it seems, wasn't a sniper, a marksman. He wasn't shooting carefully, at a distance. He wasn't, one can assume, aiming. He was shooting very much like Chow in the Woo pictures, with a gun in each hand, as witnesses state, up close, very fast."

Ultimately, says Hunter, "In at least three regards, Cho's activities so closely reflect the Woo oeuvre that it seems somewhat fair to conclude that in his last moments, before he blew his brains out, he was shooting a John Woo movie in his head."

Myth v. Reality

If, as Hunter suggests, Cho is acting out some movie myth in his head, he is dealing genuine horror from the firearms in his hands. And the most horrible element of all may be that it did not appear any of his victims fought back. Some might argue – as they did in the days following the massacre – that today's college environment chokes notions of self-reliance, and particularly self-defense.

Reality is a harsh teacher, and it is an abysmal failure on the part of college administrators to learn from past history that college campuses are not immune from violence. Administrators at the University of Utah in 2007 finally gave up fighting the state constitution and state statute in court, and now legally licensed teachers and students, and members of the public, may carry concealed handguns on that campus. But it took two years of legislative maneuvers and a lengthy lawsuit through the state courts to get that school administration to conclude that it had no statutory authority to defy a state law.

But the University of Utah is an anomaly. College campuses almost universally forbid firearms, and that remains the case at Virginia Tech.

One might reasonably question this policy after what occurred January 16, 2002 at the Appalachian School of Law in Grundy, Virginia. The incident, detailed in Chapter Five, presents an exact opposite in terms of how students responded, and how their response limited the scale of the crime.

At the Appalachian incident, students not only fought back, two actually armed themselves with handguns kept in their cars and confronted gunman Peter Odighizuwa. Though he was not as well armed as Seung-Hui Cho, Odighizuwa could have possibly shot and killed or wounded more people during his brief rampage. Instead, confronted by two armed students, he stopped shooting and was subsequently wrestled to the ground and held for authorities.

Cho took his own life before he could be confronted by armed police. In the gun rights community, it is strongly argued that had even one of the students or teachers Cho encountered in Norris Hall been legally armed, his carnage could have been abruptly halted. There is, of course, no way of knowing that for sure because it is conjecture.

What is not conjecture, though, is a body count of 32 innocent people who had effectively been disarmed by a university code of conduct.

Myth: *College (and high school) campuses are safe because they are gun-free zones.*

Reality: *College (and high school) campuses are target-rich, low-risk environments for every psychopath with a grudge, and every vicious, cold-blooded predator looking for an easy rape, robbery or murder victim.*

The notion of fighting back is not limited to just one college campus in rural Virginia. Long before Appalachian students Tracy Bridges and Mikael Gross ever dreamed they would one day have to rush for their guns to stop a killer, high school students in Springfield, Oregon set a precedent for courage under fire.

Brothers Jacob "Jake" and Josh Ryker, then 17 and 14, respectively, and brothers Doug and David Ure, 18 and 15 respectively, are in the school cafeteria on the morning of Thursday, May 21, 1998, just eleven months prior to the massacre at Columbine High School in Littleton, Colorado. Less than 24 hours earlier, a student named Kipland "Kip" Kinkel had murdered his parents William and Faith – both of whom were high school teachers – and he has now arrived on the high school campus to continue his bloody spree.

It is Jake Ryker's birthday, and one he will never forget.

Kinkel comes to class with three firearms, a Glock 9mm semiautomatic pistol that his father had illegally purchased for him, a .22-caliber rifle and a .22-caliber pistol, and opens fire, killing two classmates, Mikael Nicklauson and Ben Walker. Kinkel then heads for the cafeteria and he starts shooting as soon as he comes through the entry. Before his rampage is over, he will wound 25 students, including Jake, and Jake's girlfriend, Jennifer Alldredge.

According to the Eugene *Register-Guard*, Kinkel does his shooting with the .22 rifle. It is just before 8 a.m. when the Rykers and Ures hear the first shots, and then pandemonium erupts. Kinkel aims his rifle at

Alldredge and shoots her in the chest and neck.

Jake is immediately up on his feet and filled with rage. And then Kinkel swings the muzzle toward him and fires, sending the tiny lead bullet through his right lung. Witnesses tell the newspaper that he yells at Kinkel, "You shot me, you bastard!"

It is then that Kinkel's magazine runs dry, and instead of muzzle blasts, the Rykers and Ures hear audible "clicks" as Kinkel squeezes a trigger on an empty gun.

The Ryker brothers are familiar with firearms. In a subsequent interview on network television, their father appears, wearing a National Rifle Association cap.

Things are about to go decidedly bad for Kip Kinkel. Recognizing that his gun has "run dry" and seeing him reach into his pockets, the wounded Jake charges at Kinkel with his brother and the Ure brothers hot on his heels. Jake slams into the teen gunman, reportedly using moves he had learned on the high school wrestling team, and throws him to the floor. Josh and the Ures pounce and begin kicking and beating Kinkel, grabbing his arms so he cannot reach the two handguns he is carrying.

One of Kinkel's handguns does accidentally discharge during the fight, shattering a joint on Jake's left index finger, the newspaper reported.

In a moment, it is over. Teachers arrive to evacuate the cafeteria and take over from the four heroic young men, who proved that resistance is *not* futile.

Myth: *If someone is committing a violent crime and you could be injured, the best course of action is to comply or take cover and wait until police arrive.*

Reality: *If someone is shooting people in your presence and you can take action, do it. Remember this adage: "When seconds count, police are minutes away." If a gunman is shooting at people around you, he's going to eventually be shooting at you, too.*

And perhaps most important of all to remember, if four gutsy American teens can fight back, so can you!

Armed Students Speak Out

Twenty-four hours after the massacre at Virginia Tech, 23-year-old Chris Brown – a senior at the University of North Texas in Denton majoring in political science – founded an organization that seemed to hit the ground running, because it immediately gathered momentum and started spreading like the proverbial wild fire. In just seven days, Brown's "Students for Concealed Carry on Campus" (SCCC) attracted 2,000 members around the country.

His website, www.concealedcampus.com, attracted thousands of viewers and he was inundated with e-mails from college students like himself who are interested in personal safety on campus. Brown got lots of inquiries from students in Utah and Colorado especially, he recalled. If there were any doubt about the seriousness of students interested in their Second Amendment right, to say nothing of their ability to fight back, those doubts were erased in the wake of the Virginia Tech tragedy.

Brown told author Workman that he founded SCCC on the day after the Virginia Tech massacre. He set it up as a grassroots effort to enlist pro-gun students on campuses across the country who would ideally establish their own chapters and have them up and running by Fall 2007.

"We want this to be a student-led initiative," he explained, "because this really affects us the most."

SCCC is "pretty much an on-line organization," Brown said. The idea for such a group may have been kicking around in the back of his mind for a while, but it erupted in the aftermath of the massacre because suddenly there was an urgency. Brown would not carry a firearm on the campus even though he has been licensed to carry concealed in Texas.

This is not the first foray into grassroots politics for Brown. In 2006, he organized a national effort to send bricks to Congress to bring attention to public support for the construction of a wall along the U.S.-Mexico border to curb illegal immigration. More than 12,000 bricks were sent, he said.

Brown remains convinced that had there been an armed student at the Virginia Tech campus in Norris Hall that day, events would not have unfolded as they did. He insisted that at the very least, students should have had the option that would have allowed them, if legally licensed to do so, to carry a personal defense pistol to class.

On the University of North Texas campus, he recalled, there were "a couple of robberies" in 2006 including one in which the victim was pistol-whipped. As with Virginia Tech, personal handguns are banned on the UNT campus.

"I can take a firearm into the state capitol where our legislators meet," he marveled, "but I can't take it into my classroom."

A native Texan who grew up around firearms, Brown was a firm believer in armed self-defense prior to the Virgina Tech outrage. About a year before the incident, he actually spent time perusing state firearms laws, with an emphasis on which states allow it and which do not, and where people can carry and where they cannot. He said one of the more interesting discoveries he made was that in most states, the gun-free school zone statutes only apply to K-12 public schools.

"This is the essence of why we have concealed carry," he observed. "When this stuff happens, the police will never be there on time. If there's someone on campus with a concealed weapon, maybe it saves 32 lives."

In a statement about why he organized SCCC, Brown said, "As a college student and a concealed handgun license holder, when I step onto campus I am left unable to defend myself. My state allows me to carry a handgun in public, but there is some imaginary line drawn around college campuses for silly reasons. And those silly reasons are getting people killed, raped and robbed."

SCCC contends on its website that "it is abundantly clear that the only way to stop mass murderers is to have responsible citizens in the classroom and on campuses able to carry their licensed handguns." It is not affiliated with the National Rifle Association or other gun rights organizations.

Following the shooting, various newspapers around the country ran opinion polls concerning gun control, and from all indications, Brown was on the right track when he established the student organization. Virtually every one of these polls – which were not scientific by any means – resulted in a strong tilt away from the notion that more gun control is necessary to make campuses safer.

Brown said the organization is not limited to students. Parents and "concerned citizens" who support the right of legally-licensed students and other private citizens to carry concealed on college campuses were also invited to join.

Where this movement eventually goes remains to be seen, but it is clear that students paid attention to what happened at Virginia

Tech, and many of them are not about to let it happen at their schools. At the very least, these students are going to pay closer attention to extreme behavior, and what happened at Virginia Tech at least opened a dialogue about whether the "ivory tower mentality" should prevail over a student's right to not simply "feel" safe, but to actually "be" safe to the point that they have the option of coming to school armed.

Late in 2006, the authors collaborated on a nationally-circulated Op-Ed piece that ran in several newspapers, including the Ft. Worth *Star-Telegram*. Entitled "The dirty little secret of 'Gun-Free School Zones'," it noted that of the more than 20 school shootings since February 1996 when a 14-year-old youth strolled into a junior high school in Moses Lake, Washington and opened fire, killing two students and a teacher, the common factor in every one of these crimes was that they happened in so-called "Gun-Free School Zones."

The column hit something of a raw nerve with many Americans, especially when we noted that "the Gun Free School Zones Act transformed the public school landscape into a free-fire zone for whackos by removing any possibility, however small, that an armed teacher, student or private citizen might be present to intervene."

"As a result, monsters like Colorado's Duane Morrison or Pennsylvania's Charles Roberts, and a host of others have committed mayhem, courtesy of gun control fanatics who pressured Congress and state legislatures to pass such statutes," we wrote at the time.

Perhaps the most candid observation came from anti-gun Pennsylvania Gov. Ed Rendell, who admitted that tougher gun laws would not have stopped the gunman.

"You can make all the changes you want," Rendell said after the Amish School shooting in his state, "but you can never stop a random act of violence by someone intent on taking his own life."

What we wrote then we stand by today: "It is time to re-consider gun-free school zone laws and the zero-tolerance mentality such laws foster. Inflexible regulations aimed at keeping kids safe also place teachers in jeopardy...

"We can no longer afford the empty-headed Utopian illusion that such statutes keep anyone safe, because they don't. Like other restrictive gun control measures, this one has been a monumental failure, and it is literally killing our children."

Restrictive gun laws do not prevent crime and the notion of

a gun-free school zone is a myth. More restrictions on law-abiding citizens will never stop people like Cho, Morrison, Roberts, Kinkel or anyone else intent on committing mayhem. With each new outrage, such gunmen will prove yet again that feel-good laws have defrauded American citizens, and especially our children, of genuine safety.

But facing that, people like Chris Brown will organize opposition to gun-free zones, and perhaps more students like Jake and Josh Ryker, and David and Doug Ure will emerge from the crowd and demonstrate again that America can fight back.

CHAPTER 14

Polls Versus People: What Americans Really Want

"**M**erlony Colaco got robbed one too many times," the editorial in the Chambersburg, Pennsylvania *Public Opinion* of Sunday, May 6, 2007 began.

Colaco, a small businessman in Greencastle, got tired of being robbed and – according to the editorial – decided to do something about it. He didn't run to the police, he didn't close the doors of his business, he didn't whine to the newspaper or the city council or his state legislator or congressional representative.

He bought a shotgun with which to protect the Molly Pitcher Mini Mart, his business and his piece of the American Dream. The newspaper said he simply waited and in late March, about six weeks prior to the editorial, his patience paid off.

A woman identified as Erica Marie Lynch allegedly threw a brick through the window of Mr. Colaco's convenience store in order to steal cigarettes which she could sell to support her crack habit. But Lynch didn't get the cigarettes, she got a close-up look at the muzzle of Colaco's smoothbore. She may have been still staring at the gun when the cops arrived to cart her off to jail.

The editorial said something else about Colaco: "He used his Second Amendment rights to buy a firearm and defend his property, and he did it with common sense."

Lynch had two alleged accomplices, all of whom ended up being charged with burglary.

"If the trio are (sic) found guilty," the editorial observed, "it's because Colaco took a leading role in bringing them to justice."

Americans like Merlony Colaco are fighting back with an increasing frequency, thanks to the spread of concealed carry laws and what may be a sea change in public attitude about how to deal with criminals. People are tired of turnstile justice, early releases of violent felons, police response times that seem to stretch longer with each passing of a municipal or county budget, and most of all, by being treated as a prey base by criminals and helpless sheep by politicians and police administrators.

If some in America truly are trying to turn this country into a "nation of sheep," there is a growing segment of the public that is choosing to not be part of the flock.

These "fighting Americans" are not about to turn loose of their right to self-defense, even in the wake of a tragedy like Virginia Tech. Even the New York *Times* made vague references to the change in public attitudes about gun ownership and the right to keep and bear arms following the Virginia Tech shooting.

Reinforcing this notion were a series of public opinion polls by major media, including CNN, ABC News and MSN, along with Zogby and Pew Research. During the early 1990s in the days leading up to and immediately after the Clinton Administration pushed through the Brady Law with its background check, and the 1994 Crime Bill, with its ban on so-called "assault weapons" and large capacity magazines, the public would have supported additional gun controls in an effort to presumably prevent more such outrages as the Virginia Tech massacre.

But times change, and with the advent of a new millennium, there has been a change in public attitudes as well because the people have seen gun control for what it really is: A unilateral surrender of both a civil right to own a gun, and the more basic human right of self-preservation.

Days after the Virginia Tech tragedy, MSN teamed up with Zogby to find out what Americans thought about adding more restrictions on firearms owners, and pollsters discovered that 59 percent of the respondents reject the notion that stricter gun laws would have prevented the crime. Thirty-eight percent believe armed citizens could prevent such tragedies.

As age groups involved in that survey were separated, pollsters found that 72 percent of adults age 65 and over – people with a lifetime of experience – dismiss the idea that tighter gun control policies would prevent such shootings.

More than half (53 percent) of young adults ages 18 to 29, also reject the idea that stricter gun laws would not help prevent people like gunman Seung-Hui Cho from committing the kind of atrocity he did on April 16, 2007.

Even more revealing, the poll discovered that opinions are nearly evenly split among people living in large cities – traditionally a strong base for Democrats and gun control measures – with 49 percent of the respondents from big cities saying that tougher gun laws won't help, while 47 percent said more gun laws could prevent such shootings. Still, those people living in big cities who reject gun control now appear to outnumber those in favor.

Another revealing aspect of this survey found 89 percent of Democrats saying they do not think more guns on campus would avert such tragedies, but only 24 percent of Republicans share their opinion.

When ABC did an unscientific poll on its website, asking whether people believed the Virginia Tech shooting is ample reason to pass tougher gun laws, the reaction was staggering against the idea. By almost a 4-to-1 margin, respondents rejected the suggestion, with nearly 106,000 voting against it while only 27,000 supported the idea.

A "Quick Vote" opportunity on CNN brought a devastating rejection of gun control as a panacea to crime. Asked whether they believe the United States should have tighter laws on guns, more than 90 percent voted against the idea, while a paltry 8 percent supported the idea.

Oddly, it is almost invariable that when Americans are asked whether they support stricter gun laws, the majority says yes. Yet when they are asked whether they would support a ban on private handgun ownership, the majority opposes the idea.

Somewhere in the process, it is never quite clear whether those polled understand the question, or realize there are already reasonably strict laws in place at both the state and federal levels; including a required background check on all retail gun sales, waiting periods in some states, and so forth.

Likewise, as a Fox News/Opinion Dynamics poll found two days after the Virginia Tech shooting, the overwhelming majority of respondents turned thumbs down on the notion that tougher gun laws would help prevent such massacres. Seventy-one percent of the respondents said killers like Seung-Hui Cho will always find a gun, and another seven percent suggested more restrictions might help, but that killers will still get guns.

This suggests there may be a disconnect in the polling or in the way Americans perceive gun laws that are currently in effect.

When Americans get to cast votes on the subject of restrictive gun laws, they overwhelmingly reject the idea.

In 1976, when voters in Massachusetts, a state commonly perceived as being far left liberal socially and politically, had the opportunity to cast their ballots to ban handguns in the state, November election results held a big surprise. As recalled by David J. Bordua with the University of Illinois at Urbana-Champaign in a 1983 essay, *Adversary Polling and the Construction of Social Meaning* that appeared in the *Law and Policy Quarterly*, the measure was struck down by a 69.2 percent margin. That year, 86 percent of the eligible voters went to the polls and 77 percent of those voters cast ballots on the handgun ban.

"The voice of the people, indeed," Bordua declared.

The next major public vote on handguns came with Proposition 15 in California in 1982. From the outset, this looked to be a tough battle for the National Rifle Association and other gun rights groups. But on November 2, the proposition – which would have banned the sale and possession of new handguns, but allowed previously-owned handguns to be registered with the state, and retained by their owners – was soundly defeated 63-37 percent.

Farther north, in 1997, Washington State voters had their say when Initiative 676 was placed on the ballot as the nation's most restrictive handgun measure. Early in the campaign, it appeared a surefire win for the gun control crowd, but in November, voters descended on polling booths and rejected the initiative by a whopping 71-29 percent.

Who can forget November 1994, the first mid-term election for Bill Clinton's administration, which pushed through the Brady Law in 1993 and the ban on so-called "assault weapons" in 1994 when Democrats controlled Congress? That was the year that America took

Capitol Hill away from Clinton, and he never got it back. For 12 years, Democrats were the minority party, and their leadership, including Clinton, admitted that it was because of their passage of gun control measures.

Americans who have regained their "fighting spirit" against thugs and crazies have demonstrated repeatedly that they support efforts to keep guns out of the wrong hands, but when faced with a proposal or a politician that would take guns out of *their* hands, they follow Nancy Reagan's advice and "Just say No!"

America Votes Gun Rights

American citizens who have decided to fight back understand that they must have the tools with which to conduct that fight. While these tools include good law enforcement, tough judges and prosecutors, they also include the tool that one could have with him when a crime occurs: a gun.

Police, judges and prosecutors are not around when a crime occurs. It is only the criminal and intended victim, and in that situation, an armed citizen can more often than not turn the tables on some miscreant, as we have seen throughout the previous chapters of this book. Do not be misled into believing that the good guy always wins, because they do not. By the same token, do not believe the argument that a gun is more likely to be taken from a private citizen and used against him or her, so it is better not to have a gun.

As noted in the cases of anti-gun ballot measures in Massachusetts, California and Washington, and the public's reaction to the Democrat-controlled anti-gun juggernaut in 1993 and 1994, American citizens are not about to surrender their gun rights, which amounts to surrendering their right of self-preservation, and they are rough on politicians and political parties that champion taking those rights away.

Since 2002, the Second Amendment Foundation, working with Zogby International, has conducted opinion polls to determine public sentiment on gun rights. The results of those polls have been revealing, and they may not correlate with the results of other polling, because these polls asked specific questions that were difficult to misunderstand.

For example, a poll taken in the spring of 2002 revealed that 75 percent of Americans believe the Second Amendment protects an individual right to keep and bear arms. This poll was also revealing for another reason: A minority of Democrats (29 percent), Catholics (30 percent) and residents of the Eastern states (36 percent) were most likely to disagree that the Second Amendment affirms an individual right.

A whopping 79 percent of people living in the West, South and Central/Great Lakes regions accept the individual right interpretation, and 60 percent of those living in the East believe gun ownership is an individual right.

In April 2005, the Second Amendment Foundation and Zogby released the results of another survey. This one revealed that American voters overwhelmingly reject the notion that banning guns would reduce the threat from terrorists. Only one in five people think a gun ban will stop terrorists.

The poll was taken in reaction to assertions from gun control organizations that stricter gun laws are necessary to prevent firearms from falling into the hands of terrorists who might turn them against American citizens.

In September 2005, SAF and Zogby released the results of yet another poll, this one based on homeland security. That year, SAF's sister organization, the Citizens Committee for the Right to Keep and Bear Arms (CCRKBA), had launched a campaign to "control borders, not guns." The newspaper *Gun Week* had done an investigation and found that U.S. prisons were holding an unknown number of illegal aliens who had committed violent crimes after entering this country. This revelation inspired CCRKBA to urge its members and other gun owners to flood the White House with letters and telephone calls supporting tougher control of the U.S. border, rather than new proposals aimed at preventing people from legally buying firearms.

By a 3-to-1 margin, respondents to that survey backed the idea of more secure borders over any proposal to pass more restrictive gun laws.

Even more significant, the majority of respondents in every sub-group, including 60 percent or more in most groups, said border control is more effective at curbing crime than gun control. The question struck a nerve with people in rural areas, people in lower income brackets, high school graduates and those with some college education.

People with incomes less than $15,000 were more likely to support gun control that survey also discovered.

As Bordua recalled in his 1983 article, opinion surveys that seem to reflect overwhelming public support for gun control always seem to be "blocked by the 'gun lobby'." However, when one analyzes data and compares it with the outcomes of actual elections – arguably the only "polls" that ever really count – only then does the true public will seem to emerge.

"What blocks the public from getting strict gun control," Bordua wrote matter-of-factly, "is that the public does not want it."

What Do People Want?

If the public does not *really* want more and stricter gun laws, then the question must be asked, what *does* the public want?

Most assuredly, Americans want to live in peaceful neighborhoods, where they can feel some confidence that they and their families, and their possessions, are safe from criminals. They want to come and go without so much as a "by your leave" from government, and to not have to constantly worry about gangs, drugs, home invasion robberies, criminal assault, rape and other crimes. Perhaps people simply want to be left alone in their pursuit of happiness.

Perhaps the dilemma can be best defined not by the authors, but by people like Augusta, Georgia resident Frank Sams. Maybe someone should ask him to explain what it is that Americans want.

The 84-year-old Mr. Sams had been the victim of several break-ins and on the night of May 3-4, 2007, he decided to sit on the back steps of his home and just wait to see what happened. He did not have to wait very long.

Out of the darkness, a woman later identified by WRDW news in Augusta as Lakashia Walker showed up and tried to break into Sams' backdoor storage building at about 3 a.m. According to the Savannah *Morning News*, Sams raised his .38-caliber handgun and fired one shot, hitting Walker in the neck on the left side. She was taken to the hospital.

The newspaper noted in its coverage of the incident that this had been the third time in less than 14 days when a would-be burglar was shot by his or her intended victim.

Under Georgia law passed in 2006, Mr. Sams — who had been waiting on his steps for five long hours for the burglar to appear — had a legal right to fire. Sams, the television station reported, felt he was being attacked by the woman.

The night before, hundreds of miles away in Batesville, Arkansas the parents of Rebecca Little responded to her call for help, and when they arrived at her home around midnight, they spotted an unidentified man armed with a shotgun, running from the residence, according to an account in the May 3 edition of the Batesville *Daily Guard.*

But being good, intelligent citizens and prudent parents, the mother and stepfather, identified as Debbie and Tony Mesa, had not only the wits, but also the means, to fight back. Mr. Mesa, armed with a handgun, told deputies with the Independence County Sheriff's Office that the man was carrying a shotgun with a black synthetic stock, and that he turned around "in a threatening manner" when Mesa yelled at him.

Arkansas residents are not much for this "group think" kind of reaction. When they are faced with a problem, such as someone possibly harming their children, they deal with it.

Once Mesa fired his pistol, the unidentified man fled into some nearby woods. The Mesas left their daughter's residence, and when they returned later, it appeared someone had been inside, and had taken several items and had thrown other things on the floor.

The Mesas simply wanted their daughter to be safe in her own home. And Tony Mesa underscored that with a gunshot.

Americans have had enough. It should not take a neon sign for the social engineers and political correctness advocates to realize that a line has been drawn in the sand, and those who cross it do so at their own peril. That peril is increasing.

That much is evident in increasing numbers of confrontations between thugs and law-abiding people who have decided to stand their ground. Take the incident in the Forest Hill suburb of the greater Dallas-Fort Worth area on April 26, 2007. In that case, two 21-year-old gunmen, identified by KTVT as Michael Walker and Andrew Fobbs walked into the Fabulous Urban and Sportswear store. There, they encountered an unidentified clerk who had no intention of being robbed.

Walker and Fobbs came in about closing time, with Walker carrying what was identified as a Tech-9 pistol. But Walker and the clerk wound up in a standoff, aiming guns at one another, and suddenly they began grappling for each other's firearm. During that fight, the clerk managed to shoot Walker twice, once in the leg and once, fatally, in the chest.

Fobbs tried to run for it, but he got stuck inside the store thanks to a locked door. The clerk held him at gunpoint for police. The news report said the District Attorney declined to make any case against the clerk, calling it a clear case of self-defense.

Perhaps the answer to what people want will be found with Army Captain Barre Bollinger of Augusta, Georgia. He came home early on May 2, 2007 to find his home ransacked and firearms missing from his bedroom. Bollinger, who was stationed at Fort Gordon, was quoted by WSB in Atlanta and the Associated Press as explaining that he quickly grabbed his SKS semi-automatic rifle (identified by both news agencies as "a weapon similar to an AK-47 assault rifle"), and a telephone to call police, and then spotted a suspect coming to the back door.

The burglar, identified as 29-year-old Errol Lavar Royal, did not expect that his next steps would be his last. Bollinger fired three rounds, hitting Royal twice. He died later at a hospital.

Bollinger was an Iraq war veteran, and perhaps all he wanted was to be at peace in his own home.

When police went to Royal's parents' house, they found two of Bollinger's guns, and a stash of marijuana.

What People Won't Accept

America has grown weary of sensationalized outrages like the "gun free zone" shootings at Virginia Tech, Salt Lake City's Trolley Square, Colorado's Columbine High School and Luby's Cafeteria, and the small, almost unnoticed outrages experienced by individual private citizens every day in this country.

An Associated Press-Ipsos poll published on April 20, 2007 in the San Francisco *Chronicle* – four days after the Virginia Tech shooting – found Americans "profoundly split along gender, racial and other lines over gun violence and what the government should do to control it." The Associated Press is one of the world's leading news agencies, and Ipsos is a marketing and polling firm.

Looking over the history of gun control reveals that the

government has done very little to control violence, and an increasing number of American citizens have decided to take care of themselves. Government cannot put a policeman on every corner of every neighborhood in America. This is, after all, still the United States…not a police state.

American citizens would never tolerate such a scenario, no matter what gun control advocates believe, and more importantly, want the rest of us to believe. Our culture of "rugged individualism" goes back to the very foundation of modern civilization in this country, some 400 years. From the time of the Pilgrims, through the years of colonization while America was still ruled by England, up through the settling of the frontier and the great exploration of the West, the American spirit has always been dominated by the individuality of its citizens.

This individuality is what sets Americans apart from all others, and it might best be exemplified by the actions of a Purcell, Oklahoma liquor store operator named Butch Kluth. The proprietor of Butch's Cork and Bottle, the 63-year-old Kluth was confronted by a would-be robber on the afternoon of May 1, 2007.

According to an account of the incident in the Norman, Oklahoma *Transcript* newspaper, Kluth set a new standard in nerve when the miscreant, later identified as 32-year-old Jeremy Lloyd Cox, came through his door and told the businessman to hand over all of the money in his cash register.

Kluth's startling response: "F--- you!"

The flustered robber, certainly not accustomed to that kind of reaction, demanded to know, "What do you mean, f--- you? Give me all your money!" He then reached into his pants as though he were preparing to pull a gun.

But Kluth didn't flinch or shrink away in fear. Instead, he pulled out a Smith & Wesson .357 Magnum revolver and gave the robber what *Gun Week* called "a close-up look at the muzzle" before ordering the wannabe bandit out of his store. And he did not stop there.

Kluth followed the man outside and saw him jump into a dark green Ford Mustang and head for the road, according to the published *Transcript* account. As the car sped away, Kluth fired a single shot sending a bullet into the car. The retailer then called police, who stopped the car a few blocks away, arrested Cox and took him to jail.

According to the Norman *Transcript*, Kluth had only been in business for a year, and while he had never really expected a robbery, he obviously planned for one. Butch Kluth, like so many other Americans who work hard for their income will not accept the kind of scenario where they are expected to simply turn it over to some thug who has decided to make a career out of preying on others.

The idea of submitting one's self entirely to the care of the "Nanny State" is repugnant to an overwhelming majority of today's citizens, despite the expansion of political correctness and the philosophy of government as shepherd.

From within that realm come poll results like those revealed by the *Chronicle*, which noted, "Democrats and city dwellers (take) a far dimmer view of guns than Republicans and suburban and rural residents."

Likewise, the newspaper reported that the survey found "Women and minorities are far likelier than men and whites to view gun violence as a major problem, to worry about being shot and to want stricter firearms laws…"

That survey also found that "Nearly 60 percent of Democrats favor stricter gun laws, almost double the number of Republicans, with more women in both parties supporting tougher standards."

Yet earlier experiences in Massachusetts, California and Washington State suggest that Democrats may just believe that people *other* than themselves should face tougher gun laws. When it comes to their own personal choices, they still vote against restrictions and in favor of their firearm civil rights.

Clearly, Americans have no intention now, nor have they ever, of unilaterally disarming in the interest of some perceived greater public good. They realize, perhaps now more than ever, that police will rarely be present to intervene in the event of a violent criminal act. They have acknowledged, albeit perhaps reluctantly, that court orders are essentially useless pieces of paper against someone determined to harm another person. They admit that the justice system of today, where career criminals may be released early due to overcrowding in jails or some semblance of "good behavior" behind bars, does a pitiful job protecting the public from the predators.

The Associated Press/Ipsos poll found that roughly one person in five has known someone who was a crime victim involving firearms in recent memory. The other four out of five people have decided that they're not going to be next, and they are taking steps to prevent it, or at least survive the encounter if and when it happens.

Of the one-fifth who know a crime victim, the survey said almost 25 percent of them have considered buying a gun. One in three of these people *already have a gun.*

What does this tell you?

It suggests to the authors that after nearly a half-century of failed social experiments that wiped out parental authority by criminalizing discipline, that considered prisons places for "rehabilitation" rather than "confinement," and demonized the very notion of firearms ownership, America is slowly but surely regaining its consciousness and its conscience. The long slumber of socialization is coming to an end, and that proud American spirit of self-reliance is once again emerging.

Perhaps the contrast can best be exemplified by what occurred a few weeks after the Virginia Tech massacre when two politicians from the same state, but obviously from far different philosophical backgrounds, spoke about their solutions to such violence.

Attorney General Alberto Gonzales – hardly a man strongly devoted to gun rights – told reporters during an appearance in Oklahoma that he opposes the idea of allowing licensed concealed carry by students and faculty on college campuses. Instead, he stated, "We need to see what we can do as a government – on the federal level, on the state level – to ensure the safety of our students."

In almost the same breath, Gonzales admitted, "We can't guarantee complete security."

Compare that to remarks by Texas Gov. Rick Perry, a man widely known among Texans for his support of firearms rights. He told reporters in Dallas that legally-armed citizens should be able to carry their firearms anywhere they please, with very few exceptions. He would allow armed citizens on college campuses, in schools, restaurants and churches; all places that under many state statutes are now considered "gun free zones."

Why is it so easy for Rick Perry to understand that criminals and madmen do not make appointments in advance to commit violent acts, but this fact eludes college presidents, liberal politicians, an Attorney General and far too many pundits?

Those who lobbied in state after state against passage of

concealed carry statutes repeatedly predicted that such laws would lead to bloodbaths. In a sense they guaranteed the kind of mayhem they predicted by demanding that some areas be set aside as "gun free zones" where law-abiding citizens may not carry their firearms.

The absurdity of this position does not reveal itself until one sits down and analyzes just what a law-abiding citizen must endure in most states just to obtain a concealed carry permit. Armed citizens have gone through criminal background checks and in many states they have taken mandatory gun safety courses.

How many anti-gun liberals would tolerate such scrutiny and red tape just to exercise a constitutional right?

For too long, the nation tried things *their* way, taking the path toward greater dependence on government for our safety and security, and what was the result? The terrorist attack of September 11, 2001 was a nerve-shattering wake-up call that told America government *couldn't* protect us from a determined enemy. And, as Americans took stock of their "new world order" and found it to be very *un*-orderly, the rage began to build.

It is not just anger at terrorists, but also anger at criminals and a system that has allowed crime to flourish while condescending police officials repeatedly warn us "it is best to not take any action on your own but to call the police and let us handle it." And when America is reminded all too often that a new and cold-blooded generation of criminals has emerged upon the landscape; thugs who wantonly kill even when their victims offer no resistance at all, people tell themselves that doing it *their* way has given us nothing but a body count.

Americans will no longer accept that.

No intelligent person will ever claim that we can stop every determined criminal or madman, but a growing number of American citizens have decided that we might stop most of them, and save innocent lives in the process. Many have learned that firsthand, in the cold clarity of the moment they find themselves inescapably captured in the unfolding drama and terror of a criminal act. Others have discovered this simple truth by rushing to the aid of someone who has been victimized, and in that moment of personal heroism have been able to abruptly and sometimes permanently interrupt the career of some violent recidivist.

As a nation, we have always been in a position of having to

overcome the odds. From the earliest colonial times, through the Revolution, the conquering of the West, through two world wars, and now in a battle against crime and terrorism in our neighborhoods, America is and always has been at its best when America Fights Back.

EPILOGUE

'**I**'m mad as hell, and I'm not going to take it anymore!"

It was a line from a 1976 film called *Network*, immortalized by actor Peter Finch, playing newscaster-turned-"mad prophet of the airwaves" Howard Beale. In a gripping and hilarious scene from that film, Beale had Americans opening their windows, shouting at the tops of their lungs that they, too, were "mad as hell and not going to take it anymore."

While the title of the film, and perhaps even the name of the Academy Award-winning actor have faded from the public memory, that line of dialogue has become part of the American lexicon.

The social pendulum that took this nation on a disastrously failed trek toward the Utopian world as envisioned by the self-anointed "progressive" Far Left of the 1960s, 70's, 80s and early 90s has reversed course. It is a slow but certain change of direction, a "full 180" as some would call it.

Perhaps nowhere has this been demonstrated more vividly and graphically than in Cleveland, Ohio in the spring of 2007. A community that had long been divided by color and culture is hopefully coming together for the common good by lowering the color barrier and raising in its place a moral standard. It may be an example for all of America to follow, as crime data from the FBI shows that crime is once again on an upswing.

It is the evening of April 21, 2007 and 26-year-old Damon Wells takes a stroll to a neighborhood grocery store. Wells, by all accounts, is an average citizen merely minding his own business in a neighborhood that should be safe, where residents can go about their routines without being victimized.

Wells is returning to the home where his fiancé, Tiffany Berry lives with her mother, Justina, when he is confronted by two youths, one of whom is Arthur Buford, 15, known on the street as "A.C" or "Ace Boogie," or just "Ace." The other is later identified by police and prosecutors as 16-year-old Mardale Williams, who subsequently claimed he was an innocent bystander and had no idea that his friend had a gun or was planning to use it.

According to Regina Brett, a columnist for the Cleveland *Plain Dealer* who spoke with *Gun Week* (and author Workman), Wells had gone to the store for some cheese popcorn and cigarettes.

A small man – he is only 5 feet, 8 inches tall and weighs 130 pounds, according to a Brett column, making him just the kind of vulnerable-looking target for cowardly street scum – Wells is later described as a perfect example of the type of citizen for whom Ohio gun rights activists fought long and hard to secure a concealed carry statute. Even though the grocery is only a short distance from his front door, Wells dons a shoulder holster that holds a Smith & Wesson .40-caliber semi-automatic pistol, an act that will prove pivotal moments later, not only in his personal life, but perhaps in the life of his community.

Ace Boogie Buford is a freshman at John F. Kennedy High School, but he is hardly a model student. At this moment, he is on probation for aggravated armed robbery. Brett believes, and the circumstances suggest, that Buford and Williams have done this before. Buford is armed with a handgun, a violation of several statutes including federal and state gun laws – yet another clear example that gun laws do not disarm criminals, no matter who they are and no matter how strong the gun law is – and he is about to make that "fatal error in the victim selection process."

According to various published accounts, including those from Brett and fellow *Plain Dealer* columnist Kevin O'Brien, Buford and Williams move in on Wells as he reaches his front lawn. Buford pulls the illegally-held handgun and tells the older man, "Don't move or I'll pop you."

"He (Wells) told me there was a moment when he knew they weren't playing around," Brett recalled in the *Gun Week* interview.

Wells steps backward, moving toward his porch, when his path is partly blocked by one thug's raised arm. Wells tries to talk to the teens, and what he gets back is "F--- that" from one of these predators.

Damon Wells arrives at the moment of truth. He draws the legally-concealed handgun, swings the muzzle in its short arc toward Arthur Buford's "center of mass" and fires. The .40-caliber bullets cross their short path in all the time it takes to fatally wound a gunman; the beat of a heart, the blink of an eye. Hit three times in the chest, Buford stumbles back and his accomplice – living "down" to the reputation of

194 Gottlieb & Workman

all cowardly criminals — runs away.

Wells goes inside to do what he has learned from the mandatory course he had to take to secure a concealed pistol permit. He calls police and tells his twin brother and his fiancé what has just happened. Within minutes, police arrive, Wells hands over his gun, and Arthur Buford's criminal career, and his life, come to an end.

In the days following, something happened in Wells' neighborhood. The community grew a backbone and it stiffened fast, perhaps made more rigid by the outrage over what Buford's street gangster friends and a handful of morally-challenged supporters did. They broke every window in the house, which is owned not by Wells but by Justina Berry. There were threats. Wells, his fiancé and her mother moved away for a while.

But Cleveland had had enough. Off-duty police and members of the NAACP volunteered to provide security for Berry's home and the windows were replaced. The *Plain Dealer* reported that Cuyahoga County Sheriff Gerald McFaul ordered two patrol cars to park in front of the house. The Black Shield Police Association also offered to patrol the area around the Berry home.

The community, which is predominantly African-American, rallied not to the defense of Arthur Buford, but to the man who shot him. Damon Wells, like the dead teen, is black, and in the eyes of so many in his neighborhood, an "everyman" to whom something bad happened that could have just as easily happened to someone else.

"We have a lot of crime," Regina Brett told *Gun Week*. "This time, there was a black man trying to defend his life and home, and he was trying to defend himself against a black person."

That seemed to make a considerable difference in the community reaction. Had a white police officer, or just an average white citizen shot Buford, there might have been community uproar. But not this time.

"Black people can identify with Damon Wells," Brett said. "They didn't see the boy as the victim, they saw Damon Wells as the victim."

Community outrage. Perhaps that's what it takes. When a community grows weary of being preyed upon by vicious animals who have no pity, no conscience and sadly no societal value, the community will fight back. It may take the act of a single individual who is facing grave bodily harm or death to galvanize his neighbors to action.

Brett perhaps put it best when she observed, "People just said 'enough'."

Many in the city's black community made it clear that they were tired of being victimized by street hoodlums. The president of Cleveland's NAACP, George Forbes, was quoted as stating, "That man (Wells) had a right to do what he did. If he didn't do it, we'd be sitting here today mourning him rather than the 15-year-old."

In the May 10, 2007 edition of the *Plain Dealer*, Forbes said he turned down a request for help from the family of suspect Williams. The newspaper reported, "He said he told them it wouldn't be appropriate because the NAACP had already taken a side."

Likewise, Cleveland City Councilman Zach Reed was quoted as telling reporters, "Then you have a 26-year-old young man who had every right to protect his life, protect his fiancé and protect his property. But he has to live with the fact that for the rest of his life, he shot a 15-year-old boy."

But to live with that fact, one must be *alive*.

There may be no better person able to tell about how that feels than another Cleveland citizen, Ohio State Rep. Michael DeBose. He is an ordained Baptist minister and, until the spring of 2007, one of the Legislature's most ardent Democrat anti-gunners.

An account of his "epiphany" was also reported in the *Plain Dealer* by yet another of its columnists, Phillip Morris. That his misadventure happened so close to the incident involving Damon Wells and "Ace Boogie" Buford is, perhaps, a coincidence. Some might just call it Divine Intervention.

It was the night of May 1. Less than two weeks had passed since the night Buford was shot. While some argue that Buford's death should have sent a signal to Cleveland's street criminals, apparently two of them didn't read the newspapers or watch television or listen to the radio.

DeBose went for an evening stroll through his neighborhood and found himself confronted by two predatory street thugs. (Why does it always take more than one?) One of them pulled a handgun, which he no doubt was not legally licensed to carry.

According to Morris' account in the newspaper, DeBose said, "At first I just backed up, but then I turned around and started running and screaming."

When he had voted against gun rights and concealed carry measures in the Ohio House of Representatives, DeBose had "voted his conscience." But finding himself running and screaming evidently gave this preacher a fit of reflection about self-preservation.

Chad Baus, a veteran Ohio gun rights activist and one of the founders of the Buckeye Firearms Association, put it best when he wrote on the organization's web page, "Why, with all of the mountains of testimony legislators heard, and presentations of evidence legislators received about the urgent need to restore the right to bear arms for self-defense, did it take a violent attack on his own person before Rep. DeBose could see the light? How many thousands of other people were made victims because of anti-gunners in the decade of debate over concealed carry in the Buckeye State?"

Why, indeed?

It is easy to preach lofty morals from the safety of a pulpit or the legislative chamber, but far less so when you are facing the muzzle of a gun held by someone who doesn't care who you are, but only about what he can take from your pockets, alive or dead.

Rep. DeBose was quoted by columnist Morris admitting, "I was wrong."

"I've changed my mind," he told the newspaper. "You need a way to protect yourself and your family…I don't want to hurt anyone. But I never again want to be in the position where I'm approached by someone with a gun and I don't have one."

Every journey, even the moral ones, begins with the first step. In the case of Cleveland's experience, there may be more than one first step.

The *Plain Dealer*, considered by many Ohio activists as being ardently anti-gun, turned its columnists loose to report self-defense and the gun issue from a remarkably different – and refreshing – perspective.

An anti-gun state legislator has publicly confessed a dramatic change of heart on the gun issue, but it took a frightening personal experience to alter his perspective. Better late than never, perhaps, and Rep. DeBose, like Damon Wells, is at least alive to make that moral and ethical reflection, and to enjoy what we all hope is a long and joyful life with his family.

A community, outraged by the harassment of Damon Wells after he, like any good citizen might have, defended himself against a ruthless predator, has opened a dialogue and is re-examining its own values.

There are many ways for Americans to fight back. They can organize community block watches, they can demand good schools, they can provide support to troubled youths, and they can fight for tougher sentencing guidelines for violent crime, they can support their police and elect sensible representatives while turning the "deadwood" out of office.

All of these things can have some impact on crime in the broad scheme of things. But in those cold, empty moments when you are standing face-to-face with a violent criminal who wants to steal what you own and then, perhaps, take your life, you will realize – as did Rep. DeBose the Baptist minister – that armed self-defense may be all that separates you from this life and eternity.

Unlike Mr. DeBose, for whom the bell has not yet tolled, and likewise for whom experience has provided a proverbial moment of clarity, there remain many people whose commitment to restrictive gun control has not simply left them wearing rose colored glasses, but blinders. They will campaign hard against laws that recognize their fellow citizens' right of self-preservation by armed self-defense, yet you will never see a single one of these victim disarmament advocates erect a sign on his or her front lawn advising all who pass by that "This is a gun-free home."

For years, as we have noted earlier in this book, gun ban advocates have fought against concealed carry statutes in state after state, insisting that they would not prevent crime, but only contribute to it. After the Damon Wells incident in Cleveland, *Plain Dealer* columnist O'Brien noted in his April 25, 2007 essay, "This kind of incident proves knee-jerk gun foes wrong, and they know it."

Yes, they do know it, and they are loathe to admit it. Such "knee-jerk gun foes" live in a state of denial that is akin to the alcoholic who cannot see he has a substance abuse problem. Stubbornness leads to self-delusion, but that kind of philosophical myopia should never be allowed to become national policy.

Gun rights activists are fond of noting that "free people only surrender their rights once." That must never be allowed to happen here.

Remorseless predators with nothing to fear become ever more

ruthless and unforgiving. History has taught us that lesson repeatedly.

Some people, like Michael DeBose, learn the hard way, but soon enough to change course and perhaps use their influence to do something about it.

The good citizens of Cleveland believe their neighborhoods, and their lives, are worth fighting for.

What about the rest of you?

ACKNOWLEDGEMENTS

The authors would like to note that news accounts, essays and other reports from the following were invaluable in the production of this book.

Of particular help as resources were Wikipedia, Clayton Cramer's Civilian Self-Defense blog, KeepAndBearArms.com, FreeRepublic.com, Snopes.com and TheHighRoad.org.

In particular, we would especially like to thank Jill "J.R." Labbe, Deputy Editorial Page Editor, *Fort Worth Star-Telegram*, who applied a critical eye to our original draft manuscript.

Prologue

Hartford Courant (July 24 - August 10, 2007 selected editions)
WFSB News in Hartford, Connecticut
CBS News (July 28, 2007)

This is America

Harrison County, Mississippi Sheriff George H. Payne, Jr.
Second Amendment Foundation
WLOX in Gulfport, Mississippi
Cincinnati Enquirer (November 20, 2006)
USA Today (March 20, 2006)
Rocky Mount Telegram (August 15, 2006)
Indianapolis Star (December 7, 2006)
Shreveport Times (January 12, 2007)

The Deterrent Factor

Richard Shenkman, *Legends, Lies and Cherished Myths of American History*
Ryan McMaken, *The American West: A Heritage of Peace* (February 12, 2004)
Wikipedia
WEWS in Cleveland, Ohio
The New Gun Week

Buckeye Firearms Association
David B. Mustard, *Journal of Law and Economics* (October 2001)
H. Sterling Burnett, National Center for Policy Analysis (May 2000)
Port Huron Times Herald
KATV in Little Rock (December 28, 2006)
Robert VerBruggen, *Reason* (June 2005)

Stopping Rape and Abuse

Rape, Abuse and Incest National Network (www.rainn.org)
National Crime Victimization Survey, 2005
Wikipedia
King County Sheriff's Department
Albuquerque Journal (April 19, 2002)
Santa Fe New Mexican (July 3, 2002)
Women & Guns
Robert Waters, *Another Thug Done Gone* (June 30, 2000)
Charlotte Observer (January 22, 1999)
F. Paul Valone, *Charlotte Observer* (October 6, 1999)
Colorado Gazette (February 7, 2001)
Boulder Daily Camera (December 31, 2001, January 1, 2002
and December 14, 2002)
Denver Post (January 31, 2007)
Lumberton Robesonian (December 28, 2006)
Atlanta Journal-Constitution (May 29, 2001)
Kennebec Journal (January 21, 2007)
Mobile Register (May 30, 2001)

Arm Yourselves

University of South Carolina *Daily Gamecock* (April 2, 2001)
New York Times (January 13, 1998)
Montgomery Advertiser
Des Moines Register (December 15, 2001)
Montrose Daily Press
TIME, *Death on the Beat* (June 28, 1999)
Thank God I Had A Gun by Chris Bird (Privateer Publications)
Bremerton Sun (December 18, 2000)
WLWT in Cincinnati, Ohio (July 10, 2005)
Gainesville Times, (January 21-22, 2007)

Defending Your Livelihood

Newport News Daily Press (January 17, 2002)
John Lott, *New York Post* (January 25, 2002)
Claremont Review of Books (Fall 2003)
Ratherbiased.com (interview transcript with Bernard Goldberg)
New York Sun (February 2, 2007)
Mediaresearch.org, Geoffrey Dickens, *Outgunned: How the Network News Media Are Spinning the Gun Control Debate* (January 2, 2000)
Pat Buchanan, *The American Conservative* (September 22, 2003)
Prof. Gary Kleck, *Armed Resistance to Crime: The Prevalence and Nature of Self-Defense with a Gun*, Northwestern Law School Journal of Criminal Law and Criminology

Fighting Media Bias

Chicago Tribune (April 13, 2001)
Lexington Herald-Leader (June 11, 2006)
WCMH/NBC4 in Columbus, Ohio
Columbus Dispatch (Friday, June 30, 2006)
Burlington Free Press (February 9, 2007)
WCAX in Burlington, Vermont (February 9, 2007)
Snopes.com
News Net 5 in Cleveland, Ohio (May 14, 2002)
Miami Herald (January 9, 2007)
Hartford Courant (November 21, 2001)
Kentucky Post (November 17, 2001)
Robert A. Waters *The Self Defense Files* (February 1, 2001)
Muncie Star Press (April 5, 2002)
Florida Today (May 21, 2002)
Wilmington Star News (November 2004)

Gun Free Folly

Salt Lake Tribune (February 14-15, 2007)
Morgan Reynolds, *Intellectual Ammunition* (January/February 2001)
Buckeye Firearms Association
Gerard Valentino, *The False Hope of Gun-Free Zones,* CNSNews.com (December 16, 2004)
Columbus Dispatch (January 29, 2007)
David Kopel, Independence Institute

Cleveland Plain Dealer (May 23, 2006)
Boston Herald (January 11, 2001)
J. Neil Schulman, *A Massacre We Didn't Hear About*, Los Angeles *Times* (January 1, 1992)
Associated Press (August 30, 2005)
KRQE in Albuquerque, NM (August 25-26, 2005)
Indianapolis Star (August 19, 2006)

You're On Your Own

National Shooting Sports Foundation
National Safety Council 2007 report on "Injury Facts"
National Rifle Association
Citizens Committee for the Right to Keep and Bear Arms
WIS-News 10 in Columbia, South Carolina
Minneapolis Star-Tribune (February 27, 2007)
Rochester Post-Bulletin (February 27, 2007)

A Plague of Recidivism

Portland Oregonian (October 9, 2006)
Clayton Cramer, Pete Drum, *Civilian Gun Defense Blog*
KOTV News in Tulsa, Oklahoma (February 5-8, 2007)
Department of Justice, Bureau of Justice Statistics
New York Daily News
New York Post (December 26, 2000)
KeepAndBearArms.com
The Seattle Times (October 10-11, 2006)
The New Gun Week
Detroit News (April 2, 2002)
Charlotte Observer (April 4, 2005)
Jackson Clarion Ledger (December 20, 2003)
Macon Telegraph (December 19, 2003)

The Insanity of Public Disarmament

Benedict D. LaRosa, *Freedom Daily* (November 2002)
Sidney, Australia *Morning Herald* (October 24, 2006)
British Journal of Criminology, (October 18, 2006)
Ian Bell, *The Sunday Herald* (February 2007)
The Washington Times

National Safety Council 2007 Injury Facts
The New Gun Week (March 20, 2007)
Bradenton Herald (March 13, 2007)
Fox News Channel 13 in Tampa, Florida (March 13, 2007)
Chattanooga Times Free Press
WRAL TV Raleigh, North Carolina
Jeff Snyder, *The American Handgunner* (September/October 2001)

Lethal Self-Defense is Moral

Corpus Christi Caller-Times (October 11, 2006)
KRIS-TV News in Corpus Christi, Texas
WATE News in Knoxville, Tennessee
Knoxville News Sentinel (January 10, 2007)
The Denver Post (February 14, 2007)
KCCI NewsChannel 8 (March 19, 2007)
Des Moines Register (March 17-19, 2007)
Clayton Cramer's blog in the archives for 2004.
Beaufort Gazette (August 25, 2004)
WSAV in Savannah, Georgia on August 24, 2004

Coming Soon to a Forest Near You

Barry Yoeman, *Out* (November 1996)
Tongass National Forest, U.S. Forest Service, Department of Agriculture
The Washington Times (April 5, 2007)
Seattle Times (October 15, 2006)
Bill Berkowitz, "Patrolling the U.S. Back-Country," *Z Magazine* (October 2003)
Eugene Register-Guard (June 2003)
New York Times (February 23, 1994)
Florida Trail Association
Indianapolis Star (September 23, 2006)
Vin Suprynowicz, *Las Vegas Review Journal* (December 6, 2006)

Institutional Stupidity

NBC News
Roanoke Times (January 31, 2006)
Roanoke Times (August 31, 2006)
The Washington Post (April 20, 2007)

Eugene Register-Guard (May 22, 1998)
Fort Worth Star-Telegram (October 6, 2006)

Polls Versus Reality: What the People Want

Chambersburg, Pennsylvania *Public Opinion* (May 6, 2007)
David J. Bordua *Adversary Polling and the Construction of Social Meaning* in *Law and Policy Quarterly* (Vol. 5, No. 3, 1983)
WRDW in Augusta, Georgia
Savannah Morning News (May 5, 2007)
Batesville Daily Guard (May 3, 2007)
KTVT in Dallas-Fort Worth (April 26, 2007)
San Francisco Chronicle (April 20, 2007)
Norman Transcript (May 3, 2003)

Epilogue

Cleveland Plain Dealer (April 25, 2007)
Cleveland Plain Dealer (May 4, 2007)
Cleveland Plain Dealer (May 10, 2007)
Cleveland Plain Dealer (May 11, 2007)
Cleveland Plain Dealer (May 15, 2007)
WEWS Cleveland News Channel 5
The New Gun Week (June 15, 2007)
Buckeye Firearms Association

Suggested Web Sites

KeepAndBearArms.com

www.keepandbeararms.com

TheHighRoad.org

www.thehighroad.org

Second Amendment Foundation

www.saf.org

Citizens Committee for the Right to Keep and Bear Arms

www.ccrkba.org

The National Rifle Association

www.nra.org

Gun Week

www.gunweek.com

Women & Guns Magazine

www.womenandguns.com

HandgunLaw.us

www.handgunlaw.us

About the Authors

Alan Gottlieb

Alan is a Nuclear Engineering graduate of the University of Tennessee and attended the Institute on Comparative Political & Economic Systems at Georgetown University.

He is recognized as a member of the working press, maintaining active membership in the Outdoor Writers Association of America. His articles have appeared in the *Seattle Times, San Francisco Examiner, Washington Post, Atlanta Journal-Constitution, Cincinnati Inquirer, Chicago Tribune, Orlando Sentinel, Ft. Worth Star-Telegram* and *USA Today*.

Alan is the Publisher of *Gun Week* and The Gottlieb-Tartaro Report.

He is the Chairman of the Citizens Committee for the Right to Keep and Bear Arms, Founder of the Second Amendment Foundation, a National Director of the American Conservative Union, President of the Center for the Defense of Free Enterprise, President of the American Political Action Committee and President of NoInternetTax. org.

His handiwork has received notice in the *New York Times, Washington Post, Boston Globe, Cleveland Plain Dealer, Time, People, Rolling Stone, National Review* and *Outside* magazine.

Alan has received the prestigious Golden Eagle Award from the American Federation of Police, and was commended by the Kentucky House of Representatives for his "outstanding leadership in preserving our American heritage of freedom."

Alan has appeared on over 3,600 TV and radio talk shows, including the McNeil-Lehrer News Hour, ABC's 20/20, The Michael Reagan Show, The Ken Hamblin Show, PBS All Things Considered, CNN Crossfire, Fox TV's Crier Report, NBC Today Show, The O'Reilly Factor, ESPN, Larry King Live, CNN Special Report, Hannity & Comes, CNN All Politics, Fox News Channel and Good Morning America.

Alan is also President of four radio stations: KBNP in Portland, Oregon, KITZ in Seattle, Washington, KGTK in Olympia, Washington, and KSBN in Spokane, Washington.

AUTHORED BY Alan Gottlieb

Gun Owners Political Action Manual

The Rights of Gun Owners

The Gun Grabbers: Who They Are, How They Operate,
Where They Get Their Money

Alan Gottlieb's Celebrity Address Book

Gun Rights Fact Book

Politically Correct Guns

The Wise Use Agenda

She Took a Village: The Unauthorized Biography
of Hillary Rodham Clinton

Gun Rights Affirmed: U.S. v. Emerson

CO-AUTHORED by Alan Gottlieb

Guns for Women with George Flynn

Trashing the Economy with Ron Arnold

Things You Can Do to Defend Your Gun Rights
with David Kopel

More Things You Can Do to Defend Your Gun Rights
with David Kopel

Politically Correct Environment with Ron Arnold and Chuck Asay

Double Trouble: Daschle and Gephardt—Capital Hill Bullies with
Dave Workman

George W. Bush Speaks to the Nation with George W. Bush

Dave Workman

Dave Workman is an award-winning editor, author and nationally recognized firearms authority. The senior editor of *Gun Week* since November 2000, he is also a contributing editor to *Women & Guns*, and his work also appears frequently in various firearms periodicals including *Gun Digest* and *Gun World*.

A native of the Pacific Northwest, Workman grew up in Tacoma, Washington and graduated with a degree in editorial journalism from the University of Washington.

His newspaper career began at a small town weekly newspaper in Snoqualmie, Washington where he was recognized for his editorial columns by the Washington Newspaper Publishers Association. He spent 21 years at Outdoor Empire Publishing, where his outdoor writing garnered several awards. For 13 of those years, he was on the editorial staff of *Fishing & Hunting News*, and then was promoted to managing editor of *Small Craft Advisory*, a marine law enforcement journal, and *Hunter Education Instructor*. His work has also appeared in *Police and Law and Order*.

In addition, his byline has appeared in several major newspapers, including the *Atlanta Journal and Constitution, Chicago Tribune, Lacrosse Tribune, Seattle Times and Seattle Post-Intelligencer, Fort Worth Star-Telegram, Providence Journal, New Hampshire Union Leader, Tacoma News Tribune* and *Washington Times*.

A past associate member of the American Society for Law Enforcement Training, Workman spent nine years on the board of directors of the National Rifle Association. He is a certified firearms instructor.

Authored by Dave Workman

PETA Files: The Dark Side of the Animal Rights Movement

Shades of Gray – The Record of Gray Davis

Double Trouble – Daschle and Gephard, Capitol Hill Bullies
with Alan Gottlieb

Washington State Gun Rights and Responsibilities